An artist is a child always and sees things with childlike wonder. That is what makes him an artist.

—FEDERICO FELLINI

Fellini
the Artist

Edward Murray

SECOND, ENLARGED EDITION

FREDERICK UNGAR PUBLISHING CO. / *New York*

Copyright © 1976, 1985 by Frederick Ungar Publishing Co., Inc.
Printed in the United States of America
Designed by Irving Perkins

Library of Congress Cataloging in Publication Data

Murray, Edward.
   Fellini the artist.

   Filmography: p.
   Bibliography: p.
   Includes index.
   1. Fellini, Federico.   I. Title.
PN1998.A3F344   1985   791.43'0233'0924   85-1194
ISBN 0-8044-6537-1 (pbk.)

For Hasha

Contents

viii / CONTENTS

Part Four: Conclusion

Preface
to the Second Edition

Since the first edition of *Fellini the Artist* was published in 1976, Fellini has made four films: *Fellini's Casanova* (1976), *Orchestra Rehearsal* (1979), *City of Women* (1981), and *And the Ship Sails On* (1984). With the exception of the last mentioned, the Italian director's recent films have not been generally well received.

All the same, interest in Fellini the man and Fellini the artist has continued unabated. The world of international cinema still awaits each new Fellini film in the hope that the maestro will turn out another *La Strada*, say, or *8½*. *And the Ship Sails On* makes that hope seem less illusory than four years ago when *City of Women*—one of Fellini's worst films—appeared. Although not a masterpiece itself, *And the Ship Sails On* has enough good things in it to remind the viewer that the artist who made it has created masterpieces in the past—and could do so again in the future.

For this edition, I have added critiques of the four films cited above. The Conclusion has also been revised and the Filmography and Bibliography brought up to date.

E.M.

Preface
to the First Edition

This book has been divided into four sections. In Part One, I have attempted a sketch of Fellini's life, with particular emphasis on the early years, in order to suggest the autobiographical dimension of his art. I have not attempted a formal biography; neither have I sought to put the director on the analyst's couch. Fellini's parents, his Italian environment, his Roman Catholic education, his attitude toward his wife, Giulietta Masina, are pertinent to my concerns only to the extent that such sources of knowledge increase the reader's understanding of the films.

Part Two focuses on the manner in which Fellini constructs a picture, from his initial conception, through the scripting and casting and shooting, to the final editing; on Fellini's relationship with his various collaborators; on Fellini's own analyses and interpretations of his films; and on the question of the possible influences—cinematic and literary—on Fellini's art. In the past twenty-five years, the director has granted many interviews and commented voluminously on his work. Although Part Two draws on these dialogues, I have not hesitated to put forward my own point of view, since on occasion Fellini has been known to exaggerate. ("The only time Federico blushes," Giulietta Masina once remarked, "is when he tells the truth.")

Because Fellini is such a scintillating personality and interviewee, one is tempted to forget that the individual films must themselves be the final object of criticism. Accordingly, in Part Three twelve of Fellini's pictures are studied, from *The White Sheik* to *Amarcord*. I have not included a critique of *Variety Lights*, which Fellini codirected with Alberto Lattuada in 1950, or the three sketches he has made—namely, *A Matrimonial Agency* (1953), *The Temptations of Doctor Antonio* (1961), and *Toby Dammit* (1967). Instead, I have preferred to concentrate on those feature-length pictures for which Fellini is solely responsible and on which his reputation as a major film-maker rests. It has been my purpose to avoid a one-sided study; that is, a study exclusively concerned with formal analysis or one devoted entirely to content analysis; consequently, the reader will find here what I trust is a balanced discussion of the visual approach and structure on the one hand and of character and theme on the other.

In most chapters, I have not separated my treatment of form and meaning. Rather, I have aimed for a smooth continuity by fusing description, analysis, and interpretation, so that reading about each film might approximate a viewing of it. The reader will "see," I hope, not only *what* happens in a Fellini picture but also *how* Fellini is doing it—where the camera is, and why, for example, and the way the whole is constructed (though words, of course, can never be an equivalent for the visual experience itself). My judgments are not confined to a pronouncement in the last paragraph of each chapter; I evaluate each film throughout my treatment of it by showing Fellini's subtlety in expressing his subject, his theme, his conception of human experience. In the chapters that constitute Part Three— as in the final section in which I offer a concluding assessment— my aim has been to provide a guideline through the cinematic technique in Fellini's films to reveal the beauty and complexity of his art and the range and depth of his personal vision of life.

In the following pages I have tried, as much as possible, to avoid becoming overly technical in my analyses. It is my hope that *Fellini the Artist* will appeal not only to film students and movie buffs but also to the general reader or anyone who has ever seen a Fellini picture and who would like to know more about his films and the personality which created them.

A filmography appears at the end of the text. A bibliography of secondary sources relevant to Fellini studies—with the exception of newspaper pieces and trade papers, which are cited in the text—is also included. This bibliography is restricted to sources actually quoted or referred to in the course of my study.

I wish to thank the State University of New York for a Faculty Research Fellowship in 1974, which helped me to complete this study.

E. M.

PHOTOGRAPH ACKNOWLEDGMENTS

Frontispiece, Fellini directing *Satyricon*: Gene Andrewski (Distributor: United Artists Corp.). *The White Sheik*: Contemporary Films/ McGraw-Hill. *I Vitelloni*: International Museum of Photography/ George Eastman House (Distributor: Janus Films, Inc.). *La Strada*: International Museum of Photography/George Eastman House (Distributor: Janus Films, Inc.); Gene Andrewski (Distributor: Janus Films, Inc.). *Il Bidone*: Audio Brandon Films, Inc. *Nights of Cabiria*: Avco Embassy Pictures Corp. *La Dolce Vita*: both, International Museum of Photography/George Eastman House (Distributor: Audio Brandon Films, Inc.). *8½*: International Museum of Photography/ George Eastman House (Distributor: Audio Brandon Films, Inc.). *Juliet of the Spirits*: Available in the U. S. from Audio Brandon Films, Inc.; Gene Andrewski (Distributor: Audio Brandon Films, Inc.). *Fellini Satyricon*: both, Gene Andrewski (Distributor: United Artists Corp.). *The Clowns*: Levitt-Pickman Film Corporation. *Fellini's Roma*: United Artists Corp. *Amarcord*: both, New World Pictures. *Fellini's Casanova, Orchestra Rehearsal, City of Women, And the Ship Sails On*: private collection.

Part One

The Man

I think that an artist is like a tree. It can grow only where it has its roots.

—FEDERICO FELLINI

CHAPTER 1

Biographical and Historical

All art is autobiographical; the pearl is the oyster's autobiography.

—FEDERICO FELLINI

1

If we respond deeply to a work of art, we are naturally curious about the artist. "Who is he?" we ask. "And where did he come from? What kind of a life has he had, what manner of person is he?" To the pure formalist critic, such questions—however interesting they may be on the human level—remain irrelevant to the evaluation of a specific film. The film-maker, argues the formalist, converts the details of his personal life into an impersonal construct. There is no one-for-one correspondence between the film and the film-maker's biography. We can know what "Felliniesque" means without possessing any facts about Fellini's life; if we simply look at *La Strada* or *8½* or *The Clowns*, we will know what "Felliniesque" stands for in critical discourse. The biographical critic thinks otherwise. Because he believes that one cannot separate the man and the picture as neatly as the formalist would have it, the critic with a biographical orientation attempts to explain the form and content of a film-maker's work by reference to the film-maker's life. The artist is a human being, and he cannot help but embody in his art all that he has seen, heard, felt, and learned in the course of his existence—so argues the biographical critic.

Of course, there is no reason to take an extreme position as either a pure formalist or a pure biographical critic. A pluralist approach is the best method for "getting at" the complex reality of a film. Although the work of art itself should be the main concern of criticism, and although biographical information can never tell us whether a film is good or bad, knowledge of the artist's life can throw light on recurrent images, symbols, motifs, and patterns in the work. In short, the biographical approach—though of no help to the critic in matters of judgment—can assist him on the score of interpretation. Provided the pluralist does not confuse life with art, and provided he does not forget that the formalist approach remains central to his task, biographical information can serve the critic as protection against reading into a film meanings neither intended by the artist nor objectively verifiable in the work. "The main ideal of criticism," Kenneth Burke once observed, "is to use all that there is to use."

Concerning the autobiographical element in film, Fellini himself has been inconsistent in his remarks on the subject. On the one hand, he has said: "An artist can only be understood through his work. You can study an ant for years, photograph it in every possible way, and never understand what an ant is" . . . "What I have to say, I say in my work. My work can't be anything other than a testimony of what I am looking for. It is a mirror of my searching." On the other hand, he has also said: "I cannot remove myself from the content of my films" . . . "If I were to make a film about the life of a sole, it would end up being about me" . . . "Although some may think *La Dolce Vita* a sort of sequel to *I Vitelloni*, insofar as it is the story of a young man from the provinces who has been in Rome for ten years, there is really no connection between Moraldo and Marcello. The only connection is the autobiographical vein that is in all my work." Now, just as the camera can be both a recording instrument and a transformer of the "real world," so too Fellini's pictures have to be understood as both imitation or mimesis and subjective expression. Viewed from one angle, *I*

Vitelloni and *La Dolce Vita* are autobiographical; however, viewed from another—and, ultimately, a more important—angle, these two pictures (as well as the others) portray impersonal, artistically integrated, self-contained "worlds." Like his chosen medium, then, Fellini's art is "impure."

2

Rimini is a resort city on the Adriatic Sea, some seventy-five miles east of Florence. During the warm summer months Rimini fills up with vacationers, but the winters are quiet, monotonous, and gloomy. It was into this milieu that Fellini was born on January 20, 1920. The influence of environmental factors—climate, terrain, social organization, economic conditions, religion, education, familial relations—on an artist's development has been a matter of critical interest since the time of Taine. As Eugene Walter has remarked of Fellini's early surroundings: "The clouded beaches, the mysterious and moody sea, the windy salt marshes, the rocky slopes with rock houses—all the backgrounds of Fellini's films are here." Similarly, Eric Rhode has declared: "the provinces of [Fellini's] imagination have the bleakness of the Adriatic coast." The sea performs an important function in most of Fellini's films, from *The White Sheik* down to *Fellini Satyricon*; and there seems little doubt that the artist's experiences as a child in a seaside city left a lasting impression on his sensibility. However, the desolate aura which often emanates from a Fellini setting should not be overemphasized. "Federico has always loved comic things and crazy, unexpected things," Fellini's mother, Ida Barbiani, has observed. When Fellini was young, Rimini attracted its share of carnivals and circuses and touring vaudeville performers, and the boy could not be restrained from visiting them. His mother has said: "there was no hope of getting [Federico] to school when the circus was in town. And he'd sit through a variety show from the first matinee until closing." *Variety Lights, La Strada, Nights of Cabiria, La Dolce Vita, 8½, Fellini Satyricon, The Clowns,*

Fellini's Roma—each of these films treats to one degree or another the subject of theatrics.

Fellini's father, Urbano, was a middle-class wholesaler in groceries. Since he traveled much of the time throughout the north, the elder Fellini rarely shared his life with his son. In *La Dolce Vita*, Marcello spends an evening with his father, a traveling salesman, with whom he has never had an intimate relationship. Urbano Fellini (who died in 1956) seems also to have been the model for the father whom Guido recalls in *8½*. Apparently, Fellini has never experienced a close bond with his mother, either. "I've enjoyed [all of Federico's films]; they are full of jokes and references which sometimes only his family can see," his mother once told an interviewer. "*8½* was the saddest. It made me cry when the son says to the ghost of his father, 'Please don't go; let's talk—we've never really had a talk.' Because, you see, Federico and I have never had a talk. He's played tricks on me, and he's always made me laugh—we're good friends—but I don't feel I really know him." Fellini himself has characteristically offered contradictory views of his early past. "My father had an eye for women [in *La Dolce Vita* Marcello's father attempts to sleep with a prostitute], and this led to many bitter quarrels between him and my mother, but my boyhood in Rimini was nonetheless an exceptionally happy one," the film-maker once explained. On another occasion, however, he was quoted as saying: "As a child, I was very timid, solitary, vulnerable to the point of fainting."

Fellini has a brother named Riccardo, thirteen months younger, who enacted the part of his namesake in *I Vitelloni*. He also has a sister named Maddalena, ten years younger, who is married to a pediatrician. Of Maddalena (the name of the nymphomaniac played by Anouk Aimée in *La Dolce Vita*), Fellini has said: "I do not know her very well."

As a child, Fellini amused himself by making puppet shows. The future film-maker used to visit the Fulgor, the local movie house, and the pictures he saw there made a strong impression on him. He remembers standing for hours before a mirror at home, putting lipstick on his cheeks in order to look like an

Indian. Similarly, when he would return from watching a circus, he liked to powder his face in imitation of the clowns. From his mother Fellini appears to have inherited a talent for drawing. According to Angelo Solmi, the young Federico occasionally sketched caricatures of movie stars; he would then display his work around Rimini, and in payment for this enterprising approach, the Fulgor management allowed the boy free admission to the theater.

Fellini was educated in Catholic schools, a fact which he does not recollect with a tranquil air. One boarding academy he attended in Fano, a northern city, appears to have been run on the principle that the imposition of harsh discipline is more important to the formation of character than the teaching of the love of God. The Carissimi Fathers there punished the boys by pounding their hands with a thick ruler. In *La Dolce Vita*, as Fellini himself has pointed out, Sylvia the sex goddess ironically wears the same kind of small white collar which distinguishes the garb of the priests in Fano. Fellini believes that an "obscure" guilt feeling—which he says still weighs heavily upon him— can be traced to the years spent in that school. "I believe," he adds, "that this experience had a great deal to do with the formation of certain structures or added certain riches to my temperament." Whatever Fellini intends by such remarks, one point remains clear: the period spent at Fano undoubtedly made a contribution to that vein of anticlericalism (*not* antireligious feeling) which runs throughout the body of the director's films.

Fellini describes himself as a "terrible student, hopeless at mathematics and barely mediocre at Italian." The only subject which interested him was art history. When he was twelve, Fellini recalls, his class was once shown slides illustrating the life of St. Francis of Assisi. One of his classmates slipped an illustration of a naked girl in with the other slides, and then sat back to wait for the fun. "Suddenly, in the darkened lecture room, the picture of the naked girl appeared on the screen. I've never forgotten the shock of that moment," Fellini says, with a straight face; "and I can't help but think that this little episode planted an interest in filmmaking in my subconscious." As his mother points out, Federico always did have a great sense of humor.

Many incidents from Fellini's past have been woven into his pictures. As a boy he used to live occasionally with his grandmother in Gambettola, a small village near Rimini. One day he discovered a farm, and hidden away in an attic there he came across an idiot child, whom the peasants evidently were ashamed of and probably hoped would die. "It is something that struck me, that made an enormous impression on me," he reports, "and I put it into *La Strada*." When Fellini was eight, there lived on the shore of Rimini a huge woman named Saraghina who was a prostitute. On one occasion, little Federico and several of his playmates pooled their meager resources and paid the wretched woman to show them her genitals. Saraghina appears in *8½*, along with Fellini's grandmother from Gambettola and other memories of people and events from the artist's early years. Later, when Fellini was seventeen, he became part of a gang which found an outlet for its energies by engaging in practical jokes. This period of the artist's life is depicted in *I Vitelloni*. Fellini and his fellow loafers once stole a large clock which they mistakenly thought they could sell; that theft seems to have inspired the scene wherein two of the *vitelloni* stupidly filch a wooden angel. Fortunately, Fellini outgrew his Moraldo period . . . otherwise the world would never have heard of him.

3

In 1938, after high school, Fellini left Rimini and went to Florence, where he took a job on a Tuscan magazine called *420*. The eighteen-year-old Federico worked as a cartoonist and proofreader, earning little money, but acquiring more material for the films he would one day create. For example, he was assigned to write comic strips for *Avventuroso*; specifically, his task required him to depict the stirring exploits of Flash Gordon —Italian style. *The White Sheik* is an amusing satire on comic strips; and in *8½*, Guido and Carla discourse in a parody of comic-strip dialogue. It is interesting to note that a number of contemporary film-makers have been influenced by the comics. Alain Resnais has said: "What I know about film has been learned from comic strips as much as from the cinema—the rules of cutting and editing are the same for the comics as for the cinema." Michelangelo Antonioni has made a similar confession. Jean-Luc Godard's *Alphaville* (1965) clearly reveals a comic-strip technique; and Arthur Penn has said that in constructing *Bonnie and Clyde* (1967), he "thought in terms of cartoons—each frame changing," and that he dealt with the characters from an external perspective, "like the cartoon, more the outline." So it would appear that Fellini's training in writing for the comics not only supplied him with part of his future subject matter but may have also taught him some valuable lessons about cinematic form.

At the time, however, Fellini's ambition was to become a journalist. He told Gideon Bachmann in 1959: "I had seen so many American films in which newspapermen were glamorous figures . . . that I decided to become one too. I liked the coats they wore and the way they wore their hats on the back of their heads." Consequently, in the spring of 1939, Fellini journeyed to Rome. He has often remarked that this was not a happy period in his life. In his interview with Bachmann, Fellini explained that all his pictures up to that time dealt with characters who were searching for their true selves. He presented these people in terms of empty streets at night—perhaps because of autobiographical considerations. When Fellini first came to Rome, he could not find work; he had no money for food or lodgings; he remained lonely. Yet, in 1965, he told Lillian Ross that he wanted to go to Rome as a young man, inasmuch as his mother was a Roman. Coming to Rome, he said, was like coming home. He saw the city in a maternal light, as a symbol of protection. It would seem that Fellini's emotional life is much more complicated than he normally manages to suggest in any one interview.

During his early periods in the Italian capital, Fellini briefly reported police news for *Il popolo di Roma*. Later he published cartoons and short stories in *Marc' Aurelio*, a weekly satirical magazine; and on the basis of his success there, he proceeded to write numerous sketches for the radio. Quite likely, Fellini's background in the latter medium provided him with the discipline he needed to present characters and situations in an artistically economical manner on celluloid. As for his experience in drawing cartoons and caricatures, the film-maker himself has remarked to Tullio Kezich: "Any ideas I have immediately become concrete in sketches or drawings. Sometimes the very ideas are born when I'm drawing. Gelsomina, for example, came out of a drawing."

Fellini initially entered the cinema as a gag writer, or rewrite man; it was his job to attempt to enliven the scripts of would-be comedies by inserting jokes at random intervals. He labored on about fifty such assignments. Perhaps the most important of the trifles he was connected with during this time remains *Avanti c'è posto* (1942; directed by Mario Bonnard), a vehicle for the actor Aldo Fabrizi. From 1940 to 1943, Fellini earned good money from the movie industry; however, he did not as yet entertain any serious thoughts about expressing himself as an artist on the screen.

It was in 1943 that Fellini met Giulietta Masina, who has had a profound influence on his life and work. The actress was then featured in a radio serial written by Fellini about a young couple named Cico and Pallina; fascinated by Giulietta's voice in the part of Pallina, the author begged her for a date, took her out to dinner, and tried heroically to make an impression on her. Evidently he succeeded. They soon became engaged, and on October 30, 1943 they were married. A son was born but he lived only three weeks; Federico and Giulietta have since remained childless. "I do not miss having children of my own," Fellini has said (for the artist derives a satisfaction from his creative work that other men find in flesh-and-blood progeny). "But I have a lot of fun with little kids. They are such funny clowns."

Giulietta Masina has appeared in six of Fellini's pictures: *Variety Lights, The White Sheik, La Strada, Il Bidone, Nights of Cabiria*, and *Juliet of the Spirits*. A graduate of the University of Bologna, and the author of a thesis on archaeology, Giulietta is hardly on the mental level of Gelsomina or Cabiria, a fact which testifies to both her acting talent and Fellini's patience and genius for eliciting precisely the performance he wants from his cast. Although the director speaks of Gelsomina and Cabiria as growing inside of him and then being "superimposed" on his wife in terms of the screen, he also admits that Giulietta inspired both characters. There is no doubt about the contribution the actress has made to her husband's work. Fellini has said that Giulietta is more important to him than any person he has ever known, including his mother. "She lives in my imagination always—sometimes too much."

Fellini has given a good deal of thought to the subject of male-female relations. In a piece on Anouk Aimée, which the director wrote for *Vogue* (October 1, 1967), he argues that the time has come for a new kind of woman. This ideal woman would be completely adult, and she would be viewed by the man in an adult way (that is, not as a mother or a whore or a child). The woman Fellini has in mind would combine modesty, intelligence, responsibility, and freedom. As Fellini sees it, Anouk Aimée suggests just such qualities on the screen. Quoting Jung, the film-maker goes on to say that woman represents man's dark side, the mysterious side of him which he doesn't understand. Men of his generation, Fellini adds, are regressive, and they must be swept away by younger men and women with fresh ideas about sex.

Fellini's thoughts on women, sex, and love are associated in his mind with mystery and religion. In the Ross interview, he claims not to know how to talk about women. Italy is surrounded by water, he notes. And water symbolizes the feminine. For man, it is necessary to escape from such feminine sources of power—in other words, it is necessary to escape from the mother. Yet the woman remains central to Fellini's philosophy. With the waning of religious faith in the last two centuries, an increased emphasis on sexual love has come to be a substitute for man's relationship with God. In literature we find the situation reflected, for example, in Matthew Arnold's "Dover Beach" ("The Sea of Faith/Was once, too, at the full, and round earth's shore . . ./Ah, love let us be true/To one another!"); in D. H. Lawrence's *Women in Love* ("The old ideals are dead as nails," Birkin says. "It seems to me there remains only this perfect union with a woman—sort of ultimate marriage—and there isn't anything else . . . seeing there's no God"); and in Ernest Hemingway's *A Farewell to Arms* ("You're my religion," Catherine Barkley tells Frederick Henry. "You're all I've got"). Similarly, Fellini told Ross that, though he does not follow the teachings of any specific church, he remains religious. For him, to be religious means to love, to have faith in life: "To feel that things are going right, going exactly the way they should go. . . . I go to church only when I shoot a scene in church, or for an aesthetic or nostalgic reason. For faith, you can go to a woman. Maybe that is *more* religious."

Early in his career, when asked if his films were Christian, Fellini replied in the affirmative—if by "Christian" is meant "love toward one's neighbor." He went on to explain that his pictures depict a loveless, egotistical world; however, he added: "There is always, and especially in the films with Giulietta, a little person who wants to give love and who lives for love." Elsewhere, during the same period, Fellini declared his belief in Christ: "[Jesus] is not only the greatest figure in human history, but he continues to live in the being who sacrifices himself for his brother." Yet Fellini went on to remark that he might be a heretic, that he did not possess a sophisticated grasp of Christianity, and that he could pray only when he was unhappy and frightened ("but one should be able to pray out of happiness!"). As for the church, Fellini has said: "I see her for what she means to Catholics in Italy—a great mother, indulgent and affectionate towards the sinner. I should never dream of purposely exiling myself or opposing myself to her, for she is inseparable from my personality as an Italian." All the same, the director's films often reveal a critical attitude towards the church.

In the Ross interview, Fellini praises the younger generation for being freer in their sexual relationships than the middle-aged: "There is not this myth of a woman who must be either a virgin or a whore." However, Fellini claims not to be entirely satisfied with the young either. "The kids are without mystery," he reflects. "To me the feeling of fear, the feeling of hope, the feeling of mystery are all very important." Still, when the director was in New York to promote *Fellini Satyricon*, he told Tom Burke that young people take drugs because they long to experience mystery (*New York Times*, February 8, 1970). Finally, it is interesting to note that in his talk with Kezich, Fellini observes that an aura of mystery surrounds Giulietta, that she creates a nostalgic longing in him for innocence and perfection. Unless we understand the "mystical" side of Fellini, then, we will fail to comprehend the fullness of his art—which, in turn, is so bound up with his past.

And, as Fellini is well aware, one cannot easily overcome the past. He told Kezich that a yearning for an absolute morality troubles him; he attributes this nostalgia to his early training. As Fellini remarks, we devote the second half of our lives to erasing the taboos and damage created by faulty education in the first half.

The relationship between art and neurosis has inspired much discussion; nevertheless, the critic's temptation to psychoanalyze the artist should generally be resisted. It may be said that *if* art *were* somehow involved with sickness (and Karen Horney, in *Neurosis and Human Growth*, argues otherwise: "*An artist . . . creates not because of his neurosis but in spite of it*" [author's italics]), art must also be a form of health. But just how, precisely, a film is born from the abnormal depths of a film-maker's unconscious and then comes to have meaning for and to give pleasure to millions of viewers remains a question which is often not even raised, much less answered, by psychoanalytic critics. The past has an influence on an artist's work; and an artist creates, in part, out of his tensions, some of which can be identified in his art. It is extremely difficult to say more than this on the subject. As Freud himself wrote: "Unfortunately, before the problem of the creative artist, analysis must lay down its arms."

4

Through bribery and connections with the right people, Fellini managed to stay out of the army during the Second World War; however, when the Germans shut down the Italian film industry during their occupation of Rome in late 1943, the ex-rewrite man came near to poverty. Fellini was obliged to stay home ("home" was a corner in the flat of Giulietta's aunt) most of the time for fear of being seized by the Nazis and sent to a slave-labor camp in Germany. Finally the Americans landed in Sicily; and in June 1944, Rome was liberated. Fellini borrowed money, opened several Funny Face Shops, and made a living sketching and photographing GI's.

The turning point in Fellini's career was his meeting with Roberto Rossellini. One day early in 1945, Rossellini came into one of the Funny Face Shops and asked Fellini to help write the script for *Open City* (1945), which was to become a masterpiece of neorealism. The following year Fellini (no longer an entrepreneur) worked again for Rossellini as a writer and assistant director on *Paisan*. "That's when I began to understand—or at least to suspect—that one could express deep things too in films," Fellini says. Afterward he worked as a writer with Pietro Germi, Alberto Lattuada, and lesser directors. For Rossellini's *The Miracle* (1948), Fellini not only wrote the script but also played the tramp-hero who is mistaken by Anna Magnani for St. Joseph. From Rossellini, Fellini has said, he learned that film is a primarily visual medium, that pictures are more important than words. Gradually the urge to direct grew inside Fellini: "When one really loves films," he said, "one cannot stop at the written page." So, starting in 1950 came *Variety Lights*, and then the other pictures which have since earned the director over two hundred international awards.

Success, however, has not spoiled Federico Fellini. Although he indulges himself in some material comforts, the man from Rimini still dresses carelessly and refuses to put on airs. Today Fellini lives with his wife in Fregene, located some twenty miles from Rome, and about ten minutes from the Tyrrhenian Sea. Some scenes from *Juliet of the Spirits* were shot in Fregene. The director also maintains an apartment in the Parioli section of Rome, much to the delight of tourists.

Fellini is one of a handful of film-makers whose name is as recognizable to moviegoers as any star. His physical appearance —thinning black hair, gray at the temples; high broad forehead; dark, heavy, somewhat jowly face; big, brown, penetrating, expressive eyes; large jaws; wide shoulders; tall, rather thick body— is familiar to most viewers. Associates refer to Fellini as the "Maestro"; passersby wave at him and call out: *"Ciao, il poeta!"* He will embrace a priest in the middle of traffic, pinch an actress on the buttock, even play the clown (he is not above hamming it up in front of a camera, for instance, in order to enliven an interview). Nonetheless, there is more to this director than just an "image" or a "personality." For Fellini remains one of the greatest film-makers in the history of the medium: an artist who is constantly seeking the expressive means for transmuting the raw data of his personal experience into cinematic form.

Part Two

The Artist

Of course I call myself an artist. What should I call myself—a plumber?

—FEDERICO FELLINI

CHAPTER 2

The Artist at Work

*I have to say—with all gratitude to those who work
with me—that I consider myself father and mother
of my films. I am helped by knowledgeable
obstetricians and faithful friends, but the
conception is mine alone.*

—FEDERICO FELLINI

1

Where a novel is concerned, it is easy to determine the author.
No problem exists in declaring: *"Eugénie Grandet* was created
by Balzac," because the writing of that classic book was a one-
person operation. To speak of an "author" in terms of a film,
however, presents certain difficulties. One must not forget the
contributions made to a Fellini picture by his co-workers. Some
of writer Tullio Pinelli's ideas inevitably find their way into the
script; a portion of Marcello Mastroianni's personality is expressed on the screen; since cameraman Otello Martelli is not
always given precise instructions, some of the shots in the
completed films are traceable to his vision; and composer Nino
Rota is not wholly an organ on which the director plays his
personal theme. Yet the idea for the movie is always Fellini's.
Furthermore, he helps write the script; does his own casting;

coaches the performers; tells the cameraman, the set designer, and the composer what he expects of them; takes an active part in the dubbing as well as the editing; and so forth. In short, Fellini is very nearly the complete film-maker.

The birth of a film starts, according to Fellini, with a spontaneous but vague feeling. A film never begins in a calculated, intellectual way, he insists. Inspiration is all. By "inspiration," Fellini means the artist's ability to make direct contact between the conscious and unconscious levels of his mind. The healthy artist is one who translates what lies in his depths into the forms of his art with the least amount of interference from the rational side of him. Unfortunately, because of the artist's upbringing, his art often suffers; for the movement from the artist's unconscious to images on celluloid involves some degree of rational manipulation. And consciousness, Fellini contends, cannot help but contain intellectual biases which threaten creativity. Hence the finished work of art is never as good as the dream film in the artist's mind. When an image remains in the unconscious, it possesses all the charm of the ineffable; its vagueness makes it exciting. When the image finally appears on the screen, however, it has lost its mystery.

Fellini always uses a script. But this stage in the development of a film he regards as mere preparation for the real task— the creation of the action by the cameras. Nonetheless, whether Fellini realizes it or not, this conscious preliminary labor seems to be essential in any kind of genuine artistic work; for there can be no art—as opposed to pure dream—without conscious "interference." Although Fellini denies that his method is improvisatorial, he refuses to allow himself to be hobbled by a script. With his love of "mystery," he understandably has to leave room for changes in the course of shooting a film. He told Gideon Bachmann: "for me, to make a picture is like leaving for a trip. And the most interesting part of a trip is what you discover on the way."

An important step in Fellini's preparation for making a film— he once called it *the* "most important single element in film-making," and on another occasion described it as perhaps "the most serious phase of my preparative work"—is casting. "Faces are more important to me than anything else," he observed to Eileen Hughes, "more important than the set designs and the costumes, more important than the script itself, even more important than acting ability." Fellini has over thirty thousand photographs of faces in cabinets, on walls, on the floor, everywhere in his offices. When he begins a picture, an ad is put in the paper, and the next day a crowd appears. Fellini experiences agony when he must decide on one actor over four or five others for the role he has in mind, since he realizes that the face he chooses will influence his conception of the characters, and each one of the faces offers an interesting possibility. As Fellini sees it, he has no recourse but to decide on irrational grounds. Sometimes the choice is salutary, sometimes not. According to Fellini, faces on the screen are a film's "human landscape." In his piece on Anouk Aimée, he writes: "Face is always the first clue one has to understanding of a person. My profession concerns images. A director has to entrust to a face everything he wants to say . . . [I]n a film, if one wants to express certain feelings, one has to use faces. Even the face of the least important bit player has to be chosen with infinite care. It's like a writer choosing one adjective over another." Manifestly, Fellini's emphasis on faces has contributed to that warm, humanistic quality of his art.

2

In an interview with Enzo Peri, Fellini likens his relations with his co-workers to that "of the craftsman and his disciples." And he adds: "It may be a leftover of the Middle Ages, but it is colorful and useful for the close cooperation necessary in producing a work of art."

Tullio Pinelli and Ennio Flaiano were co-writers with Fellini on his first eight full-length films, i.e., from *The White Sheik* through *Juliet of the Spirits*. Beginning with *Fellini Satyricon*, Bernardino Zapponi and, later, Tonino Guerra took over their function. Numerous commentators have suggested that Pinelli's contribution expressed Fellini's mystical side, whereas Flaiano's represented the director's comical or irreverent side. In his talk with Tullio Kezich, Fellini lauds Pinelli's ability to create dialogue; but at the same time, the film-maker detracts from the praise he gives the writer by pointing out that words are "of little importance" on the screen, whereas faces, or even a tic, command more interest. Pinelli himself once remarked: "The basic idea for the film comes from Fellini. . . . I have seen things I have written attributed to one of the others, and things that I hadn't written attributed to me . . . When I have finished the scenario, my work is over. I don't see how I could be useful on the set, especially with a director like Fellini, who creates his film as he shoots it."

Five cameramen have worked with Fellini: Arturo Fallea (*The White Sheik*); Otello Martelli (*Variety Lights, I Vitelloni, La Strada, Il Bidone, Nights of Cabiria, La Dolce Vita,* and *The Temptations of Doctor Antonio*); Gianni di Venanzo (*A Matrimonial Agency, 8½,* and *Juliet of the Spirits*); Dario di Palma (*The Clowns*); and Giuseppe Rotunno (*Toby Dammit, Fellini Satyricon, Fellini's Roma,* and *Amarcord*). Fellini believes that if a scene isn't correctly lighted the effect resembles a sentence with adjectives wrongly placed. The cameraman represents a hand of the director; and the best cameraman is one who does precisely and skillfully what he is told. For such a task, the technician should not have strong beliefs of his own; he needs to be open to whatever the artist wants done. Fellini has been fortunate in having the best cinematographers in Italy available to him.

When Fellini was a boy, he thought the movie actors made up the story and dialogue as they went along; it was only later that he realized the role played by the director. In his own films, Fellini strives to create a sense of spontaneity, of life-likeness. To accomplish this end, he refuses to allow his cast to see their lines until they appear on the set. Fellini does not want his actors to be self-conscious about their job, or to intellectualize their part, or to create their own characters, or to memorize dialogue. No "method" director, Fellini rejects the theory that the actor should become the character he is playing. "On the contrary," he says, "I always try to do the opposite, namely, to let the characters take on the color of whatever actor I have available for the part." Although Fellini considers his approach to be "fun," some actors and actresses would disagree—especially those who have been forced to go through fifty or even a hundred takes. On occasion, Fellini's demands for perfection have elicited hysterical reactions from exhausted players. Yet all the first-rate actors who have worked with the director have had high praise for him. For example, Anthony Quinn calls Fellini "the most talented, intelligent, sensitive, and perceptive director I'd ever worked for. . . . I learned more about film acting in three months with Fellini than I'd learned in fifty movies I'd made before [*La Strada*]."

Nino Rota—whom Fellini describes as "a man made of music, an angelic friend"—has been the composer for all the director's films with the exception of *Variety Lights* and *A Matrimonial Agency*. "My fondness for Rota as a musician comes from the fact that he himself seems very much akin to my themes and my stories," Fellini remarks. "I do not suggest the music to him since I am not a musician. However, since I have a fairly clear idea of the film I am making, in all its details, the work with Rota proceeds as exactly as the work on the scenario. Nino sits down at the piano; I stand by his side and tell him what it is I wish." As Fellini rightly observes, Rota knows "that the music for a film is a marginal, secondary element that can hold first place only at rare moments and that, in general, it must simply sustain the rest." Echoing not only Fellini's other collaborators but also the film-maker himself, Rota says: "You must have an affinity of spirit to work with Fellini."

Fellini helps cut his films, working along with his chief editor, Ruggero Mastroianni (Marcello's younger brother), until the completed movie is ready for distribution. How different the situation is in America, where few directors have the right of final cut, where producers can alter endings and remove scenes and in other ways destroy the integrity of a film. Fellini—who has had his own difficulties with producers—speaks few kind words about the breed. "There are no bad movies that were not made because of some fault of the producer or through intellectual affectation, or good films that were not made *despite* the producer," he argues. "My only regret is to have allowed my producers, who have made mints out of my films, to pay me too little." Eleven producers refused to back *La Dolce Vita*, Fellini remembers; but after the picture became a box-office success, they wanted the director to make a sequel to it, just as they had previously begged him to do a *Sons of the Vitelloni* and a *The Daughter of Gelsomina*. "The producer is an authoritarian figure who risks nothing, presumes to know public taste, and always wants to change the end of the film," Fellini writes in *Variety* (January 5, 1972). "If the film is a hit, he makes even more money while the film author receives nothing in addition. . . . For many years, my conflicts with producers have at least obligated me to keep my work in sharp definition against their spurious judgments, betrayals, and clumsy interference. But it has also helped me generate an extra measure of energy to keep going."

And for *that*, at any rate, we can all be grateful to producers.

CHAPTER 3

The Artist on His Art

*I have no vocation for theories. I detest the world
of labels, the world that confuses the label
with the thing labeled.*

—FEDERICO FELLINI

1

Fellini does not espouse a theory of film. Indeed, as the quotation
above makes clear, he has little respect for what he conceives
to be the emasculating operations of the intellect. "I am not a
cerebral artist," Eileen Hughes quotes him as saying. Fellini
views the technique used in a picture as a rational process (the
how), but he regards the inspiration behind that process as
irrational (the *why*). An artist cannot wholly explain what his
art means; moreover, if he attempts to do so, he destroys what
is vital in the work. Hence Fellini has an antipathy for criticism:
"Why reevaluate something that has moved you, water it down,
control it, kill it?"

Although Fellini rarely utters a remark which might be con-
strued as a generalization on the subject of film art, and although
he normally resists offering explanations on the score of *why*
he did such and such in a particular movie, he has been extremely
voluble on *how* he makes a film.

Because cinema is basically a pictorial medium, Fellini believes that a director must be curious about what he calls "the multiple aspects of reality." Working with Rossellini, as noted earlier, taught Fellini that pictures are more expressive than dialogue on the screen. "I believe I have the internal rhythm of the sequences in mind well before shooting begins," he informed Tullio Kezich; however, he added: "If I find that a scene assumes a significance because the camera has started rolling around a glass and goes on to the discovery of all the rest, I adjust my way of shooting to the discovery I have made." Fellini denies that he chooses deliberately to use certain individuals or places for visually symbolic purposes. "Things happen," he informed Gideon Bachmann. "If they happen well, they convey my meaning." The Italian director would agree with the American critic James Agee that "there is only one rule for movies," namely, "that the film interest the eyes, and do its job through the eyes"; and that symbols should "bloom from and exalt reality, not be imposed on and denature reality."

According to Fellini, a black and white film allows the viewer a more imaginative engagement with the characters and story than a color film because viewers tend to project onto the screen the colors they desire. Nonetheless, aside from the fact that most spectators prefer color, and that almost all films today are in color in order to meet audience expectations, the color picture can make a positive aesthetic contribution to screen art. To do so, however, color must be an integral feature of the picture; color must be born with the film in the film-maker's imagination; color should *not* be a redundant duplication of reality but a vehicle for artistic values. Naturally, a color film is harder to make than one in black and white. As Fellini put it to Pierre Kast: "cinema is movement, color immobility; to try to blend these two artistic expressions is a desperate ambition, like wanting to breathe under water." Lighting is the secret to bringing out the distinctive qualities of a face or a landscape. Yet once the director calls for the camera to move, the light changes. Although the cameraman shot a green room, the screen later shows a rose room. Of the thirteen feature-length films Fellini has made, five—his last five—have been in color.

"Film is only images," Fellini claims. "You can put in whatever sound you want later and change and improve it." In most instances, the actors we see on the screen in a Fellini picture are not the sources of the voices we hear on the sound track. Fellini contends that it is rare to find an actor whose voice remains as true to the artist's conception as his face; consequently, he feels compelled to dub his pictures. In spite of the fact that Fellini believes (or pretends to believe) that the image is all in film, he works carefully on the dubbing, music, and other sounds, often running a scene one or even two hundred times in order to achieve precisely the effect he wants. The experienced filmmaker, Fellini maintains, learns to alternate sound and silence in an expressive way. Undoubtedly, film is a combination of sight and sound and silence—though of the three elements, it is true, sight remains by far the most important.

"I cannot make a picture without knowing exactly who wears this shirt, that tie, a moustache," Fellini told Tom Burke. "I must know intimately everything I put in a shot." Yet Fellini is no partisan of the documentary approach. For to him, the imaginative world is in no way inferior to the phenomenological world; indeed, if a choice had to be made between imagination and actual events, he would even argue that his filmic transformations of the world "out there" possess more truth value than the empirical domain. Fellini is well aware that art and life are not identical; he also knows that there remains a subjective realm and an objective one. Selectivity on the part of an artist presupposes interpretation—with the obvious result that complete objectivity, even if it were desirable, is impossible.

Since Fellini performed as a scriptwriter for a number of neo-realist directors before making pictures himself, his films reveal traces of the neorealist approach. Location shooting, the use of nonprofessionals in the cast, close attention to "this shirt" and "that tie"—all this is reminiscent of Rossellini's *Open City* and De Sica's *The Bicycle Thief* (1949); however, the stark "objective" style—that fidelity to external appearances—which distinguishes the cinema of those directors is not the dominant feature of Fellini's work. Fellini's attempts to define neorealism historically have not been successful. For example, he informed Enzo Peri: "The really important contribution of neorealism is that it suggested a way to look at things—not with the narcissistic glasses of the author, but with equilibrium between reality and subjectivism." The foregoing statement would seem to be a more accurate description of Fellini's pictures than of neorealism. "For me," the director told Bachmann, "neorealism means looking at reality with an honest eye—but any kind of reality: not just social reality, but also spiritual reality, metaphysical reality, anything man has inside him." Again, Fellini's remarks on neorealism tell us more about *l'universe fellinien* than about neorealism.

Because of Fellini's respect for the mysterious, for the indeterminacy of being (in spite of his gloomy utterances about the harmful effects of past conditioning), and for the viewers intelligence, he never really ends his films or presents ready-made solutions. He feels that if he did provide a closed ending, he would be guilty of dishonesty, since he has reached no lasting solutions in his own life. Fellini prefers to let the viewer imagine how the story will ultimately conclude, what will happen to the characters at last; for unless the viewer is permitted to construct his own conclusion by actively participating in the film, he will be handed a trite or rosy denouement, and thus will be discouraged from seeking remedies for the problems in his own life. Although some of Fellini's characters change and some do not, the conclusions of the films are never wholly determined, the endings are never final, there are always question marks left in the viewer's mind at the last fade-out.

Jean-Paul Sartre has written: "A fictional technique always relates back to the novelist's metaphysics." The same can be said of a cinematic technique. "I do not want to have a fixed idea about life," Fellini told Lillian Ross. "The only thing I want to know is: *Why am I here? What is my life?*" The motion picture is both an art form and an industry. Although Fellini likes to leave his endings open, he realizes that many viewers *want* smooth answers to thorny questions. What Fellini offers the viewer is art; what the director with a solution gives the viewer is entertainment. Generally, Fellini prefers not to express the problem in such a crude manner, however, because "art" and "entertainment" are not necessarily antithetical terms. Rather, he divides films into those with an author and those produced merely for consumption: films in the first category express an individual personality and vision; films in the second category express nothing and consequently are popular because they leave the audience undisturbed.

In his article for *Variety*, previously cited, Fellini argues that the film-maker must have faith in the public, otherwise he will never develop but will only go on repeating himself, giving the audience what it wants instead of what he wants to give it. Fellini believes that his films, personal though they are, relate to other people's lives; but he also holds that "salvation" is a state of being to be endlessly sought after, not a narcotic in the form of a conventional happy ending. Naturally, Fellini wants his films to make money. Art, however, comes first with him, pecuniary concerns second. If the viewer rejects Fellini's "truth," so be it: the artist has done what he has had to do. After a picture is made, Fellini remarked to Charles Thomas Samuels, "it becomes a prostitute, lives a commercial life; what it does for the public is the public's business. Working for the public doesn't interest me. I think that my films are produced by a wholehearted sense of vocation."

2

To the pure formalist critic, as noted earlier, only the aesthetic object matters, not the conditions under which the film-maker struggled or his self-confessed intentions. Of course, one must avoid the error of the "intentional fallacy"; that is, of confusing the picture with what the director says about it. But one must also avoid the error of the "unintentional fallacy"; that is, of paying no heed to anything the film-maker says about his films. We learn much about Fellini's work not only from acquaintance with the facts of his life but also from his own statements on the themes of his pictures—or the *what* of his art as opposed to the *how* and the *why*.

In part, Fellini creates out his inner conflicts; for example, he is both Gelsomina and Zampanò (*La Strada*). That is, Fellini is torn between love for others and indifference, the resultant strain dictating the subject matter in many of his films. He told Ross that he was not a sociable person; yet he informed Bachmann that the longing to establish a deep relationship with others remained a spiritual problem of our age—adding that this very problem could be seen in all his pictures. Although Fellini enjoys surrounding himself with people (when he is shooting a movie his sets resemble a huge family picnic or even a carnival), there is still within him the shy, timid boy from Rimini who detested competition and who found his keenest pleasure in solitude, whether it involved going off alone to a circus or movie, or imitating the clowns and Indians later at home. So it is not surprising that Fellini added in his interview with Bachmann that the stories he puts on celluloid point to tensions in the relationships between people who ought to love one another. Thematically, Fellini is always "saying": Look, the relations between human beings must be improved. It is Fellini's contention that if he had solved this problem in his own life there would be no creative unrest in him, no motive for making pictures.

Related to the themes of love-versus-indifference, and communication-versus-alienation (themes that dominate modern thought, and hence are by no means in themselves peculiar to Fellini's creations), is another idea. The director explained to Pierre Kast that a recurrent motif in his pictures is the endeavor on the part of some characters to free themselves from conventional patterns of behavior; such characters attempt to oppose an authentic mode of existence against an inauthentic one. In the same conversation, Fellini remarked that the characters in each of his pictures are involved in a search for self-discovery, personal identity, and a more meaningful existence.

As Fellini sees it, the Church stands for an inauthentic way of life, since it tends to thwart man's expansive capacities. Fellini regards his art, at least on one level, as a reaction to his Roman Catholic education. He also realizes that on occasion he may *over*react to his past, with a consequent warping of his artistic personality. Because of the various psychological tensions that burden every artist, Fellini holds that the critic should not try to pigeonhole him or to identify him completely with that which arouses his hostility. Art, for Fellini, seems to represent a search for wholeness. However, not all artists, Fellini believes, can be comprehended in similar terms. In order to function creatively, one artist requires ideology; a second, love; a third, hatred; and so on. For the real artist—that is, for the man of personal vision —ideas merely trigger his imagination. When a specific film is completed, the idea that inspired it is exhausted. The artist can then turn to another idea—even one entirely at variance with the first—provided it will trigger a second narrative.

For Fellini, ideas are obviously much less important than feelings. Although he generally does not have cheerful words to say on behalf of intellectuals, he remains too well disposed toward all manner of men and all forms of existence to qualify as an anti-intellectual, or indeed as an anti anything. Fellini the artist seriously attempts to love the totality of existence. Where we detect a hostility in his work toward, say, some institution, the negative feeling is simply one factor in the artist's complicated response to experience. As Fellini has often noted, to give one example, his attitude toward the Church is a rebellious one; more accurately it could be described as ambivalent; consequently, his perspective on Roman Catholicism provides a complex psychological soil conducive to filmic creation. Since life is also complex, the polarities that distinguish the Fellinian universe guarantee the director a sufficiently rich assortment of themes with which to capture the interest of the intelligent viewer, who invariably likes to be shown the different sides of every experience.

3

Because he is afraid of being influenced by other directors, Fellini rarely goes to the movies. Many critics believe that *8½* was influenced by *Last Year at Marienbad* (1963), but Fellini has never seen that famous Resnais film. Nor has he viewed any pictures (incredible as it seems) by Eisenstein, Murnau, or Dreyer. Similarly, he has not read Joyce; so *Ulysses* could not have had —as has sometimes been claimed—a direct influence on *8½*. Of course, Fellini doesn't rule out the oblique influence of great film-makers, novelists, and other artists on his work. A writer like Joyce transforms culture. The stream-of-consciousness subject matter of *Ulysses* is in the air every modern artist breathes.

Fellini makes no secret of his love for the poetic realism of the French cinema during the thirties, freely admitting to a possible indirect influence on his own creations. John Ford was another early favorite of Fellini's, possibly because of the warmth and sentiment in the American director's work. As anyone who has seen *La Strada* might well imagine, Fellini is also a fervent admirer of Chaplin; he singles out *City Lights* (1931) as a masterpiece among the silents, and he considers *Monsieur Verdoux* (1947) to be the most beautiful film he has ever seen. In *La Strada*, Giulietta Masina's performance has been justly praised as an example of screen acting at its finest. With immense sensitivity, she develops the character of Gelsomina largely in nonverbal terms through her changing facial expressions, the way she moves and gestures, smiles and stares, dances and plays the trumpet. A few critics, however, have registered disapproval over what they regard as a Fellini-Masina imitation of Chaplin's Tramp. In *Essays on Elizabethan Drama*, T. S. Eliot writes: "Immature poets imitate; mature poets steal; bad poets deface what they take, and good poets make it into something better, or at least something different. The good poet welds his theft into a whole of feeling which is unique, utterly different from that which it was torn; the bad poet throws it into something which has no cohesion." Can anything more intelligent be said on the subject of influence? Eliot's comments as applied to comparisons between the Tramp and Gelsomina—or between any Chaplin film and any Fellini film—refute, I believe, criticism of *La Strada* on the score of imitation. For in that film a brilliant director and an outstanding actress preserve certain qualities of another great artist, namely Chaplin, while at the same time creating a singular work of art and a highly individualized performance.

Fellini denies, however, that Rossellini taught him anything except the primacy of the visual on the screen. Still, the director of *Open City* and *Paisan* helped Fellini to discover his native land—the people, the landscape, the special cultural atmosphere —and also the cinema as a serious art form. Thanks to Rossellini, Fellini discovered that film was the ideal means of expression for him.

The contemporary directors who elicit the most praise from Fellini are Kurosawa and Bergman. He has boundless respect for *Rashomon* (1950) and *The Seven Samurai* (1954), both of which make him feel like a boy again. *Wild Strawberries* (1957) and *The Magician* (1958) are Fellini's favorites among Bergman's pictures. Completely lacking in jealousy, Fellini loudly proclaims his Swedish contemporary a great film artist. Back in 1968, Fellini and Bergman were supposed to collaborate on a movie about love; but the project never materialized . . . which, considering the different temperaments and stylistic approaches of the two men, was probably all to the good.

Fellini admires the tight structure of Hitchcock's thrillers, though the form of his own pictures is entirely different. He has lauded *The Birds* (1963) because of its neat, perfect construction; and he has expressed a desire to shoot a film some day in the Hitchcock manner—that is to say, one whose structure would progress causally rather than episodically. The prospect of Fellini making such a picture in the near future appears rather remote . . . as remote as the prospect of Hitchcock making a film in the Fellini manner. *Le style est l'homme même.*

It is interesting to note that Fellini praises Antonioni's eye for visual detail; at the same time, however, he calls the films of his distinguished contemporary bloodless: "The allure of his pictures is very exterior and very elegant. They have a strange result, like *Vogue*: sophisticated, but cold." Elsewhere Fellini has said that he misses the "humanity" in Antonioni's films.

Fellini's favorite writers are Dostoevsky and Kafka; outside of these the books he mentions most often are *Don Quixote, Gulliver's Travels, The Thousand and One Nights,* and *Orlando Furioso.* As can be seen, Fellini's taste does not tend in the direction of "realism." For the most part, the film-maker limits his reading to newspapers, science fiction, history, a little philosophy, and treatises on the occult (he is extremely fond of Eliphas Levi*). His favorite painter is Botticelli; his favorite composer, Stravinsky.

Although Fellini is an extremely intelligent and sensitive man, he is neither well read, highly cultured, nor even particularly knowledgeable about the history of his chosen medium. Inevitably, there have been some influences on his work, both direct and indirect. . . . No matter. Fellini goes his own way, creating great films out of his own sources, as original an artist as one might realistically expect in a world such as ours, where so much art (and what passes for art) is almost too abundantly obtainable. Unlike Joyce, then, Fellini is not a learned man; however, like Joyce he remains a major figure: one of those exceptional individuals whose art, rather than merely reflecting culture, helps to shape it. If one is not quite the same after reading *Ulysses,* one is likewise not quite the same after watching *La Strada.* Ever after one will see the world, at least in part, through the Italian director's viewfinder. Fellini's best films exist at that rare level at which cinema becomes experience.

---

* 19th-cenury philosopher of the occult.

Part Three

The Art

*Realism is neither an enclosure nor a panorama that
has just a single surface. A landscape, for example,
has several textures, and the deepest, the one that can
be revealed only by poetry, is no less real. It is said
that what I wish to show behind the epiderm of things
and people is the unreal. It is called my taste for the
mysterious. I shall readily accept this description if
you will use a capital "M." For me, the mysterious
is man, the long, irrational lines of his spiritual life,
love, salvation. . . . For me, the key to the mystery—
which is to say, God—is to be found at the center of
the successive layers of reality. . . . Man is not only
a social being; he is also divine.*

—FEDERICO FELLINI

CHAPTER 4

The White Sheik

An artist evolves; he goes through changes like
any other man. . . . The seasons of a creative nature
are conditioned by the seasons of the man himself.
Impoverishment, enrichment, falling in love with
certain styles and ideas—these changes occur,
but I don't find them important. To myself, I
seem always to be making The White Sheik.
—FEDERICO FELLINI

A brilliant social comedy, *The White Sheik* (1952) is probably
Fellini's most tightly constructed film. The time sequence covers
roughly twenty-four hours (day-night-morning); most of the
story takes place on a national holiday; and the action is further
unified by a consistent method of parallel editing or cross-cutting.
"*The White Sheik* is a satiric film," Fellini told Charles Thomas
Samuels. "Thus while Wanda follows the White Sheik as her
dream romantic hero, the husband follows his own mythology,
consisting of the Pope, decorum, respectability, *bersaglieri*
(soldiers), the nation, the king." In other words, the structure
of the film grows out of character contrasts and remains a vehicle for thematic values.

The White Sheik is an early treatment of what has become a familiar subject in the Fellini canon: the conflict between illusion and reality. From the beginning of the picture, when the provincial couple arrive in Rome by train for their honeymoon, Fellini emphasizes the distance which separates Ivan Cavalli (Leopoldo Trieste) and Wanda Giardino Cavalli (Brunella Bovo). For example, we see the groom first as he stares out the window at the Roman countryside; we do not see the bride until the train pulls into the station, and then Ivan is on the platform and Wanda is still on the train, visible in a window as she hands her husband their suitcases. At the hotel, while Ivan calls his aunt and uncle on the telephone in the lobby, Wanda disappears upstairs with the porter to their room. Then later, when Ivan takes a nap, Wanda pretends to be bathing but instead leaves the hotel in pursuit of the White Sheik (Alberto Sordi). Throughout the picture, as noted, Fellini alternates scenes depicting Wanda's adventures with her magazine hero and Ivan's search for his bride. The couple are not reunited until the end of the film.

Except for composing a little "poetry" for Wanda during their engagement period ("She's a pretty and sweet and tiny little pearl . . . "), Ivan represents the antithesis of the romantic. Indeed, throughout the film, he seems more interested in his relatives's approval of Wanda than in Wanda herself. Very un-Fellinian, the protagonist of *The White Sheik* evinces no love for mystery and leaves nothing to chance; his entire existence is regularized and routinized: "respectability" is all. "The porter! . . . The porter! But it looks so bad . . . a lady alone . . . with the porter," he tells Wanda in their room. However, Ivan soon gets over his anger and outlines the day's activities: "Everything's scheduled down to the last minute, without any time left over. Seven o'clock, arrival in Rome . . . Seven to ten, rest in hotel; ten to eleven, meet and socialize with relatives . . . Eleven o'clock, visit Pope . . . Then dinner at my uncle's . . . And from one P.M. to midnight, everything's set up perfectly; not one minute free." Similarly, Ivan has his future mapped out: in two months he expects to be town secretary. Even after Wanda has disappeared, and even after he has been reduced to despair and near lunacy,

Ivan can still take pride in the fact that he got his bride to Rome that morning "right on schedule."

Wanda's romanticism is suggested early in the film when, during Ivan's call to his relatives, she pays no attention to what her husband is saying but instead directs her attention to two Indian women seated in a corner of the lobby. Like all romantics, Wanda is fascinated by the exotic. At the office of *Blue Romance*, the magazine in which the photo-cartoon depicting the adventures of the White Sheik appears, Wanda agrees with the editor that "dreams are our true lives," adding: "I'm always dreaming. . . . There's nothing else to do in our town. . . . The people are so common. . . . The boys don't even know how to talk, you know? Once you've walked a few times up and down the main street, there's nothing else to do." No wonder *The Starry Abyss, Souls in Torment, Hearts in the Tempest,* and *In the Whirlpool of Love* —titles of stories featured in *Blue Romance*—appeal to Wanda. "All week long I just wait for Saturday to come and bring me my little magazine," she tells the editor. "I go pick it up at the station, then I run home and lock myself in my little room. . . . And then my true life begins. . . . I read all night long." In her correspondence with the White Sheik, Wanda refers to herself as "Impassioned Doll."

Throughout *The White Sheik*, Fellini juxtaposes the romantic and the realistic, the serious and the comic, in a manner reminiscent of Flaubert. In their hotel room just as Ivan is suggesting to Wanda that they might squeeze into their busy schedule some midnight lovemaking, for example, a maid rudely enters without knocking and prosaically announces: "The towels!" On the beach as Wanda plays opposite the White Sheik—she has been cast as a "faithful slave," romantically transformed from a plain-looking girl into a beautiful heroine—the director off-screen cries: "Ready, shoot!"; Fellini then cuts to a restaurant where Ivan and his relatives are dining and we hear a waiter off-screen cry: "Three tripes!" Later in the same scene, Ivan recites the poem he wrote for Wanda—"She's a pretty and sweet and tiny little pearl."—and the waiter appears, remarking: "Here we are with the noodles!" Three musicians come up behind Ivan and sing a romantic song: "O sea . . . O sky . . . O sun . . . ," while the uncle declares: "This is a hearty dish; sticks to your ribs!"

There is a striking resemblance between the famous agricultural fair scene in *Madame Bovary* and the key scene in the boat between Wanda and the White Sheik in Fellini's film. In the Flaubert novel Emma and Rodolphe converse on the second floor of the town hall, while down below awards are given to farmers for the best manure. The novelist not only plays off the romantic verbiage of the lovers against the coarse language on the platform, but he also ironically suggests the lust concealed behind the high-flown sentiments of Emma and Rodolphe. (I believe it was Eisenstein who first noted the cinematic technique in *Madame Bovary*.) In Fellini's film the White Sheik—whose real name is Fernando, and who used to work as a butcher's boy and a barber—tells Wanda a romantic tale about how he was drugged by his wife into marrying her against his will, because in reality he loves another—the beautiful, and lost, Milena. Poor Wanda believes every word. "But now that I've met you, what does it matter," Fernando sighs—staring down Wanda's dress. "What's past is past. . . . C'mon, gimme a kiss." Meanwhile, on shore the unpoetic director and his troupe wait impatiently for the White Sheik to return. Fellini concludes the scene by showing Fernando and Wanda about to kiss—when all at once the sail boom swings free and smashes against the sheik's head, thus fortuitously preserving Wanda's chastity. Immediately the action shifts to an opera house where Ivan and his relatives are watching a performance of *Don Giovanni*, a scene that is obviously a romantic parody of the previous one in the boat between the would-be lovers. (The reader will recall that chapter in *Madame Bovary* in which Emma and Charles attend an opera, and in which the heroine, dreaming Wanda-like dreams, meets Leon again and commences an affair with him.) Later in the film, Wanda decides to kill herself. Speaking to the porter at the hotel on the phone, she composes a farewell note to Ivan: "Dreams are our true life. . . . But sometimes dreams plunge us into a fatal abyss . . ." The porter is a poor speller. "What?" he asks. "Abyss? . . . 'A' as in 'Able'? . . . 'B' as in 'Baloney'?"

THE WHITE SHEIK: *Wanda and the White Sheik in the boat.*

In a masterful way, Fellini mixes objective and subjective shots, so that the viewer can see both the humor and the ugliness of many scenes (such as the previously described boat scene), and comprehend both the facts of the events and the ways in which the characters experience those events. When the frightened Ivan walks toward his relatives in the lobby, Fellini uses a subjective camera, forcing the audience into an identification with the distraught husband. The relatives are nearly always shown in a tight group, as though they were ready to pounce on Ivan because his wife has failed to appear. On one occasion, Fellini employs a high angle shot as Ivan seems to be swarmed over by his family in their determination to batter down the hotel door which separates them from Wanda. The angle makes Ivan look small and helpless, suggesting his response to the situation, and hence it can be described as subjective. The viewer gets still another impressionistic simulation of the character's feelings in the shot of Ivan fainting—he appears to be whirling around—when he hears on the phone that Wanda is in a mental hospital. Like the group shots of Ivan's relatives and the high angle shot, the shot of Ivan passing out is not, in the strict sense, a subjective camera because we see the character.

Fellini likewise permits the viewer to witness the scenes involving Wanda's pursuit of the White Sheik from two points of view. When the troupe leaves the office of *Blue Romance* and boards the truck that takes them to Fregene Beach, the audience can see the shallowness of the performers and their crude professionalism because the camera gets up close to them and the microphone picks up their banal comments. For Wanda, however, the departure is nothing less than a Joycean "epiphany." By alternating shots of the troupe (objective) with shots of Wanda wide-eyed and sighing ecstatically (subjective), Fellini conveys a complex perspective on the action. The director accomplishes the same feat later as the photo-romance is being shot by the sea.

Relevant to any discussion of viewpoint and the visual dimension in *The White Sheik* is the scene in which Wanda for the first time encounters her dream hero. It is day, and the sun is shining through the pine trees near the shore. Alone, Wanda steps deeper into the woods. Suddenly she hears someone singing. And there in a small clearing ahead—swinging from a tree high in the air above her and displaying a self-satisfied smile—is the White Sheik himself. For Wanda the moment is a revelation: It is the word—or the photo—made flesh. For the viewer the moment is an occasion for laughter, since the White Sheik is obviously a flabby, ludicrous imitation of Rudolph Valentino (himself a ludicrous imitation). Later, after the events of the day, and after Wanda has been disillusioned by the White Sheik, Fellini shows her passing the now empty swing, swaying in the night breeze. The contrast between the two images underscores the conflict between appearance and truth, or between romance and reality.

The White Sheik is filled with imaginative reversals and note-worthy visual humor. At the beginning of the film, as previously observed, Ivan is disturbed because Wanda has been seen alone with the porter; later in the film she is alone in a boat with the White Sheik—an outing that is not quite as innocent as the experience with the porter, and one which Ivan would find even more unsettling. When Wanda exits from the hotel to find her hero, she leaves the tap running in the bathtub; it overflows and Ivan is forced to splash around ankle-deep in water. At Fregene Beach, Wanda sails on the sea with the White Sheik. Later, disillusioned with her hero, Wanda attempts suicide by jumping into a river—only to land ankle-deep in mud. Near the end of the film, Wanda is taken to a mental hospital—where, presumably, all romantics belong. But Ivan—who remains unromantic—is suspected by his relatives of being insane; a police inspector considers him a "nut," and a cab driver calls him a "lunatic." Inside the mental hospital, Ivan is seen just about to enter Wanda's room; right behind him is an immense nun with a mustache which clearly resembles Ivan's own, so that the two faces absurdly mirror each other. It is also important to observe that the two prostitutes who talk to Ivan at night in the piazza (one of the prostitutes is named Cabiria, and she is played by Giulietta Masina) are, like Wanda, devotees of romance. "You

gotta see it . . . the end of Part One. . . . It's out of this world.
. . . He says to her, 'Do you love me?' " Cabiria relates to her
companion. "She tells him yes, so come dance with me. So they
start dancing like this . . ." Yet these are the two creatures who
some critics would have us believe help Ivan to face his illusions!

Fellini has said of *The White Sheik*: "It's an ironic story and
Italians don't like irony—sarcasm and buffoonery, but not irony."
Throughout the action, Fellini ridicules both the rustics and the
urban masses. As Gilbert Salachas points out: "Fellini castigates
the provincial bourgeoisie (the class into which he was born)
with an affectionate compassion that in no way attenuates his
ruthless powers of observation. The synthesis between the extremes of Fellini's duality is sadness. The pusillanimous husband
and wife in *The White Sheik* move us with their unfailing stu-
pidity. The complicated tangle of their adventures makes us
laugh, for it reveals the most futile reactions of the mediocre
provincial in such situations: the idea that respectability must
be preserved at the price of perilous lies, naïveté, affectation, and
incurable conformity." Much of the humor in *The White Sheik*
stems from Ivan's attempts to conceal from his relatives the
fact that Wanda has mysteriously disappeared. Instead of telling
his relatives the truth, Ivan desperately invents one silly excuse
after the other for his wife's absence (Wanda has a headache,
she fell asleep, she has no appetite, etc.).

But if Fellini is hard on the country people, he is equally
critical of the Romans. From the start of the film, the city is
seen as a confusing madhouse: the station platform is crowded
with people of various nationalities—all shoving and shouting—
and Ivan loses his hat when he is struck on the head by a flying
knapsack. In the hotel, when the bath water overflows, a black
priest compains to Ivan of the flooding in a language which the
troubled provincial cannot understand. On the street, a platoon
of *bersaglieri* appear behind Ivan, blowing bugles, and before
he can get to safety on the sidewalk a mob of civilians following
the military troupe force him to run along with them. Once again,
Ivan loses his hat (symbol of his "dignity"); and once again, he
is thoroughly confused by the bedlam surrounding him. At the

police station, where Ivan goes to report the disappearance of Wanda, the inspector appears to be more interested in lighting a cigarette and mixing a Bromo Seltzer for himself than in the citizen's complaint. Later, outside in the hall, a clerk asks Ivan to carry a stack of papers for him; when Ivan deposits the papers on the floor clouds of dust arise—a comment on the machinery of Roman bureaucracy. Then, downstairs in the courtyard where a squad of policemen are being drilled by an officer, Ivan is again caught up by the masses and buffeted about until he is finally able to make his escape. And so it goes, Fellini satirizing both romantics and realists, both provincials and Romans, with an even hand.

"In each of my films there is a character who goes through a crisis," Fellini once remarked. "It seems to me that the best atmosphere with which to underline this moment of crisis is a beach or a piazza at night; for silence, the emptiness of night, or the feeling that the sea is close by, brings the characters into relief; this isolation allows him to be himself without any special effort." Some critics have concluded that every time a Fellini character goes through a crisis in a piazza at night there is insight and transformation. According to such critics, then, Ivan and Wanda by the end of the film are two different people. There is not a shred of evidence in the scene between Ivan and the two prostitutes to justify the interpretation that Ivan faces up to his shortcomings; when the scene terminates, Ivan is just as stupid as when it commences. Nor does Wanda appear to enjoy a moment of recognition. Consider the nonsensical farewell note she dictates for her husband; consider also her suicide attempt. Waving goodbye to the statues of angels that line the bridge, the reader of *Blue Romance* throws herself melodramatically into the river. True, Ivan and Wanda both suffer in a piazza at night; however, neither character comes to grips with the truth. To think otherwise is to badly misunderstand Fellini's ironic satire.

In the last scene of *The White Sheik*, as Wanda and Ivan, followed by his relatives, move towards the church, Fellini has the bride say: "Ivan, I didn't do anything wrong, believe me.

It's the truth. . . . It was ill-starred destiny." *Ill-starred destiny* —this is the language of romance. Then, with a sob, Wanda adds: "Now . . . you're my White Sheik." According to John Simon in *Private Screenings*, "this is, on a humble level to be sure, the beginning of true wisdom. . . . Wanda has learned that in a world where illusions crumble into reality, the only happiness is to raise reality to the level of illusion by seeing it with loving, forgiving eyes, grateful that it is at least as much as it is. White Sheiks do not fall into our laps ready-made; we must fashion them patiently and fondly out of the brown or grey ones life provides." Simon's view of the ending is a sophisticated one. Nonetheless it is wrong. Immediately after informing Ivan of his changed status, Wanda gazes blissfully off at the statue of an angel on top of the colonnade. Can there be any real doubt that Wanda remains just as romantic as before when she pursued the fat sheik, and just as romantic as when she waved farewell to the angels on the bridge prior to her abortive suicide leap? Isn't Wanda simply projecting onto the dull Ivan now the same unrealistic expectations she had formerly projected onto the rotund Fernando?

Similarly, Ivan remains the same: "At eleven," he tells Wanda at the hospital, "we have to see the Pope. . . . I don't want to hear any explanations now. First comes the honor of the family." Ivan takes pride in the fact that he has arrived with Wanda for the papal audience on time. Just as Wanda seems to have no real value in herself in Ivan's eyes (he brags to the prostitutes that in the first grade Wanda got all A's!), neither the Pope nor the church have any intrinsic significance for him. "Seen from the perspective of Ivan," Fellini observed to Samuels, "the church is a spectacle, like the Colosseum or the Quirinal, something to tell others about back in the provinces." According to Eric Rhode, the ending of *The White Sheik* is unsatisfactory because the couple's "reconciliation is childlike and seems an unlikely basis for a happy marriage." Such a shallow judgment of the picture certainly does injustice to Fellini's artistry and intelligence. The supreme irony of the film is the characters' belief in their future happiness, and the alert viewer's knowledge of the boring, dismal, regimented lives in store for both Ivan and Wanda Cavalli.

The White Sheik is a remarkable film, especially when one realizes that it was the first picture Fellini directed without help. Structurally, the action remains consistently unified and the parallel developments neatly balanced. Although in general the camera work and editing are unobtrusive, the film is noteworthy for the manner in which Fellini projects a dual view of experience. The characters are not explored in depth, but the three chief personages are clearly established in terms of their main traits and they are not easily forgotten. Finally, the thematic content of the picture is rich and broad enough in scope to lift the particular into the realm of the universal.

All the same, *The White Sheik* is not wholly satisfying. It lacks those "Felliniesque" moments that distinguish some of the film-maker's other works—such as the pathos of the scene between Cabiria and the music-hall hypnotist in *Nights of Cabiria* or the final scene in *Il Bidone* that shows Augusto dying at the side of the road. It possesses none of the warmth of *La Strada*, none of the intellectual complexity of *La Dolce Vita*, and none of the visual brilliance of *8½* or *Juliet of the Spirits*. Though a minor work in relation to some other films in the canon, the relatively unknown *The White Sheik* is still a worthy contribution to the development of Fellini's art.

CHAPTER 5

I Vitelloni

I Vitelloni *is the story of adolescents who cannot see
anything more in life than satisfying their animal
desires—sleeping, eating, fornicating. I was trying
to say there is something more, there is always
more. Life must have a meaning beyond the animal.*
— FEDERICO FELLINI

One of Fellini's most autobiographical films, *I Vitelloni* (1953)
was released in the United States with the ludicrous title *The
Young and the Passionate*. The word *vitelloni* literally means
"big slabs of veal"; idiomatically, the word describes men in
their late twenties and early thirties who have never outgrown
their adolescence; hence the title of the film should be translated as *The Big Loafers* or *The Overgrown Teenagers*. In a
letter to Angelo Solmi, Fellini confessed that Rimini was the
model for the drab provincial town in the film, that Moraldo
was "partly" himself, and that the other *vitelloni* were based on
his boyhood friends, but added that "a little" of himself went
into them, too. As noted earlier in this study, Fellini left Rimini
after high school. Consequently, Moraldo and the other *vitelloni*
in the picture represent what the film-maker imagined *could*
happen to him and his young friends, based on his observation
of older idlers in his home town.

I Vitelloni focuses, with varying degrees of emphasis, on five of the title characters: Fausto (Franco Fabrizi), Riccardo (Riccardo Fellini—the director's brother), Alberto (Alberto Sordi), Leopoldo (Leopoldo Trieste), and Moraldo (Franco Interlenghi). As Fellini has observed, none of the *vitelloni* "really knows what he wants to do." Unemployed and without ambition, the men "borrow" money from their fathers and working sisters, pass their days shooting pool, going to the races, and staring at the sea, spend their nights drinking and chasing women. It is a mean manner of existence.

The character who receives most of Fellini's attention is Fausto, described as the "leader and spiritual guide" of the *vitelloni*. Sex is Fausto's consuming—or rather compulsive—interest in life, perhaps because he has no other interests. By conquering women, the man reassures himself that he is worthwhile and significant. (As Karen Horney remarks in *The Neurotic Personality of Our Time*: "just as 'all is not gold that glitters,' so also 'all is not sexuality that looks like it'.") Fausto gets Sandra (Moraldo's sister) pregnant; but, though he insists on his "love" for the girl—"It was destiny," he says—he does not offer to marry her; instead he decides to head for Milan (and he even urges Moraldo to accompany him!). When Fausto asks his long-suffering father for five thousand lire to finance the trip, however, the older man not only pommels him but also forces him to go to the altar. "That girl's father is a decent man like me!" Fausto's father shouts. "He's slaved his whole life long like me! Like me! To raise his family with honor! But I'll take you to the church. You'll see—I'll kick you all the way there. You bastard!" Similarly, Alberto observes: "If we want to be objective about it, Fausto's a real bastard—a filthy-minded wencher." Later in the film, Alberto repeats these sentiments to Fausto's face: "You coward, you rotten pig—you bastard!" Aside from the naïve Sandra, the only character in the picture who verbally supports Fausto is the would-be poet and dramatist Leopoldo: "No, he's not a bastard. . . . I'd say he was an instinctive type . . . ruled by passion . . . like a beast of the wilds." Nevertheless, even the faithful Moraldo eventually admits the truth about Fausto to himself and, by the end of the film, can even say to his friend: "You're a coward!"

After Fausto and Sandra return from their honeymoon, the bride's father arranges for his son-in-law to work in a store owned by his friend Michele. Ironically, the business involves the sale of religious articles. Not surprisingly, Fausto proves to be an indifferent employee—he is repeatedly late in the morning, and he constantly has to be told what to do. Furthermore, he makes advances to Michele's wife, Giulia (in spite of the fact that she is fifteen years older than him); and for his pains, he loses his job. To get revenge on Michele, Fausto and Moraldo steal a large angel carved out of wood that is stored in the basement of the shop. However, the two men are unable to sell the angel, and when the theft is discovered they narrowly escape a beating at the hands of Moraldo's father.

In one scene, which is both funny and revolting at the same time, Fellini shows Fausto and Sandra at the movies. The improvident Fausto (who depended on Sandra to furnish the ticket money) cadges a cigarette from his wife. Just as he is about to throw away the match which he has used to light their cigarettes, a woman sitting on the other side of him asks: "Would you please hold that?" Her voice and gaze are inviting. With one arm around Sandra and with his lips occasionally brushing her hair, Fausto also watches the strange woman beside him and even manages to touch her foot with his own. When the woman leaves, Fausto tells Sandra: "I'll be right back. . . . Watch my seat." Pursuing the woman (who is not only older than the pretty Sandra but also coarse looking), Fausto kisses her in the lobby of her apartment house, where he receives some vague encouragement from her about their future relations. When the newly-wed returns, his bride is waiting for him in front of the theater. "Where were you?" she asks. "I saw a fellow," replies Fausto. "I forgot I'd said I'd meet him . . . but I was late." Even the ordinarily gullible Sandra senses the truth behind her husband's transparent lie. "How did the picture end?" Fausto inquires. "Did the heroine die?" To which—significantly—Sandra replies: "No . . . they got married."

Near the end of the film, after Fausto has spent the night with a chanteuse, Sandra takes her baby and disappears. The *vitelloni* help their frightened friend in his search. At one point, Fausto encounters the woman from the movie theater. "Destiny!" she cries, echoing Fausto's romantic sentiment to Moraldo about the "love" which led to Sandra's pregnancy. "I'm going home," the woman continues. "Would you like to come along?" For once, the distraught Fausto refuses: "No, I'm sorry. No, Ma'am. I really can't; I have to go." Finally, Fausto discovers Sandra and the baby at his father's house. Before the happy reconciliation, however, Fausto is subjected to a beating with a belt wielded by his outraged father. Afterwards Fausto tells Sandra: "You made me feel so bad. I'll never do it again." With a new show of strength, Sandra declares: "If you get me mad another time, I'll do just like your father—even worse! I'll beat hell out of you!" Fausto looks pleased. "That's the way I like you," he says. "Here, give me the baby!" Has Fausto learned to be a faithful and responsible husband, or will he soon begin to pursue his old ways? As Fellini normally does, he allows the viewer to construct his own future for the character.

If Fausto is the most extensively treated of the *vitelloni*, Riccardo is the least fully realized. Aside from his ability to sing, the character played by the film-maker's brother is indistinguishable from the rest. Riccardo is not presented in any scenes apart from his fellow loafers, so that whatever individual traits he might have are left unexplored.

Alberto is probably the most immature member of the group. A daydreamer who longs to travel, he allows his sister Olga to support him and their mother. Nevertheless, Alberto feels empowered, in the absence of his dead father, to lecture Olga about the immorality of her affair with a man who is separated from his wife. During the scene at the carnival, Alberto is dressed as a woman—certainly a comment on his lack of masculine initiative —and, in the early hours of the morning, he drunkenly dances with a symbolic dummy to the equally symbolic tune of "Yes Sir, That's My Baby." As Moraldo attempts to help Alberto home, the latter questions his friend: "Who are you?" But when Moraldo identifies himself, Alberto revealingly asserts: "Uh-uh. You're nobody. All of you. All. . . . We've got to get married!" However, the emotionally arrested Alberto immediately changes his mind: "You know what we'll do instead? We'll take a boat to Brazil. Think of it. *Brazil!*"

Aside from Moraldo, Leopoldo is the most sensitive of the *vitelloni*. The aspiring artist (in a speech reminiscent of Wanda's discourse with the editor of *Blue Romance*) explains to the actor Natali: "It's hard, you know, to live in the midst of people who cannot understand, in this deadly provincial life, deaf to all art, to every voice. . . . One's all alone . . . even one's friends don't really understand; their interests are more material . . . more contingent . . . women . . . money. . . . Winter never passes. Look, everything's all over by midnight. How can an artist dream his dreams here, how can he live? . . . And so the years roll by, and one morning you wake up. . . . You were a boy, and you're a boy no longer." However, Leopoldo has little artistic talent —the dialogue we hear from his play is filled with romantic claptrap. (Sample: "*Frida*: In the silence of your desert, do you not hear a voice calling you? *Roberto*: Your voice, Frida? *Frida*: No, God's!") Instead of taking a serious and practical view of his art, Leopoldo speaks of waiting for "poetic inspiration," while dallying with the next-door maid. He seems to enjoy striking the attitude of an artist ("Let's go to Africa," he says at one point, "and hunt like Hemingway") rather than actually *being* an artist. In short, Leopoldo is sensitive but also somewhat superficial. His ideas about life are derived, not from life, but from literature.

The youngest of the *vitelloni*, Moraldo is also the most humane and the most responsive to simple, natural beauty. When the other men taunt an aging prostitute in the street, Moraldo attempts to make them desist. In the course of the film, Moraldo grows increasingly sympathetic towards his sister and increasingly critical of the unfaithful Fausto. When the picture opens, Moraldo is gazing absorbedly at the sky; turning to his friends, he exclaims: "Look how beautiful it is out here!" And later in the same scene, during a rainstorm, he observes: "It's just beautiful outside. . . . Like the end of the world. It's beautiful!" Moraldo is always the last of the *vitelloni* to leave the deserted nighttime streets. Quiet and withdrawn, he enjoys listening to the whistle of a train and the tolling of church bells. When Fausto and Sandra leave for Rome on their honeymoon, Moraldo is the only one to remain on the platform, staring after them with a faraway expression on his face. Throughout the picture, Fellini prepares the viewer for Moraldo's eventual departure. At one point, early in the action, Moraldo looks up at the starry sky and, hearing the distant train, remarks to himself: "Suppose I left, too?" Just then, a boy appears and Moraldo engages him in conversation:

> MORALDO: Where are you going at three A.M.?
> THE BOY: I work at the railroad station.
> MORALDO: What do you mean, *work*?
> THE BOY: I work at the station.
> MORALDO: Well . . . tell me, are you happy?
> THE BOY: Oh, it's pretty good.

Later in the film, Moraldo again meets the railroad boy. Together they stare at the stars.

> THE BOY: There must be people on Sirius, like here.
> MORALDO: Well, I don't think so.
> THE BOY: Would you go live there?
> MORALDO: Sure.
> THE BOY: Oh stop it.
> MORALDO: Sure I would.
> THE BOY: Coming along with me to the station?
> MORALDO: Sure, I'm coming along.

At the end, Moraldo decides that he must leave his home town in order to find some work that will give meaning to his life.

> THE BOY: Where are you going?
> MORALDO: I don't know. I'm just leaving.
> THE BOY: But what are you going to do?

I VITELLONI: *In the middle of the night, Moraldo encounters a boy who is going to work.*

MORALDO: I don't know. I have to leave. I'm just going away.
THE BOY: Tell me. Were you happy here?

Moraldo remains silent, and the train pulls away, taking the young man with it.

Structurally, *I Vitelloni* follows a clearly defined pattern: a scene or action engendering an illusion in one or more characters is followed by a scene or action in which reality destroys the illusion. At the beginning of the film, there is a beauty contest at the Kursaal, a local nightclub. In an atmosphere of much gaiety, Sandra becomes Miss Siren of 1953: people crowd around, offering congratulations, assuring her that she has an enviable future ahead as a movie star. Suddenly she faints, however, and a doctor is summoned. One look from the man to Sandra's mother is enough to reveal that the girl is pregnant. Now Sandra will have to marry Fausto, and the only way she will be able to get into the movies will be to purchase tickets for two. When Fausto and Sandra return from their honeymoon, the bridegroom is so happy that he performs a mambo in the street: he still exudes an air of holiday irresponsibility, of romantic escape from care. In the next scene, Fausto's father punctures his fantasy by getting him a job in the religious store. "Frankly, I really need a boy, or a handyman," Michele says. And Fausto—who stands much taller than Sandra's father and Michele, and who is dressed in the latest fashion—is forced to don a smock that makes his nose turn up. "What's the matter?" exclaims Michele. "It's clean. I just had it washed."

Similarly, the scene depicting the carnival at Bertucci Hall opens with the orchestra playing a mambo. Everyone is drinking and dancing and laughing. On the following morning, however, Alberto staggers drunkenly through the piazza and discovers that Olga is running off with a married man, leaving him as the sole support of their mother. Earlier in the picture this development is prefigured skillfully by Fellini in a minor variation of the pattern. On the beach, Alberto, in a carefree mood, is shown playfully chasing a dog; but the game ends unhappily when the animal leads Alberto behind a shack, where the romantic dependent finds Olga talking surreptitiously with her lover. In like manner, the scene involving the appearance of the actor Natali at the Bertucci Theater commences with music and singing and dancing girls. The *vitelloni* are very excited, particularly Leopoldo, whose play has been read by the "great actor." Afterward, Leopoldo's hopes are smashed when the homosexual Natali reveals less interest in the play than in the playwright. Seeking to lure Leopoldo down to the deserted beach, Natali smiles: "Are you possibly afraid of me? . . . Poldy! Poldy! Where are you going? I was just fooling. Come here. Poldy!" Without answering, and with a bitter and disgusted expression on his face, Leopoldo heads back for town, clutching the play to his chest.

At certain points throughout the action, Fellini uses an off-screen narrator who speaks for the *vitelloni* as a group. For example, the narrator introduces each of the *vitelloni* at the beginning of the film as the camera reveals them in a characteristic posture. Sometimes the narrator functions like a Greek chorus by commenting on the theme: "What else can we find to do? Another day's over, and we can only go back home, just as we do evening after evening." At other times, the speaker's voice bridges transitions in time, providing a link between sequences: "And one fine day, when we'd almost forgotten all about him . . ."; and on the screen, Fausto appears, back from Rome. In at least one instance, Fellini cleverly juxtaposes the narrator's words with a visual image. We hear: "So Fausto was forgiven for stealing the statue, and he settled down to looking leisurely for a new job," while we see Fausto shooting pool with the other *vitelloni*. On occasion, however, Fellini's use of the narrator device becomes obtrusive and redundant—such as when we are told: "By now the seaside is deserted" or "Fausto begins to be frightened," when it is plain as plain on the screen that the seaside is deserted and that Fausto is frightened.

Fellini is expert at involving the audience in the actions of his characters through imaginative use of the camera. During the beauty contest at the Kursaal, for instance, there are numerous quick cuts and pans and tilts, together with many tracking shots, in order to project the excited mood of the crowd. Time—like

Fellini's camera—moves swiftly here. Afterward, in the scene
between Fausto and his father, the camera is largely stationary.
Once again, Fellini correlates his visual technique with the emotional and thematic context of the scene. Where the illusions of
the characters prevail, the camera is dynamic; where reality
takes the place of illusion, the camera remains static. In *I Vitelloni*
clock time is not observed.

A different kind of "subjectivity" is conveyed by Fellini when
he has the crowd encircle Sandra and stare directly into the
camera—that is, directly into Sandra's face (and the viewer's)—
just before she faints. When Sandra gets married, the camera
tracks down the aisle, past the faces of the spectators, as though
it were part of the bridal procession. Likewise, when Sandra
hears that Fausto has stolen the angel, the camera trucks quickly
in—then out—in order to suggest her shock and dismay. By
making his camera an active participant in the story, Fellini
forces the viewer into a closer identification with his characters.

Perhaps the most brilliant example of subjective shooting
occurs at the end. As Moraldo leaves town, Fellini shows us the
young man's thoughtful face: four quickly edited shots reveal
Leopoldo, Riccardo, Alberto, and Fausto and Sandra, all sleeping in their beds, and all shown, as it were, from Moraldo's point
of view. Since the transition from "objective" to "subjective"
is facilitated by having the camera move like the train itself
through the *vitelloni's* rooms—in other words, as though the
moving train, the moving camera, and Moraldo's stream of consciousness were all one (unified by the sound of the train
whistle over the shots)—the basically "realistic" surface of the
film remains undisturbed.

It would be impossible to discuss all the ways in which Fellini
makes use of the camera to convey meaning symbolically in
I Vitelloni. While the credits are being shown there is a shot of
a piazza at night, followed by shots of the five *vitelloni* walking
arm-in-arm, toward nowhere. Right from the start, then, an
atmosphere of emptiness and loneliness is adumbrated. However,
even though the predominant mood of the film is one of spiritual
poverty—accentuated by the bleak light in the day scenes, and

the wind and rain in the night scenes—the picture ends at dawn with Moraldo's escape from his fellow *vitelloni*. The last shot of the film is an image of the railroad boy walking along one rail, deftly attempting to balance himself without toppling off. The symbolism seems clear: In order to succeed in life, Moraldo will have to be as careful and as determined as the boy, whose cap, earlier in the film, the young man jokingly placed on his own head.

On the deserted beach where the lost *vitelloni* wander aimlessly, strange-looking structures—apparently also without purpose—jut up out of the sand, seeming to mirror the ineffectuality of the five men. When Fausto and Moraldo steal the angel, the latter's arm protrudes stiffly from underneath the sack in their wheelbarrow, as though it were protesting against this indignity. Later the idiot Giudizio—who assists Fausto and Moraldo in their attempt to sell the statue—removes the angel from the wheelbarrow and carries it out onto the beach, where he places it on a mound of sand, the better to gaze at it with adoration. As is frequently the case in Fellini's films, the idiot is nearer to genuine feeling than the more "normal" and intelligent characters. It is also interesting to note that the image of the angel resting on the sand calls to mind the image of those structures which looked so peculiar and out of place on the beach earlier in the picture. Is Fellini "saying" that the "death of God" has left modern man without the capacity to love, an alien in the natural world, lacking a proper function and a meaningful goal?

"I was portraying, not, as people have claimed, the death throes of a decadent social class," Fellini has remarked of *I Vitelloni*, "but a certain torpor of the soul." True enough, there is "social consciousness" in the film. Whereas neorealist directors like Visconti and De Sica stressed economic conditions, Fellini has always concentrated on the problem of boredom. With the rise of modern industrial society, man's days have grown progressively regimented and routinized; for most people in our era, work has lost its significance, and leisure time offers neither true relaxation nor a worthwhile compensatory meaning. "In a sense the *vitelloni* are right not to want to settle down," Suzanne

Budgen argues. "[Fellini] knows that organized life as we know it has no room for the quality of ease and freedom and companionship which he has shown in his young men. He sees that they are not even adequate in their family lives, and that they must alter if they are to survive; that they must accept a procrustean diminution as individuals before they can be enlarged into social beings." There is some validity in what Miss Budgen writes. Fellini is certainly aware that contemporary forms of social organization tend to destroy man's ability to experience life with joy, that custom too often deadens the soul and results in an impoverished, inhuman existence. Still, Fellini's art remains more complex than Miss Budgen—who overstates the case in her defense of the *vitelloni*—allows.

Consider the scene in which the men search for Sandra. Delighted by the countryside and the singing of a bird, the *vitelloni* suddenly cease looking for Fausto's wife and baby:

RICCARDO: Hear the wren?
ALBERTO: What do you mean "wren"? That's a robin.
RICCARDO: What do you mean a "robin"? The robin makes a noise like this.
ALBERTO: How does the robin make a noise?

As Miss Budgen sees it, this scene "is presented, not as a sign of irresponsibility alone, but as an instance of that naturalness and spontaneity which are a part of [the men's] moral rightness." Granted that there is a modicum of truth in Miss Budgen's observation, her interpretation as a whole misses the point. The *vitelloni* are superficial; human relationships are more important than the singing of birds, and life should add up to more than "sleeping, eating, fornicating." In the same scene, Sandra's wet nurse offers the *vitelloni* food:

RICCARDO: What were you saying about some eggs?
WET NURSE: Yes.
RICCARDO: With salami?
WET NURSE: Yes.
RICCARDO: Alberto! . . . With salami.
ALBERTO: With salami?
RICCARDO: Yes.

And immediately, the *vitelloni* make a dash for the kitchen.

Fellini laughs with his characters, and he compels the audience to laugh with them, too. All the same, the artist does not flinch from judging the *vitelloni*; though he scorns preachment, he nevertheless assumes a moral stance. With Chekhov (at least as interpreted by Gorky in his *Reminiscences**), the creator of *I Vitelloni* "says": "You live badly, my friends. It is shameful to live like that." Fundamentally, the problem that besets Fellini's characters, here and elsewhere in his work, is man's inability to love. "Carnival will be better this year," Riccardo says. "The people are more anxious to have a good time." However, the illusion of "a good time" is always superseded by the reality of boredom. The unloving Fausto, surrounded by crucifixes and statues, attempts to seduce Giulia in the back of her shop; but the simple idiot Giudizio, who respects the holy and the mysterious, reveals true love for what the angel represents. Perhaps the closest Fellini comes to putting his meaning into words occurs in the scene where Michele fires Fausto: "[Giulia and I] are not young any more," the store owner says, "but we get along fine together. We have only a few friends, so we're almost always at home in the evenings. . . . Sometimes we even play cards! That should make you laugh, shouldn't it? Playing cards? Or else I read a book and my wife knits. And we don't bore each other. You know why? Because we love each other."

Because we love each other. As the reader has been told often enough, modern society has alienated man from nature, from the means of production, from God, from other men, and even from himself. In spite of that, and until the millennium arrives (Fellini seems to be telling us), man must somehow find a way to resist dehumanization. Man must continue to believe in the possibility of a Moraldo finding some form of meaningful work, but at the same time still retaining his capacity to enjoy the sight of a beautiful sky. And finally, as Fellini once put it to Gideon Bachmann, man must also continue to "desire to have a real, authentic relationship with another person."

---

* Maxim Gorky, *Reminiscences of Tolstoy, Chekhov, and Andreyev* (New York: The Viking Press, 1959) p. 85.

With good reason, *I Vitelloni* remains one of Fellini's most highly regarded films: it has a cast of unforgettable characters, a rhythmic structure, an expressive visual approach, symbolic richness, and a profound theme. A "torpor of the soul" is, indeed, what *I Vitelloni* is all about. But, though the picture remains open-ended and undidactic, Fellini suggests at least a partial remedy for the spiritual apathy from which most of his characters suffer. Unless he cares for others, man is an animal; unless he cares for others, man is bored—neither work nor play has any value for him. "All our anguish and mistakes occur," Fellini has said, "when there is no love."

CHAPTER 6

La Strada

La Strada *is really the complete catalog of my*
mythical world, a dangerous representation of my
identity, undertaken without precautions.... The
point of departure of that film, apart from the
spectacle of nature and the fascination of the
gypsylike travels, was the story of an enlightenment,
of the shaking of a conscience, through the sacrifice
of another creature.

—FEDERICO FELLINI

La Strada (The Road), which was made in 1954, opens by the
sea. In the pale sunlight children shout across the dunes to
Gelsomina (Giulietta Masina), telling her to come home.
Zampanò (Anthony Quinn), an itinerant strongman, wants to
buy Gelsomina, a young girl, for 10,000 lire so that she can
help him in his act. Once before the impoverished mother had
sold a daughter to Zampanò, but that girl died on the road; now
destitution again forces the woman to surrender a child, perhaps
to the same fate as the previous one. From the start, Fellini visually contrasts the two main characters of his film: Gelsomina
—blonde, diminutive, pixy-faced, humble in bearing; Zampanò
—dark, huge, glowering, arrogant in demeanor. On one level, *La*

Strada is a fable about Beauty and the Beast; in this case, however, Gelsomina's beauty is interior, not exterior, and it is Beauty who loves the Beast, not the other way round—at least for most of the picture. Before leaving the place of her birth, Gelsomina turns and kneels in the direction of the sea, in a silent farewell communion with those waters that throughout the film are identified with her. Revealing his usual sullen expression, the strongman watches the simple-minded girl on her knees. Then Gelsomina climbs in the back of Zampanò's motorcycle-driven trailer and the two depart on what is to become a spiritual odyssey for both of them.

Zampanò's main act consists of breaking an iron chain with the muscles of his chest, a performance that impresses not only the country people along the road but also Gelsomina. Over and over in the course of the picture, Zampanò utters the same words ("Sensitive souls are advised not to look. In Milan, Ettore Montagna lost his sight through this trick, since there is an enormous strain on the optic nerve . . ."), struts in a circle—stomach in, chest out—waving his chain in the air, prior to bursting its links by inflating his lungs. The repetition of this performance underlines Zampanò's monotonous, self-enclosed manner of existence. He is an animal, and he treats other people as though they were animals. On their first evening together, Gelsomina cooks soup that is so bad even she can't eat it; although Zampanò devours the soup—as he devours everything—he still calls it "slop for pigs." At the beginning of the film, Zampanò assures Gelsomina's mother that he "can even teach a dog to perform." Now he proceeds to teach Gelsomina. Her job is to announce his act by intoning: "Zam-pan-ò is here!" followed by drumbeats as the chain is broken. Unfortunately, Gelsomina is not a fast learner. The audience laughs at the attempts of Zampanò to make the girl understand the simple requirements of her role; but when the lout proceeds to strike Gelsomina on the leg with a switch in order to make her concentrate, the laughter dies. What starts like a kind of Abbott and Costello vaudeville turn, then, ends far from comedy. Just as Fellini juxtaposes beauty and bestiality, just so he alternates gaiety and

LA STRADA: *The Fool taunts Zampanò as Gelsomina looks on.*

sadness, the complex structure of his film moving from the serio-comic (up to about the middle of the picture) to the serious (there are few laughs in the second half of La Strada).

Fellini does not indulge in fancy camera work or bizarre compositions. Whenever he moves his camera, the movement is well motivated in terms of mood, action, and theme. For example, on their first night together Zampanò tells Gelsomina to sleep with him in the trailer. She wants to sleep outside. He repeats his order. The camera-eye has been recording the scene impassively in front of the motorcycle. The characters step out of sight and start around to the back of the trailer. Slowly, the camera glides forward, makes a turn to the left, and gazes downward at the mattress. Zampanò pushes Gelsomina roughly inside the trailer and closes the flap on the tarpaulin, causing the screen to go dark. This incident remains one of the few times in the film when the viewer becomes aware of the camera. Since Gelsomina is frightened, the camera seems hesitant, unwilling to look at what is to follow; the camera's eventual intrusion—with its serpentine downward motion—is both intimate and faintly ominous.

The structure of La Strada can be described as episodic. As Zampanò and Gelsomina journey from town to town, characters are introduced and then seen no more—which is lifelike, but unlike plotted films, where characters who appear at the beginning must also function in the middle and reappear at the end. The episodes are unified thematically; a scene that at first sight might strike the viewer as a digression later reveals its relevance to the overall design. Although Fellini structures his action vertically by concentrating on character development and idea, he also provides horizontal movement or story interest. Indeed, it is almost impossible to separate vertical and horizontal movement, or character exploration and story, so closely has Fellini woven together the various elements of his picture.

Like all his films, Fellini's La Strada is open in structure, thus reflecting his view of life as a mystery filled with unpredictable possibilities. Throughout the movie, Fellini alternates a day scene with a night scene, a rhythmic pattern that finds its musical parallel in the recurrence of Nino Rota's famous tune. A scene enacted in bleak, sometimes cold sunlight gives way to a scene involving an empty street or a market place at night, while the music comes and goes throughout; hence, the score not only augments the happy-sad thematic approach but also functions as a structural device for unifying the whole. The result is an exquisite blending of realism (the location shooting, the numerous nonprofessionals in the cast, the holes in Zampanò's sweater and pants) and a kind of "poetic," "lyrical" expressionism or surrealism (the numerous symbols, the fablelike quality of the action, the stylized conception of the three chief personages).

Fellini rarely puts his meaning into words; when he does, as we shall see, it is generally because certain ideas cannot be expressed in any other way. However, through his associational manner of linking scenes, Fellini not only gives his form continuity but he also supplies nonverbal commentary. After the screen goes black in the trailer, for instance, there is a scene in which Gelsomina wakes up in the night and begins to cry. Zampanò—his sexual appetite satisfied—is sleeping. Even though she has been taken against her will, even though her body has been used without respect for her person, Gelsomina stops weeping momentarily to gaze fondly at the unconscious male who has somehow, in spite of himself, aroused her love and inspired her hope. But the next shot makes clear how little Gelsomina can really expect from the future. It is the following day; and on the screen we see the strongman with a chain stretched across his chest: food, drink, breaking the chain, sex, sleep— Zampanò knows only these physical activities and needs.

Evening. The couple visit a café. Zampanò is in his customary surly mood, but Gelsomina remains delighted with the experience. When Zampanò, before eating, pokes a toothpick around in his mouth, Gelsomina imitates her hero; likewise, she mops her plate greedily with a crust of bread as he does, and she even tries to drink as much wine as the strongman. To no avail. Zampanò ignores the clownish little creature who shares his mean existence, constantly foiling her attempts at intimacy with disdain:

GELSOMINA: Where do you come from?
ZAMPANÒ: From my part of the country.
GELSOMINA: Where were you born?
ZAMPANÒ: (Sneering) In my father's house.

Drunk now, Zampanò notices a buxom, red-headed woman across the room and calls her over to their table. During this scene the strongman shows off his muscles and makes the woman laugh, treating her in a way he never treats the faithful wretch who assists him in his act. All the same, Gelsomina fails to understand what is happening, fails to grasp the fact that Zampanò intends to spend the night with the fat redhead; so she naïvely laughs along with the other two, with no trace of jealousy apparent on her innocent countenance. However, in order for the viewer to see the scene from Gelsomina's perspective—or, rather, to see what Gelsomina would see if she had eyes to see—Fellini shoots the action partly from her viewpoint. The camera-eye does not actually "see" what Gelsomina sees; nevertheless, although her skull remains visible on the screen, the shot is clearly angled from her point of view, since the camera is situated just in back of her head. Outside the café, Zampanò helps the other woman onto his motorcycle and instructs the confused Gelsomina to wait behind for him, "But where are you going?" she cries. There is no reply, only the sound of the motorcycle fading into the night.

Dissolve. It is dark and quiet . . . and Gelsomina is still waiting for Zampanò. As she sits at the curb with a morose expression, a horse suddenly emerges and noisily clipclops past. The appearance of this stray, riderless animal has occasioned much comment. John Russell Taylor, for example, observes: "the effect is positively surrealistic: totally arbitrary, yet giving an instant visual reinforcement to the mood of the scene. The lost horse might well be a figment of Gelsomina's imagination, an image of her own state. But it is also a real horse, and its appearance here at this time is not impossible, only mildly peculiar." Is Fellini "saying" that Gelsomina is like a horse without a rider? Certainly the strongman treats her no better than he would a horse. In *La Dolce Vita*, Marcello—who has some traits in common with Zampanò—rides on the back of a woman who is down on all fours. During a later scene in *La Strada*, Zampanò says to a woman with whom he has sexual relations: "Do you always eat standing up like a horse?" In the same scene, Gelsomina worries about a sick horse; and near the end of the film, just before he deserts her, Zampanò tells Gelsomina that she too is sick. The sequence in which Zampanò leaves Gelsomina to wait for him while he sleeps with the redhead (who, not surprisingly, robs him of all his money), together with the shot of the riderless horse, not only rehearses the final desertion but also suggests another scene in *La Dolce Vita*. In the later film, Emma accuses Marcello of not being able to love; he concurs—but argues that he does not want to spend his entire life caring for her. After slapping Emma, Marcello pushes her out of his car. Hurt and angry, she tells him: "You've lost the only thing of value in life—a woman who really loves you. Someday you'll be old. There'll be no more women. And you'll die alone like a dog!" Later Marcello comes back for Emma— who, like Gelsomina, has waited for her man on the road—but the couple have no future together. The situation is the same in *La Strada*.

Morning. A child sits on the curb beside the petulant Gelsomina. Also beside her is a plate of food, which a compassionate woman has left for Gelsomina, but which she has not touched. When the woman returns, she informs Gelsomina that a man is sleeping in a field down the road, near a moto-trailer. Happily, Gelsomina returns to her brutal master. Dancing lightly across the desolate landscape, she suddenly pauses before a single bare tree. A child passes, watching her. With arms outstretched, a smile lighting up her small puffy face, Gelsomina imitates the tree. A boy approaches. "The dog died in there," he informs her, pointing to an area beyond a fence. Standing before the dog's burial ground, Gelsomina looks inside, wonderment evident in her expression. She listens for something. For what? Gelsomina communicates intuitively with the sea, with trees, even with the spirit of a dead dog. She is witness to a reality beyond the one that can be seen or touched. Yet, at the same time, she is very much a part of that natural world whose inner being she mysteriously apprehends. Because she longs to see the various manifestations of the Good—be it love or a tree—take root and grow, she plants tomato seeds by the side of the road, even though Zampanò plans to move on again. To her astonished question: "Are we leaving already?," Zampanò contemptuously replies: "Think we're going to stay here 'till your tomatoes come up? *Tomatoes!*" The brute's lack of understanding remains abysmal.

Fade in to a shot of an open area where a wedding celebration is taking place. On one side there is a long banquet table with happy people eating and drinking; on the other side Zampanò and Gelsomina are performing. Seated on the ground, Zampanò is beating a drum, while Gelsomina, wearing a bowler hat and a clown's makeup, goes through a simple dance number. Except for some children watching Gelsomina in the background, the act goes largely unnoticed. A man offers Gelsomina a glass of wine; she takes a sip, then unselfishly passes it along to Zampanò. During this scene, Fellini again moves his camera to advantage. There is a long tracking shot the length of the banquet table: faces of happy celebrants, a priest eating, wine glasses raised, confetti, the bride and groom; cut to a momentary shot of other celebrants again—followed by a shot of Gelsomina and Zampanò, set apart from the others. The visual juxtaposition of the bride and Gelsomina speaks for itself; the contrast between the boisterous fun along the table and the dreary routine of Gelsomina's life with Zampanò requires no verbal underlining. It tells us something about Fellini's tact that he does not starkly play off the image of the bride with a shot of Gelsomina, but instead separates the two images with a brief shot of a few guests in order to convey the relational nature of his editing in a more subtle manner.

Zampanò and Gelsomina are called by a woman to the farmhouse to eat. The children who have been watching Gelsomina perform intercept her, however, and lead her around to the side of the building and up a narrow flight of stairs. Skillfully employing a subjective camera, Fellini takes the audience (via identification with Gelsomina's field of vision) along a series of dimly lighted corridors. Shot of a tiny boy in a black cape; he looks made up to resemble a priest, or perhaps a magician. An air of the uncanny suffuses the scene. And when Gelsomina is led into a dark room, the subjective camera intensifies the viewer's sensation of entering the unknown. In a large bed, propped up on pillows, sits an idiot boy named Oswaldo; he stares at Gelsomina with a frightened gaze. The children want her to amuse the lad. Yet Gelsomina's imitation of a bird only seems to increase Oswaldo's fright. Tentatively, she steps closer to the bed, exchanging a silent, wide-eyed gaze with the strange boy opposite her. All at once, a nun enters the room and angrily chases Gelsomina and the children away.

As noted in an earlier chapter, the scene involving Oswaldo is based on an experience from Fellini's boyhood when he visited his grandmother in Gambettola. The film-maker has provided his own interpretation of the episode:

> I probably used it to give Gelsomina an exact awareness of solitude. There is a feast at the farm, and Gelsomina, who ultimately is a creature who likes to be in the company of other people, and who wants to take part in the singing and in the general gaiety, is led off by this host of children who, shouting, take her to see the sick boy. The apparition of this creature who is so isolated, and a prey to delirium—and who thus has an extremely mysterious dimension—it seems to me that uniting him in a close-up with Gelsomina, who comes right next to him and who looks at him with curiosity, underlines with rather great suggestive power Gelsomina's own solitude.

While Gelsomina has been making her discovery of solitude, Zampanò has been making the acquaintance of the woman who called the performers to eat. Positioned outside the kitchen, Zampanò and the woman are discoursing on sex and swallowing their food ravenously. (This is the woman to whom Zampanò remarks: "Do you always eat standing up like a horse?") The woman has buried two husbands; she would now like to give Zampanò some suits and a hat left behind by her first mate, in exchange for some lovemaking on the part of the strongman.

Gelsomina joins them; but when she tries to explain to Zampanò about Oswaldo, the brute ignores her. As he does so often, Fellini here makes use of contrast. Gelsomina's encounter with the mysterious boy represents a discovery of her own loneliness: she yearns for Zampanò to recognize her as a person, to genuinely share his life with her—not merely to exploit her in his act and to use her body for sexual purposes. To be sure, the farm woman also knows solitude; like Zampanò, however, all she thinks about are her physical needs (stuffing her face with macaroni, for example, she refers to sex as a "sweet"). Finally, Zampanò disappears with the woman, leaving Gelsomina to wait for him once more. . . .

Dusk. The wedding party is over, except for one last couple, still dancing to the accompaniment of a remaining musician. A lone tree is prominent in the composition. Next Fellini reveals Gelsomina, from within a barn, studying the scene we have just witnessed. The tree outside reminds the viewer of the single tree that Gelsomina imitated in the previous sequence; later in the film, as Zampanò's moto-trailer journeys down a road, a bare tree again appears in the distance. The lonely Gelsomina and the motif of a bare, isolated tree are what Kenneth Burke calls "equations." Humming the tune that is likewise associated throughout the film with her, Gelsomina asks Zampanò to teach her to play it on the trumpet. The strongman is too absorbed, however, in trying on his newly acquired clothes to reply. Preening himself in a pin-striped suit and snapping the brim down on his fedora, Zampanò mutters scornfully: "Women!" the way he had previously muttered: "Tomatoes!" Angry at Zampanò's refusal to respond, Gelsomina strides back and forth across the barn—until she falls into a deep hole. Zampanò is amused but Gelsomina obstinately decides to spend the night below. Although the scene is played in a seriocomic fashion, Gelsomina's confinement in the ground represents one of the numerous ways Fellini foreshadows her death.

Dissolve to morning. As though reborn, Gelsomina removes the clothes Zampanò had given her and proceeds to set off in her original garb on a journey by herself, thus leaving the sleeping brute (in the clothes the farm woman has given *him*) to seek another slave for his act. . . . Shot of Gelsomina sitting by the side of the road, examining a bug with curiosity and wonder. Suddenly three musicians appear out of nowhere, marching along in a single file, and Gelsomina, stirred by their spirited playing, jumps up and follows them. The procession involving the three musicians and Gelsomina gives way in the next scene to a conventional religious procession. Shots of a bishop coldly and mechanically blessing the enthusiastic faithful. Shots of the crowd. Shots of a huge cross and other traditional symbols. When Fellini shows us Gelsomina, who is thrilled by the event, he keeps his camera up close and moving with her; hence we tend to identify with Gelsomina, we experience her own emotions, we too are caught up in the excitement. In one long shot Fellini reveals the procession on the right-hand side of the screen, while on the left-hand side he presents a sign reading: BAR. The film-maker is fond of such polarities (consider, for example, the opening of *La Dolce Vita*, wherein the statue of Christ suspended from a helicopter remains juxtaposed to bikini-clad girls sunbathing on a rooftop). In *La Strada* "procession" equals "quest for love and spiritual meaning" (the Gelsomina motif), whereas "BAR" equals "drunkenness, brawling, and casual sex" (the Zampanò motif). When Gelsomina and the other members of the procession enter a church, Fellini again uses a subjective camera, a visual strategy that calls to mind the experience at the farm when the children led Gelsomina into the mysterious room of Oswaldo. By using the same kind of camera technique in both scenes, Fellini links up the two events thematically.

But if Gelsomina learned something about solitude from her meeting with Oswaldo, she is not blessed with a similar discovery upon stepping inside the church. From a low-angle subjective shot of the church interior, Fellini dissolves to the next scene: a shot of Il Matto (Richard Basehart), or The Fool, on a tight-rope above a piazza at night. "In a moment," a woman working with the acrobat says into a loudspeaker, "Il Matto will perform the most dangerous of his stunts. Sitting forty meters above the earth, he will eat a dish of spaghetti." Gelsomina looks up to

God, but the answer to her prayer comes in the next scene when she again looks up . . . this time at Il Matto. Fellini has said that The Fool is "Jesus." And not surprisingly, critics have managed to ferret out the "Christ symbolism": suspended high overhead, the acrobat is equipped with angel's wings; in one scene, he rides a donkey, just as Jesus did on Palm Sunday; also like Christ, The Fool predicts his own death; and when Zampanò finally kills the equilibrist, he drags the corpse over the ground in a cruciform manner. In religious art, Christ is never depicted with wings; still, one could argue that both Christ and angels are associated in a spiritual way.

Unlike Christ, The Fool does not willingly sacrifice his life for Zampanò; Gelsomina performs that function, though partly as a result of what she learns from The Fool. Christ provoked his executioners, and Il Matto torments Zampanò; however, Christ was motivated by the desire to show men how to live a more authentic existence, whereas The Fool taunts Zampanò out of irrational malice. The "Christ symbolism" is present, then, but it appears in an ambiguous way. Near the end of the film, just before his recognition scene, Zampanò shouts: "Ho bisogno di nessuno"; but twice in the picture, Il Matto repeats the same words to Gelsomina: "I don't need anyone." In short, Fellini avoids a too neat symbolic dovetailing of Christ and Il Matto. Yet, as noted, the link *is* there.

Fellini suggests that Jesus must be sought outside the Church, that in the present age Christ appears to men under different manifestations, even in the guise of a circus performer. ("Today, we are finished with the Christian myth, and await a new one," Fellini observed to Tom Burke in 1970. "Maybe the myth is LSD? And the new Christ comes to us in this form?") As suggested previously, Il Matto is associated with another fool—namely Oswaldo—in that Gelsomina learns something from both of them. Of course, Gelsomina is a simpleton herself; and Il Matto is not really a fool—he merely plays the part of one. Furthermore, there is a sense in which Fellini's method of representation remains solidly traditional: individuals who have truly sought to live according to the teachings of Christ—that is to

LA STRADA: *Gelsomina and Zampanò perform for a crowd.*

say, individuals who have taken seriously such injunctions as: "Thou shalt love thy neighbor as thyself"—have frequently been called "fools for Christ." And Fellini has always had a weakness for such people. Clearly, then, the symbolism involving Il Matto in La Strada cannot be reduced to a single pat explanation.*

Following the scene in which Gelsomina sees The Fool for the first time, Fellini presents the gloomy square after the performers and the crowd have gone. Scraps of paper blow fitfully in front of an ancient fountain; looking feverish, Gelsomina pats a few drops of water on her brow. Some men, who are huddled nearby in the darkness, watch her; one of them grabs at her, muttering the word "balmy," but she slips away from him. Suddenly Zampanò appears. Descending from his motorcycle, he slaps Gelsomina several times and forces her into the back of his trailer. Then, gazing belligerently at the onlookers, he asks: "Any objections?" No reply. "That's what I thought," he growls. And off he goes, taking Gelsomina with him once more. . . .

Daylight. Zampanò and Gelsomina are discovered in the act of signing up for work in Colombaioni's Circus. Here Gelsomina also finds The Fool again, for he too is now a member of the troupe. Gelsomina is delighted with the acrobat (who plays a tiny violin with a cigarette fastened to its end) but she remains dismayed by his habit of teasing the vicious Zampanò. When Gelsomina asks the strongman what The Fool has against him, he replies: "I don't know." Nor can his tormentor offer a rational motive: "I can't help it," Il Matto confesses. "Zampanò's such a brute!" Unmindful of the danger, The Fool heckles

---

* The following remarks by Fellini seem worth quoting in the present context: "One day I met an angel who stretched out his hand to me. I followed him, but after a short time I left him and went back. He stopped and waited at the same place for me. I see him again in difficult moments and he says to me, 'Wait, wait,' just as I do to everyone. I am afraid that when I call him one day, I shall not find him. It is the angel who has always awakened me from my spiritual torpor. When I was a boy he was the incarnation of an imaginary world, and then he became the symbol of a vital moral need."

Zampanò during his performance with the chain, in an attempt to disparage his strength; he also tries to use Gelsomina in his own act, much against Zampanò's wishes; and once, he even throws a bucket of water in the strongman's face. Finally, Zampanò pulls a knife on The Fool—which results in his being jailed, and in both of them being fired by Colombaioni.

While Zampanò is locked up, Gelsomina has a fateful conversation with The Fool. It is night, and around the couple the circus tents are half-dismantled, for Colombaioni has decided to leave town; Gelsomina, if she chooses, can remain with the circus. She asks The Fool for advice. And it is here, because of the abstract nature of his theme, that Fellini must rely on dialogue to carry the meaning:

> THE FOOL: So, go on, do it! It's a good chance to get rid of Zampanò, right? Can you imagine the look on his face tomorrow! He gets out and sees that you have gone off! . . . You want me to tell you whether or not you should stay with him. Isn't that so? . . . I can't tell you what to do.

Gelsomina explains how Zampanò, once before, had prevented her from leaving him.

> THE FOOL: Why didn't he let you leave? No, no, all things considered I wouldn't take you with me, even if you wanted me to. Who knows . . . maybe he loves you?
>
> GELSOMINA: Me, Zampanò?
>
> THE FOOL: Inside, he's a dog. He looks like a man . . . but when he tries to talk, he barks! . . . If you didn't stay with him, who would? I am ignorant, but I've read some books; so, you are not going to make me believe . . . and yet everything in the world is good for something. Take . . . take this stone, for example.
>
> GELSOMINA: Which one?
>
> THE FOOL: Uh, this one—it doesn't matter which. Even this little stone has a purpose.
>
> GELSOMINA: What's it good for?
>
> THE FOOL: Well, it's good for . . . How do I know? If I knew, you know who I would be?
>
> GELSOMINA: Who?

THE FOOL: God. He knows all. When you are born, when you die
... I don't know what it's good for, this pebble, but it certainly
has its use! If it were useless, then everything else would also
be useless—even the stars! That's the way things are, you know.
You too—you have your reason for being here. . . .

Convinced now that her purpose in life is to remain with
Zampanò—to teach him how to love, to teach him how to be
a human being—Gelsomina, the next morning, bids farewell to
The Fool as she waits outside the jail near the moto-trailer for
the strongman. Separating from Il Matto is painful for Gelsomina,
inasmuch as a spiritual affinity exists between the two (in some
scenes Fellini visually suggests this close relationship by match-
ing Gelsomina's striped jersey with The Fool's striped trousers),
but she naïvely believes that Zampanò will soon change in his
attitude towards her. When the brute appears on the sidewalk
beside her again, however, he has little to say and the two
resume their travels.

At about the midpoint in the structure, Fellini shows Zampanò
and Gelsomina pausing by the sea. "Where's my home?" Gelsomina asks. Wading into the water and nodding indifferently off
to the right, Zampanò answers: "Over there." Gelsomina smiles
warmly in the sun. "I wanted to leave you once," she tells him.
"But now *you're* my home." Zampanò only laughs. "Sure," he
says. "With me, at least you eat regularly." Gelsomina explodes.

This scene by the water reminds the viewer of the film's
opening, but it also prepares him for the ending.

Shot of Zampanò driving his motorcycle; behind him sit
Gelsomina and a beautiful nun. Dusk is closing in, fast. The
strongman asks the sister if he and his "wife" can stay at her
convent for the night; once there, the Mother Superior agrees
and the nun brings food to her guests. After eating, Zampanò tells
Gelsomina to play something for the sister on her trumpet. The
simple, haunting tune—so expressive of Gelsomina's soul—
delights the nun. Close-up of Zampanò's face. Anthony Quinn's
eminently plastic features reveal the complex feelings suddenly
experienced by this inarticulate boor. For the music seems to
touch something heretofore undiscovered in Zampanò: he looks

uneasy, humble, softened, bashful, embarrassed. Positive forces appear to be stirring inside him. However, perhaps Zampanò also feels threatened—not only by love, which would alter his whole personality, but also by jealousy, for he has always mocked Gelsomina and here she is playing in an admirable way. When the nun begins washing the dishes, Zampanò offers to do them for her, but she won't let him. When an elderly sister begins to split some wood, Zampanò jumps up and takes the ax away from her. "Here, let me do that," he says. "That's a man's work." Again, Zampanò's motivation would seem to be complex. By offering his help, the strongman reveals an embryonic goodness in his nature; yet, such physical activities as washing dishes and —especially—chopping wood also permit him to be the star of the show again. It is hard for a man like Zampanò to change.

Night. Zampanò and Gelsomina are bedding down in the convent granary. The composition—Zampanò in the foreground, lying on his side with his back to his "wife"; Gelsomina in the background, facing him across a space of ground—comprise a visual statement on the nature of the couple's relationship. Gelsomina yearns for Zampanò to take an interest in her but he only wants to sleep. "If I died," she asks, "would you be sorry?" He replies: "Why? You thinking of dying?" Exasperated, Gelsomina asks: "Don't you ever think?" He replies: "What's there to think about?" Perhaps hoping to stir him again, as well as to give vent to her feelings, Gelsomina blows on her trumpet; this time, however, Zampanò merely growls: "Knock it off!"

Later that night. As lightning flashes in the granary and thunder booms outside the convent, Gelsomina wakes up. She discovers Zampanò trying to squeeze his hand through some narrow bars in an attempt to steal a few silver hearts from the wall of the adjacent chapel. He tells her to help him. Shocked by his behavior, Gelsomina refuses. The brute strikes his tiny companion, who slides down against a wall, sobbing. The scene fades out.

Fade in on the following morning: Zampanò and Gelsomina are preparing to leave the convent. The strongman utters a pious, hypocritical farewell; however, Gelsomina is reluctant to leave this place in which women are happy because they feel useful.

"Do you want to stay with us?" the young nun asks. No reply . . .
for Gelsomina knows her fate. The nun attempts to console her:

> THE NUN: We change convents every two years, so as not to for-
> get what's most important. I mean, God. You see, we both
> travel. You follow your husband and I mine.
> GELSOMINA: Yes, each one has her own.

And once more, Gelsomina drives off with Zampanò . . .

Bright sunlight. On an empty country road Zampanò and
Gelsomina encounter The Fool, who is repairing a tire on his
car. Still angry with the equilibrist, the strongman punches him
several times, threatening him with more violence the next time
they meet. Unknown to Zampanò, his blows snapped The Fool's
head against the car, causing a fatal concussion. "He broke my
watch" are the only words The Fool can say, as he staggers
off and collapses on the ground, his fingers clawing spasmodic-
ally at the earth. Gelsomina becomes hysterical. Even Zampanò
is frightened. "Now I've done it!" he says. "Now I'm in for it!"
Dumping the body and the car down an embankment, Zampanò
quickly drives off with Gelsomina.

Significantly, the next shots—showing the couple in flight—
are enacted under a wintry sky, with bare trees shaking in the
wind and snow falling on distant mountain tops. Zampanò
attempts to continue with his act, but Gelsomina is unable to
utter: "Zam-pan-ò is here!" or to beat the drum; instead, she
constantly mutters: "The Fool is hurt! The Fool is hurt!" Gelsomina is distraught because she has seen the man she loves kill
another man—the very man who had given her a reason for
staying with the killer. Although her words attempt to belie the
reality of The Fool's death (he is merely "hurt," not dead), deep
down of course she knows the truth. At night, Gelsomina refuses
to allow Zampanò to sleep with her in the trailer; and in a
reversal of the earlier situation, Zampanò—who is not only afraid
that Gelsomina will report his crime but who is also ashamed of
the guilt he sees reflected in his companion's eyes—agrees to
sleep outside on the ground. Ten days go by. On a cold, sunny
afternoon, while the couple are sitting against a wall of rocks and
cooking soup, Gelsomina appears to return to her old self. "It's

about time," Zampanò sighs, with obvious relief. But then, off in the distance, very faintly, comes the sound of a dog barking. And suddenly, Gelsomina remembers the past: "The Fool is hurt!" she begins again. Frightened by her illness, Zampanò decides to go off alone. While Gelsomina sleeps, he gathers up his few belongings, stuffs some money beside the embers of their fire, and leaves her trumpet nearby. Pushing the moto-trailer down the road a distance, so as not to awaken Gelsomina, Zampanò vanishes from her life.

Five years pass. And we next find Zampanò working in a seaside town: his hair is gray; his stomach bulges. Although he has a new woman—a more attractive woman than Gelsomina —he doesn't seem to be happy with her. After one performance, he insists on going out for a walk, alone. On the street Zampanò hears someone humming the tune Gelsomina used to play on her trumpet; he stops, looks around expectantly—but the humming suddenly ceases. Disappointed, he moves on. Then, just as suddenly, the humming is resumed. Beyond a fence, Zampanò discovers a young woman hanging sheets on a line in the sun.

ZAMPANÒ: Where did you learn that tune?
THE WOMAN: From a little creature my father found on the beach one night. She was always playing it on her trumpet. We took her in for a time, but she was always crying, and she never ate.
ZAMPANÒ: What happened to her?
THE WOMAN: Oh, she died.

During this scene, Fellini's camera rarely shows us the woman. Either we hear her words as we watch the wash flapping in the breeze, or we watch a reaction close-up of Zampanò's face. For what is important here is not what the woman looks like, but what she is saying and the effect of what she is saying on Zampanò as he stands on the other side of the fence.

Elsewhere in the film, as noted, Gelsomina stands by a fence to see where a dog is buried. The reader will also recall that The Fool describes Zampanò as a dog who possibly loves Gelsomina, but who can't express his love except by barking. And it was the sound of a dog barking that made Gelsomina think of The Fool again, right before Zampanò decided to desert her.

It is impossible to wholly reduce the associations just catalogued to the dimensions of rational understanding. Certainly love and death are common to the scenes and dialogue involving fences, dogs, and Gelsomina; but Gelsomina communes with the spirit of a dead beast, whereas Zampanò grieves over the loss of a creature whom he had treated like a beast. (In one scene, Gelsomina plays a quail who is shot to death by Zampanò, for the amusement of the crowd.) On one level, Fellini seems to be "saying" that, ontologically, everything that has being should be regarded as holy. On another level, he appears to be "saying" that there is a chain of being, and that animals must not be confounded with persons.

Long shot of a carnival, later that afternoon. The strongman enters the arena and proceeds to plod listlessly through his routine with the chain. Medium shot of Zampanò, as he treads in a circle, his posure slack, his gaze turned inward. Long shot of the strongman, looking small amid his surroundings. . . . Fade out.

That night. Zampanò is discovered in a cafe, drunk and belligerent. The owner, with the help of some customers, succeeds in tossing the strongman outside. Enraged, Zampanò heaves some barrels at his assailants and, shouting "I don't need anyone," staggers down to the beach. What follows is surely one of the most powerful and cathartic moments in the history of the cinema. Zampanò wades into the water, reminiscent of the scene in the middle of the film when he stopped with Gelsomina at the sea. As observed in an earlier chapter, Fellini said: "In each of my films there is a character who goes through a crisis. It seems to me that the best atmosphere with which to underline this moment of crisis is a beach or a piazza at night; for silence, the emptiness of night, or the feeling that the sea is close by, brings the character into relief; this isolation allows him to be himself without any special effort." At the beginning of the film the children call Gelsomina, who is standing near the water, to come home. But isn't Gelsomina's real home the sea? And, by wading into the sea at the end of the film, isn't Zampanò trying to find Gelsomina again?

Turning, the strongman stumbles back up the beach and collapses on the sand, breathing heavily. Once more, Anthony Quinn's face portrays a number of reactions: Zampanò gazes out at the water, then up at the sky, and then—suddenly frightened by some thought—back out to the sea. What is going through his mind? Is he thinking of The Fool and Gelsomina, and the guilt he feels for having destroyed both of them? Is he afraid that God is looking down at him? Has the thought of committing suicide flashed through his consciousness? Pitching forward, Zampanò begins to weep, his hands clutching at the sand the way The Fool clutched at the earth when the strongman killed him. At last, Zampanò knows that he loved Gelsomina and needed her as much as she loved and needed him. Edouard de Laurot has remarked that Zampanò "is finally struck down by a cosmic terror and realizes, in his anguish, man's solitude in the face of Eternity."

Slowly, the camera recedes and rises, leaving Zampanò looking small and alone on the beach at night. The film begins and ends by the sea; but, though the structure is in one sense circular, the opening and closing are in sharp contrast. When we first meet Zampanò, he is standing tall and strong in the sunlight, arrogantly watching Gelsomina on her knees facing the water. When we take leave of Zampanò, however, he remains prostrate before the sea, no longer proud of his strength but humbly enduring his dark night of the soul.

Gilbert Salachas has declared that Zampanò's sorrow will be ephemeral, that "fleeting remorse is perhaps the furthest moral development a Fellini hero can make." Yet Fellini himself has said that La Strada is "the story of a man who discovers himself." One is free to speculate about the specific details of Zampanò's future (to the extent that it is legitimate to raise such questions about a character in a work of art); but the film-maker's own comments suggest that "enlightenment" and self-discovery" will lead to change. As Emile G. McAnany and Robert Williams observe: "The cry of Zampanò as he claws the sand at the end of the film is not that of a wounded beast but the anguish of a human being in his birth pangs." What Zampanò has done to

Gelsomina can be described as "tragic"; for no amount of tears will ever bring back the love that she once offered him and which he blindly trampled beneath his feet. Nonetheless, Gelsomina's "sacrifice" (as Fellini puts it) eventually becomes the means of Zampanò's "redemption," for man is useless and lonely before "Eternity" *only* if he does not know how to love everyone and everything in the universe. Such is the meaning of Gelsomina's life and death, and such is the lesson Zampanò has begun to grasp at that final moment that Aristotle called the *anagnorisis.** Of course, what helps to make *La Strada* so unforgettable is that Fellini subjects not only Zampanò but also the viewer to the same recognition.

"From a sentimental point of view," Fellini has remarked, "I can say that the film I am most attached to is *La Strada*. Above all, because I feel that it is my most representative film, the one that is the most autobiographical; for both personal and sentimental reasons, because it is the film that I had the greatest trouble in realizing and that gave me the most difficulty when the time came to find a producer. Gelsomina is, naturally, my favorite among all the characters." Elsewhere, Fellini has added that, of all the imaginary beings he has brought to the screen, he feels closest to the three principals in *La Strada*, "especially to Zampanò."

Winner of over fifty international awards (including the Grand Prize at the Venice Film Festival and the New York Film Critics and Academy Awards as the Best Foreign Film), *La Strada*, after twenty years remains, in my judgment, Fellini's masterpiece and one of the greatest films ever made by anyone, anywhere.

---

* Fellini's conception is Dostoevskian. In *The Brothers Karamazov*, Father Zossima preaches: "Love all God's creation, the whole and every grain of sand in it. Love every leaf, every ray of God's light. Love the animals, love the plants, love everything. If you love everything, you will perceive the divine mystery in things. Once you perceive it, you will begin to comprehend it better every day. And you will come at last to love the whole world with all-embracing love. . . . 'What is hell?' I maintain that it is the suffering of being unable to love." In his interview with Tullio Kezich, Fellini admits that Dostoevsky has always "fascinated" him. It is worth noting that the character of "the holy fool" also appears throughout the work of Dostoevsky.

CHAPTER 7

Il Bidone

*I don't like people who pretend to save
humanity with a picture.*

—FEDERICO FELLINI

Il Bidone (The Swindle),* which was released in 1955, opens
with a shot of a confidence man (a *bidone*) named "Baron"
Vargas seated beneath a tree in the country. Before him lies a
winding road. Presently a black limousine appears on the road
and stops near a small bridge, not far from Vargas. Three other
confidence men are in the car: Roberto (Franco Fabrizi), who
has on a chauffeur's uniform; Picasso (Richard Basehart); and
Augusto (Broderick Crawford), who, like Picasso, is wearing
an overcoat with the collar turned up.† When the men get out

---

* Released in the United States under the original Italian title.

† Fellini has said that in *Il Bidone* the character he feels closest to is
Augusto; and he has added that Zampanò (with whom the director also
identifies) and Augusto are "related." "But Augusto is guiltier," Fellini
explains. "He is the most dishonest because he is the most lucid." At first,
Fellini tried to get Humphrey Bogart to play Augusto, but the late actor was
not available. Fellini had never seen Crawford perform. "Thus," he says,
"I had to adapt the character to suit Crawford, to suit his potential as an
actor, and his massive silhouette, which is completely different from Bogart's,
who looked more like a famished wolf, with his hollow face, and would have
perhaps more effectively conveyed the despair of a wasted life. In short,
Bogart's deep melancholy would probably have been more effective than
Crawford's." Fellini's comments notwithstanding, Crawford is extremely
capable in the role of Augusto.

of the car to join Vargas, it is discovered that under their coats Augusto and Picasso are both garbed like priests. "We nearly lost Roberto this morning," Picasso laughs. "That guy's got a woman in every village." Since Roberto is played by the same actor who performed as Fausto in *I Vitelloni*, one has the impression that Fellini might be suggesting how the loafers from the earlier film turned out. Picasso, like his namesake, is a painter, though apparently one of small talent; however, like Moraldo in *I Vitelloni*, he is sensitive to nature. "Hey, look how beautiful it is out here!" he exclaims. (In the earlier film, Moraldo, like Picasso, is introduced almost identically: "Hey, look how pretty it is out here!" he says.) "Resembles a Corot landscape," Picasso adds. "Doesn't it?" His associates ignore him.

Although a number of confidence men appear in the film, and although the viewer is given a good look at how such characters hoodwink people, Fellini focuses mainly on Roberto, Picasso, and Augusto. And of the three, Augusto is by far the most important. Fellini makes this point right from the start, as well as throughout the film, by camera placement and composition. For example, while Vargas upbraids Picasso for wearing brown shoes under his cassock, Fellini's camera watches Augusto in the foreground as he winds a cardinal's ribbon around himself, the two other men in the background. Similarly, as Vargas coaches Picasso on the operation, the viewer contemplates Augusto hanging a pectoral cross and chain around his neck. Crawford's tough, beefy face perfectly suggests Augusto's cynicism, weariness, and increasing disgust with himself, his associates, his mode of existence. Roberto remarks: "Augusto's on his last legs, the old man. He's about to drop dead." Thus, Fellini skillfully prepares the viewer for Augusto's spiritual conflict, redemption, and death.

After finishing their costume change, the swindlers get back into the limousine and drive off. Fellini shoots the car head on as it moves toward the camera; in this way, the viewer is made to feel that the confidence men are entering into his life, that in the fraud about to be perpetrated he is going to be a participator. Throughout *Il Bidone*, Fellini manages the difficult feat of making the viewer identify with both the exploiters and the exploited. Even though the confidence men perform evil deeds, the artist presents Augusto and Picasso as human beings who are not without valuable qualities. And even though the bilked are poor and hard working, swindlers could not exist if men and women were not greedy and gullible. As he so often does, Fellini maintains a seriocomic approach through much of *Il Bidone*. Consequently, the film-maker avoids mawkishness, depicts character in the round, and abstains from oversimplifying the moral issues involved in his story.

The swindlers stop before a farmhouse on land that is flat and bare. Two elderly women appear. In the ensuing scene, one can scarcely blame the women for being deceived by Augusto and Picasso, so well do the latter play their parts. Whereas in the opening scene the crooks handled the ornaments of the clergy with disrespect, in the present scene they project an almost faultless image of the priesthood. Clothes make the man. Unfortunately, the peasant women respond to the uniform of the clergy—as most of us respond to such symbols, either positively or negatively—without knowing the man underneath the dress. Perhaps the anticlerical Fellini is also suggesting that a priest and a *bidone* are one and the same.

Augusto tells the farm women a tale about how a sinful man confessed on his deathbed to having killed his accomplice in a theft and buried the corpse near a tree on their property. All this supposedly took place during the war. Of course, some jewels were buried along with the corpse. (And, of course, the swindlers previously planted the "treasure" before visiting the farmhouse.) Unctuously, Augusto explains that it is his duty to dig up the corpse, bury it again in consecrated ground, and dispose of the jewels. "Because," he says, "the deceased man expressly declared that if it is found, it shall remain the property of the owner of the land." After the digging up of the remains and the jewels is completed, and after the swindlers and the two women have returned to the farmhouse again, Augusto informs the latter that they can keep the "wealth"—easily five or six million lire—on condition, as stipulated by the late murderer, that they shall pay to have five hundred masses said for the salvation of the sinner's soul. Picasso smiles: "Five hundred masses at one thousand lire each . . ." The two women rush off to sell their cows in order to pay the five hundred thousand lire to the "priests."

Later that night, having returned to Rome, the swindlers part. Fellini's camera follows Picasso to his apartment, where we meet his daughter Silvana, age five, and his wife Iris (Giulietta Masina.)* In the previous scene, Picasso was shown playing with a baby on the farm: "Cute little kid," he says once; and later, "Hi, little cutie. Oh, you look like a real little rascal, you know?" Here Fellini shows us that Picasso was not shamming before: he genuinely loves children. As a matter of fact, Picasso —who is about thirty—is childish himself; he appears less wicked than irresponsible. For example, after cheating the two women, he whistles going up the stairs of his apartment; he brings presents for his wife and daughter bought with the stolen money. He insists on taking his family out to dinner, though he owes money right and left, and he lies to Iris about how he earns his money (he claims to be a traveling salesman). He dreams of one day finding time to express himself in his painting (like Marcello, in *La Dolce Vita*, who promises himself throughout most of the film that someday he will give up his immoral life and write a novel). "Ah, Iris," Picasso says, "I've seen more landscapes! We have to go together one day, you know? Some countryside out on the hills that not even the Dutch could dream of . . ." And the scene fades out.

Next Fellini shows us how Augusto and Roberto spend their leisure time. In a cabaret the two men drink champagne, gloat over the simpletons whom they have cheated, make the acquaintance of some women, and plot further swindles. Again, Fellini prepares the viewer for Augusto's inner struggle and death by having Roberto taunt him: "Listen to this, Augusto. This is for you." And Roberto beats out a funeral march. At this point,

* It is interesting to note that in *Juliet of the Spirits* the spirit who tells the title character, played by Giulietta Masina, to have "love for everyone" is named Iris.

however, Augusto seeks to justify his way of life. "I've been all over the world and I always conned everybody," he says. "Because the world is full of fools. I could even sell ice to the Eskimos." Before *Il Bidone* ends, Augusto will come to the realization that of all the fools in the world he is the biggest one, that he has conned himself more cruelly than he has anyone else.

Day. Shot of the black limousine pulling up before a group of old houses, crowded with people. Dressed in a chauffeur's attire once more, Roberto gets out and opens the back door for Augusto and Picasso, both of whom are dressed like government officials. Picasso sees a child crying on top of one hovel and picks him up. "Hey, what's wrong with you?" he says. "Don't cry." All the same, Picasso—no less than Augusto and Roberto—evinces scant compassion for the parents of the child, or for any of the poor wretches here, including the children. This time the swindlers take money from the poverty-stricken by pretending to assign them public housing apartments. Although the deception is brutal, the deceived are presented in an unattractive light. They push and shove and curse one another in their desperate urge to find better accommodations for themselves. One can understand their plight; one cannot, however, wholly sympathize with them. Nonetheless, one does not completely identify with the swindlers, either. With subtle inventiveness, Fellini has Augusto push through the crowd, the camera nearly —but not quite fully—subjective: people shout toward the camera-eye without looking directly into the lens. Hence the viewer sees the mob somewhat as Augusto sees it, yet without actually becoming the *bidone*, as would be the case if the shot were strictly a subjective camera.

Night. It is New Year's Eve. On the street, Augusto and Picasso are seen carrying packages. Picasso stops before a vendor who is blowing soap bubbles. "Oh, I like that!" he says. With much animation, Picasso proceeds to blow bubbles, too. "I want to bring it to Silvana," he says. "I'm sure she'll get a bigger kick out of this than anything else." To which Augusto replies: "You're the one who's getting a kick out of it. You're just like a little kid." This short scene perfectly sums up the life chosen by these swindlers. *I'm forever blowing bubbles—pretty bubbles in the air.*

Suddenly Augusto encounters a former associate, Rinaldi, who is much more affluent than himself, thanks to the drug traffic. Since Rinaldi is giving a party to celebrate the new year, he invites Augusto, Picasso, Iris, and Roberto. The party turns out to be typical of the ones Fellini presents in his films: an incongruous assortment of people; much noise, confusion, and drinking; desperate, faked gaiety, with a terrible void, an aching loneliness, just beneath the surface; and a stupid, voluptuous woman turned into a mere sex object by basically undersexed, unloving men. For example, a woman named Marisa at Rinaldi's party tells everyone that she plans to enter a beauty contest. When she claims to have perfect breasts, the leering men taunt her into undressing in order to prove her case. Charles Thomas Samuels complained to Fellini that the scene is disappointing because the film-maker couldn't "think of anything more squalid than those men who ask the girl to strip so that they can see if she's wearing falsies." To which Fellini wearily replied: "You want something more corrupt; that's your problem. I don't want to shock. I only want to be true to the story I'm telling." (Later in the same interview, Samuels also complained that Fellini, in *Fellini Satyricon*, fails to show the homosexuality directly enough: "All we see is one man kissing another's wrist." Exasperated, Fellini remarked: "What, did you want to see the prick going in?" Too many sexually explicit films by bad directors seem to have destroyed the imaginations of some critics.) In *Il Bidone*, Marisa's stripping is fully expressive of Fellini's intentions. By exposing her body, the woman reveals not only the emptiness of her own soul but also the emptiness of the on-looker's souls. The actions at Rinaldi's party—and this is, of course, precisely Fellini's point—are not so much squalid as pathetic.

Throughout the party scene, Fellini contrasts Augusto and the merrymakers. When Augusto, worried about the advancing years, tries to persuade Rinaldi to set him up in a loan office, the latter pays no attention to him. At one point in the conversation, Fellini shoots the two men from a high angle, in order to emphasize Augusto's plight by making him appear small. Rinaldi asks Augusto his age. "Forty-eight," Augusto replies. "And at your age you're still thinking about fooling around?" It's disgraceful!" Augusto is crushed. And he is further humiliated when, later in the evening, Rinaldi catches Roberto stealing a women's gold cigaret case. "Augusto, what the hell kind of friends do you have anyway?" Rinaldi says. "And you go around with them too?" By the end of the scene, the troubled Augusto has traveled further along the road toward eventual salvation.

Outside, Augusto is tempted to hit Roberto; however, the younger man stops him with insulting calm: "Augusto. At your age you shouldn't . . ." Iris is angry with Picasso, too; but he promises to give up seeing Augusto and Roberto. "I swear I'll change my ways. I swear it to you, Iris. Believe me, my love. . . ."

Nevertheless, when we see Picasso again he is still working with Augusto and Roberto. In Fellini's world—in the real world as opposed to the world of bad art—human beings do not generally undergo instantaneous transformations. The sun is bright. And Augusto looks happy, even though he is about to embark on still another swindle. Fellini's strategy of presenting Augusto in this light not only is a concession to realism (in moral matters, humanity tends to take two steps forward, then one step backward, and so forth), but also, because of contrast, possesses an aesthetic justification or rightness. For in this scene on Rome's Piazza del Popolo, Augusto has a fateful meeting with his daughter Patrizia. "Oh, how you've changed!" he says, as his daughter's schoolmates wait for her a few steps away. "I wouldn't have recognized you . . . really." Obviously, Augusto is separated or divorced from his wife; and just as obviously, he has not been, at least up to this point, a devoted father. "You know," he says, "one of these days I'll come see you . . . or . . . I'll call you." Patrizia, who has the face of an angel, seems doubtful. "Fine," she says. "Really, I will," he insists. "I promise you." Before parting, Augusto kisses Patrizia in a way that seems awkward, as though he had never embraced his child before. For a long time, the *bidone* stares after Patrizia, his expression thoughtful. Hence, this scene begins with Augusto seemingly reconciled again to his unsavory occupation, but ends with him left visibly disturbed by his encounter with innocence.

Dissolve to the inside of the limousine. Roberto is driving along the Via Flaminia, Augusto and Picasso with him. However, Fellini's camera either isolates Augusto or keeps him in the foreground, in order to emphasize the fact that the stirrings of a profound change are going on inside him. The car stops in front of a gas station in the country. Here, Roberto gets an old man to fill up the gas tank and lend him ten thousand lire—a total of eleven thousand three hundred and eighty lire—by promising to pay him thirteen thousand lire when he returns from Rome, where supposedly he will collect some money. The man agrees when Roberto lets him hold as collateral a coat that looks expensive but is in reality little more than paper. Next, Roberto stops at another gas station; and this time, Augusto is obliged to perform the coat trick. Tactfully, Fellini does not show the swindle repeated. Fade out on a shot of Picasso handing a coat to Augusto, who then folds it neatly so that its basic cheapness remains less easy to detect.

Later in the day, the trio of swindlers are discovered in the piazza of a country town, where a traveling amusement show has stopped. The men have been drinking; in fact, Picasso is drunk. Augusto, however, appears relatively sober and patently removed in spirit from the other two men, an impression that is conveyed by both Crawford's acting (he remains silent while his companions indulge in buffoonery) and Fellini's camera (which again calls attention to the protagonists's estrangement by either detaching him visually from his surroundings or by keeping him in the foreground).

Night. And Picasso is even more drunk than before. The streets are empty. "Can it be that there's not a single woman in this whole town?" Roberto shouts. The men pass an image of the Virgin set into the wall of a house; stunned, Picasso gazes at

IL BIDONE: *Picasso and Roberto in the piazza of a country town.*

the statue penitently. Suddenly Augusto declares: "We have to think about doing something more serious. We certainly can't go on this way." Augusto then attempts to sober up Picasso by holding his head under a water fountain, an operation that some critics have interpreted as a symbolic purification rite. Picasso expresses a fear that one day Iris and Silvana might leave him if he does not change his habits. Deeply troubled by his own spiritual condition, Augusto jealously and defensively attacks his comrade: "What got into your head anyway, to get married at eighteen? You ruined yourself. In our kind of work you can't have a family. A man's got to be free to come and go. You can't be tied to your wife's apron strings. You have to be a loner." In a shot revealing Picasso on the right hand side of the screen and Augusto's shadow on the left hand side, Fellini has Picasso ask: "But Augusto . . . how do you do it . . . How can you keep it up at your age?" By framing his shot in this way, the film-maker suggests that Augusto, instead of having substance, is merely the shadow or the semblance of a man. Like Zampanò, Augusto insists: *"Ho bisogno di nessuno"*; and like Zampanò, the *bidone* grows increasingly aware that everyone needs someone, that it is not good for a person to be alone. All the same, Augusto now goes off with Roberto and a married woman of loose morals, whereas Picasso refuses to accompany them in any further debauchery. Instead, he flings aside the cheap coat he has been carrying and starts running toward home. . . . We do not see Picasso again, and we can only speculate about his future.

In the next scene, which takes place on a Sunday, Augusto takes Patrizia to lunch on Monte Mario. When his daughter tells him that she loves school but that she cannot be a burden any longer to her mother, Augusto feels ashamed of himself. He fumbles in his jacket pocket for a pair of sunglasses. A tiny wristwatch is caught in them, which Patrizia mistakenly believes that her father has bought for her, though she pointedly says nothing. Obviously even more ashamed of himself now than before, Augusto gives the watch to the girl.

Later, Fellini's camera discovers father and daughter entering a movie theater, an usher showing them to their places.

Augusto, after they are seated, smiles at Patrizia: "She thought you were my girl friend!" Then, with difficulty, but trying to appear offhand, Augusto says: "If you want to keep on with your studies, I'll take care of the deposit." Patrizia is thrilled. "Oh, papa," she exclaims, and she suddenly gives him a kiss. (In his treatment of the tender relationship between a father and daughter, Fellini is reminiscent of F. Scott Fitzgerald in "Babylon Revisited"; in his treatment of the gradual moral awakening of a sinful man, Fellini is reminiscent of Tolstoy.)

There now follows one of the most painful scenes ever created by a film artist. A few rows in front of Augusto and Patrizia sits a man combing his hair. With a start, the *bidone* recognizes him. What is worse, the man—who has begun looking around—also recognizes Augusto. Frightened, Augusto tells Patrizia: "I'm going to get some cigarettes." In the back of the theater, however, the man confronts Augusto: "I've been looking for you for six months," he says, grabbing the swindler's lapel. "Bastard! I'll wring your neck!" Fellini alternates medium shots of the fracas with long shots from inside the theater—Patrizia in the foreground, Augusto and the angry man in the background—in order to make the viewer experience not only Augusto's fright and humiliation but also Patrizia's. Outside in the lobby a policeman shows up. A friend of the angry man informs the officer: "You know what this crook's done? He sold some fake Terramycin, and my brother almost died!" Patrizia also appears now in the lobby. As the policeman leads Augusto away the deeply embarrassed thief tells his daughter: "Go home!"—his voice harsh, because he loves her and feels humiliated in her eyes.

A few months pass. A noticeably older Augusto is released from prison. Immediately he returns to his old haunt, the Café Canova, and begins asking for "Baron" Vargas and Roberto. . . . Next we find Augusto dressed like a priest, working his former routine with new associates, except for Vargas. Like some other Fellini pictures, *Il Bidone* is circular in structure. Like Zampanò at the end of *La Strada*, Augusto now goes through his act in a mechanical fashion, taking neither pride nor interest in his ability to deceive people.

In one farmhouse, Augusto has another crucial encounter with a young girl—this time a crippled peasant's daughter. The girl's father explains that he has three hundred and fifty thousand lire for masses because he had saved it to buy an ox: "It would make the work so much easier. I have to think about putting something aside. Not for me, but for these two poor girls. One works for me like a man, but the other one, poor thing, is paralyzed, and when I die who'll take care of her?" Distractedly, Augusto says: "The Lord never abandons his creatures. Have you got the money with you?" Before leaving with the peasant's savings, however, Augusto has a talk outside with the girl, the stone wall of the house symbolically part of the visual composition. "You must have faith in God, you know, my dear girl," the *bidone* tells her. "I understand, it's a terrible thing for you, but we must resign ourselves to His will. This is a vale of tears, and each of us bears his own cross." Although Augusto has reached into his bag of tricks for the usual clichés, the girl is too innocent to be critical. "I know, and I don't complain," she says. "If it weren't for them, . . . if I weren't a burden for my family, I wouldn't care at all. . . . I sit here with my embroidery, I listen to music. . . . I feel like a queen. For my sister life really is hard. She's been down in the field working since four this morning." The girl tells Augusto that only a miracle would cure her, but that she still has faith in miracles. "My misfortune has made me find God," she says. "I'm always happy, even when I feel so bad I could die." For the first time, Augusto reveals genuine emotion; he speaks with sincerity, from the heart, with no more pretense at being a priest. "You don't need me," he says. "You're much better off than a lot of people. Our life . . . the life of so many people I know . . . has nothing beautiful in it. You're not losing much. You don't need me—I have nothing to give you." The girl begs Augusto to pray for her; she tries to kiss his hand. Ashamed of his deception and embarrased by her devotion, Augusto pulls away. "Stop it!" he says—in the same tone of voice he used earlier, outside the movie theater, when he told Patrizia: "Go home!" The scene ends with Augusto walking off into the shadows of the house.

Afterward, when the swindlers meet on a country road to change clothes and divide the money, Augusto informs his associates that he did not take the three hundred and fifty thousand lire. "I couldn't do it, Vargas," he says. "The man was a poor old coot with a paralytic daughter. . . . I have a daughter of my own and I couldn't do it. . . . Can't I have a conscience, too?" However, when the men attempt to search Augusto, he fights them off and runs. Here Crawford's face is a memorable study in panic, as he begins slipping down a steep hillside, the crooks pursuing him. Here, too, Fellini obliges the viewer to identify fully with Augusto (unlike the scene earlier in the film when the *bidone* walked through the mob that demanded government housing), because the rocks hurled at the hero come straight towards the lens, in an inspired use of the subjective camera. One rock hits Augusto on the forehead; as he falls, he crashes against a boulder. "My back is broken!" he cries. Unmoved, Vargas and the others search Augusto and find the money hidden in his shoe. The fact that Augusto did not refuse the peasant's money saves *Il Bidone* from sentimentality; however, the fact that he intended to give the money to his daughter shows at least that he remains capable of an unselfish act.

Left alone to die, Augusto finds himself crippled like the girl on the farm, surrounded by stones emblematic of a previously sterile, unloving existence. Slowly, very painfully, he begins to crawl up the side of the hill, church bells ringing in the distance. In the hands of a lesser artist than Fellini, this symbolic Golgotha with its redemptive sound effects would be offensive; yet, as photographed by Otello Martelli, the scene possesses the utmost realism. Fellini's treatment of Augusto's final agony—an agony in which the man, like the crippled girl, finds God in the depths of his suffering—is credible, austere, profoundly moving. When he finally reaches the road (Fellini's symbol of life), Augusto sees some children walking with two peasant women. They do not, however, see him. And as the tiny procession disappears up the road—sunshine bright all around them— Augusto cries out: "Wait for me . . . I'm coming . . . I'm coming with you. . . ." Then, with a strange smile on his face, he dies.

Throughout *Il Bidone*, Fellini's camera often moves in close on Augusto, with a zoomlike effect, in order to suggest how developments are having a moral influence on him. At the end of the picture, the camera—which during the ascent remained generally tight on Augusto—begins to move back, and up, leaving the protagonist's body on the side of the road. It is a touch again reminiscent of *La Strada*. Like Zampanò, Augusto experiences a dark night of the soul in which he at last becomes human. However, whereas Zampanò must go on living, Augusto's struggle is over. The rising camera at the end of *La Strada* makes Zampanò appear small, humbled; the last shot of *Il Bidone* resembles a benediction—it is a short, gentle movement, one that seems to confer upon the dead man a peace that perhaps only those who have faith can truly comprehend.

The rest is silence.

CHAPTER 8

Nights of Cabiria

I am not a pessimist. I believe there is a slow
conquest toward the divine state of man.

—FEDERICO FELLINI

Nights of Cabiria (1956) opens silently with a long shot of
Cabiria (Giulietta Masina) and her lover frolicking in a field
near the Tiber. Although the sun is bleak and the terrain flat,
Cabiria seems delighted with life. She kisses the man, runs
ahead, returns, kisses him again, strolls hand in hand with him.
Presently the couple stop at the river bank. Swinging her pocket-
book in a carefree manner, Cabiria contemplates the water.
Shot of her lover gazing right and left surreptitously. Then,
all at once, the man grabs Cabiria's bag, pushes her into the
river and disappears.

Unable to comprehend what has happened, Cabiria—who
obviously cannot swim—shouts: "I'm all right! I'm over here,
Giorgio!" Swept further and further away from the shore, the
tiny young woman begins to go under. She is saved from
drowning, however, by several boys who manage to drag her
limp body back to land. Some men then pump water out of
Cabiria's lungs, handling her no less roughly, in spite of their
good intentions, than had Giorgio. Once she is revived, Cabiria
springs to her feet and dashes wildly about, calling: "Giorgio!
Giorgio!"—but to no avail. Ashamed of the position she finds

NIGHTS OF CABIRIA: *Cabiria, after being thrown in the Tiber by a lover.*

herself in, Cabiria projects her resentment onto her rescuers, who evince indignation at the woman's lack of gratitude. With her hair plastered muddily against her moon-shaped face, her striped dress (calling to mind Gelsomina's striped jersey in *La Strada*) clinging oozily to her girlish-looking body, Cabiria starts for home in one shoe, an object of derision for the crowd which has gathered. "That's Cabiria," a boy observes. "She's one of those night birds."

Thus begins *Nights of Cabiria*, Fellini's unforgettable study of a lonely prostitute who longs to love and to be loved, whose story (as the film-maker once remarked) gives expression to "an irresistible and providential force, innate in us; an incoherent, intermittent force that cannot be gainsaid—the anguished longing for goodness."

Cabiria lives in a squalid part of Rome, her house a square stone box, her surroundings bare except for a few other hovels like hers, a gas works, and some odd-looking, apparently functionless structures which call to mind the *mise-en-scène* on the beach in *I Vitelloni*. Because her keys were in the handbag that Giorgio relieved her of, Cabiria is forced to enter her house in an undignified manner by climbing through a window. Wanda, a huge prostitute who lives nearby, tries to console Cabiria but the latter will not admit the truth. "I slipped and fell into the water," she explains. "Giorgio was holding my bag—he got excited and ran off." When Wanda reacts skeptically to Cabiria's story, the latter directs her anger toward her friend. Indeed, aggression as a concealment for an injured ego remains one of Cabiria's main character traits.* All the same, as Wanda is

---

* *Nights of Cabiria* had several sources. Cabiria first appeared briefly in *The White Sheik*, but Fellini felt he wanted to develop the character at greater length. In an interview with Arthur Knight, the film-maker observed that he kept turning the character over in his mind, without as yet seeing her as clearly as he wanted: "And then, while I was shooting a sequence on location for *Il Bidone*, suddenly there she was in the flesh—an independent creature with a hard cover of anger for her terrible lonely pride. We had put down rails for a traveling shot right up to the door of her little shack. She came out furious and ordered us to take them away. Nevertheless, at the lunch break I carried one of our baskets of food to her. When she wouldn't

leaving, the heroine is finally driven to reveal the extent of her hurt: "Why did he do it?" she asks. "Why? I gave him everything. Why would he shove me in the river for a mere forty thousand lire? I loved him." To which Wanda replies: "*Love. . . .* You only knew him a month—you know nothing about him." After Wanda leaves, the frightened Cabiria sits with a chicken on her lap, caressing it. "Suppose I should die?" she whispers to herself. "Then what?" Burying her need for love again, however, the "night bird" gathers up all of Giorgio's pictures, takes them outside, and burns them.

In the following scene, which takes place at night on the Passeggiata Archeologica, Cabiria is discovered with Wanda and a number of other prostitutes, together with their pimps. One of the girls, Marisa, has a new car, but her lover only reluctantly allows her to drive it. Cabiria is making a determined effort to forget Giorgio and to pretend that she no longer feels pain or humiliation. Consequently, as a mambo is heard on the car radio, Cabiria proceeds to dance with one of the men. Nevertheless, when an aging prostitute named Matilda begins to taunt Cabiria, her suppressed rage flares up and an unseemly brawl takes place between the two women. Although Fellini's camera keeps its distance from the action by not involving the audience through a subjective approach, the point is made that Cabiria's existence—as well as that of the other girls's—is shallow, mean, not far removed from the bestial level. One is reminded of Fellini's observation which might be applied to almost all of the director's films: "Life must have a meaning beyond the animal."

Afterward, Marisa and her pimp drive Cabiria away from Matilda and the Passeggiata Archeologica. The pimp wants Cabiria to work for him, but she refuses to turn over her money to him or to any other man whom she does not love. When the

---

open the door, I left it on the step. Two hours later she crept out and carried it off to the woods to eat. After that she began to come closer and closer to us, like a little animal, and finally we could talk. This girl, Wanda, ultimately served as a sort of technical advisor on *Nights of Cabiria*" (*Saturday Review*, November 9, 1957).

car arrives at the Via Veneto, Cabiria gets out and is left alone
by her companions. The high-class tarts in this section of the city
regard their less prepossessing sister—who wears bobby socks,
and who looks almost sexless—with studied contempt. Cabiria
wanders in front of the Kit-Kat, a nightclub, where she tries to
solicit an elderly doorman, who instead chases her away.

Suddenly a well-known movie star (Amedeo Nazzari) and an
attractive blonde (Dorian Gray) emerge quarreling from the
Kit-Kat. With a quick tracking shot, Fellini moves in close for
Cabiria's reaction: her eyes fairly bulge as she recognizes the
actor. When the blonde goes off by herself, the man gets into
his Chrysler convertible and gazes across the street at Cabiria.
It is clear that the actor has no sexual interest in the humble
prostitute, but it is equally clear that he does not wish to be
alone. "Get in," he says, with an indifferent air. Stunned, Cabiria
looks around before replying: "Who, me? The actor nods. Convinced that he is serious, the young woman casts a haughty
glance at the doorman and joins the movie star.

The car stops in front of another nightclub. Inside, Cabiria
attempts to act with disdain for the patrons who obviously awe
her, but instead she pathetically reveals her low economic and
social position, as well as her general ineptitude. She hands her
cheap umbrella to the hatcheck girl as though it were a scepter.
When she attempts to enter the interior of the club, she gets
hopelessly entangled in the silk drapes and has to be extricated
by two attendants. Although she is patently fascinated by the
gyrations of two scantily clad black dancers, Cabiria comically
affects nonchalance. And when the actor dances a mambo with
her, she seems oblivious to his abysmal boredom. Outside again,
on the way to the man's house, Cabiria stands up in the convertible and taunts the better-paid tarts, who merely stare in
disbelief at her client.

The star's villa, located on the Appian Way, similarly impresses
Cabiria with what she conceives to be its splendor, though a
more discerning eye—like Fellini's—detects all the signs of the
nouveau riche: a fountain that rivals the Trevi, a flight of stairs
long enough to challenge a mountain climber, and a collection

of birds sufficient for a menagerie. During this scene Fellini invites the viewer, through camera placement, to experience the event in close identification with Cabiria. For example, when the little prostitute climbs the staircase, the camera is behind her, thus conveying a subjective impression of her steep ordeal. When Cabiria examines the birds, Fellini sets up his camera on the far side of the cage, so that the viewer can see his heroine's expression of wonderment, thereby further emotionally involving him in the scene. (Truffaut has argued that film becomes truly subjective, not when the camera simulates what a character sees, but when the character is shot head-on and in close-up.) Playing Beethoven's Fifth Symphony on the phonograph, the actor reclines histrionically on a couch and informs Cabiria that he is "fanatical" about the piece. Although the movie star is never deliberately unkind to Cabiria, he strikes the viewer as a phony—no less superficial, in spite of his wealth and fame, than the wretched tarts and greedy pimps who frequent the Passeggiata Archeologica in Rome.

Next, the butler spreads a lavish dinner for Cabiria, who asks the actor to autograph his picture and to inscribe the words: "For my friend, Cabiria, who was a guest in my home," so that she can show it to her companions. When the actor's blonde mistress returns, he locks Cabiria in the bathroom, assuring her that she will be released in a few moments. Unfortunately, the couple make up and the prostitute is forced to spend the night in the bathroom. Again, Fellini sees to it that the viewer identifies with his heroine. When Cabiria peeks through the keyhole to observe what is going on in the next room, for instance, we see precisely what she sees—thanks to a subjective camera in combination with a mask. Moreover, Fellini keeps his heroine in character; for, just as Cabiria consoled herself by caressing a chicken after Giorgio deserted her, here she strokes the actor's dog before falling asleep on the floor.

In the morning, the actor quietly lets Cabiria out and leads her past the sleeping blonde, whose naked shoulders are visible above the sheets. Cabiria gazes at the woman with admiration and envy. When the actor hands the prostitute money for services unrendered, her pride obliges her to refuse but the man insists. Still overwhelmed by her experience and surroundings, Cabiria nearly gets lost in the labyrinthian villa, finds difficulty in locating her umbrella, and crashes into a glass door before finally making her customary awkward exit.

Next Cabiria and her companions are found engaged in a visit to the Madonna of Divine Love. One of the pimps, a cripple, wants the mother of Jesus to make him whole again; hence, in expectation of a miracle, he has tendered an offering of thirty thousand lire. His nephew, Marisa's pimp, assures him that divine help is on the way. All that remains necessary—now that the money has been paid—is for his uncle to have faith. For her part, Cabiria wants the Madonna to show her the way to be reborn, to enjoy a new life. So, like the other pilgrims, Cabiria buys the largest candle for sale. As an unseen priest addresses them impersonally over a loudspeaker, the faithful surge forward; when a sufficient number are admitted into the sanctuary, the clergy shove back the rest, shutting a gate against them as though they were cattle. Throughout this scene, Fellini's attitude toward the action remains a mixture of irony, compassion, and disgust. As the crowd grows increasingly hysterical, Marisa's pimp encourages his uncle to abandon his crutches and to walk forward toward the shrine. When the cripple attempts to do so, however, he falls down on the ground, still broken in body and spirit. Similarly, Cabiria is disappointed because no sign appears from the heavens guaranteeing her a changed mode of existence.

After the fiasco at the shrine, Cabiria and her friends hold a picnic in a field near the church. Disillusioned with her recent experience, and still longing for a better life, the heroine gets tipsy and belligerent. She upbraids the others for not having been regenerated by the Madonna, ridicules a procession of believers that passes by, and boots a football belonging to some young men playing in an adjacent field. Finally, weary of her associates, Cabiria wanders off alone.

In a cheap vaudeville house and movie theater, Cabiria watches a magician hypnotize some young men, who are made to believe that they are sailing through a storm in a boat. Afterward the magician asks Cabiria to come up on stage. At first she refuses, and the uncouth spectators jeer; but when the old ham insists, the heroine acquiesces. The viewer is then treated to one of the most beautiful scenes in all of Fellini's films. Whereas the shrine was unable to provide a proper setting for Cabiria's spiritual transformation, the third-rate theater now becomes the occasion for a true revelation. When the magician removes his top hat, he is seen to be wearing horns. (One is reminded of *La Strada*, in which Gelsomina follows a procession into church, and in which she receives spiritual guidance, not from a priest, but from a circus performer—namely, The Fool.) "So, you're not married yet," the magician says. "But you'd like to find a husband wouldn't you?" Defensively angry once more, Cabiria replies: "Think I'm crazy? Hah! Why should I want to get married?" The audience sends up a barrage of rude comments. Unobtrusively, the magician proceeds to hypnotize Cabiria . . . and in so doing, to carry her back into the past, so that her innermost being can be revealed.

By setting up his camera directly in front of Cabiria, and by shooting upward toward the spotlight beaming behind her, Fellini makes his heroine literally glow. The prostitute now looks like a saint—an image that is accented by the wreath of artificial flowers that the hypnotist places on her head. As the strains of "The Merry Widow Waltz" commence, the magician introduces Cabiria to an imaginary lover named "Oscar," who now speaks to her through the lips of the conjuror: "There hasn't been any man in your life? I thought so. I've watched you many times at your window, and Sundays at Mass. You always have your eyes modestly fixed on the ground. I see you love flowers—like all sensitive souls." Cabiria and "Oscar" waltz together around the stage. "You should have known me when I was eighteen—I had long, beautiful black hair," Cabiria remarks; to which "Oscar" replies: "For me, you are still only eighteen." Cabiria demands: "Do you love me? Be honest. Do you truly love me?" While this heart-breaking scene is enacted on stage, the boorish spectators are temporarily mesmerized too.

However, when the magician ends the act and snaps Cabiria back into present reality, the audience starts to hoot again. Once more, Cabiria experiences anger and humiliation.

After the show, Cabiria is approached on the street in front of the theater by a seemingly timid young man (François Périer), who introduces himself as "D'Onofrio," a bookkeeper. The loquacious stranger tells Cabiria:

> I understand what you must feel. . . . It's a question of sympathy. . . . One can pretend to be cynical and calculating—but when, unexpectedly, one finds oneself faced with an example of purity, candor, then the mask of cynicism falls away. Everything that is best in one is reawakened. I want to thank you, because you've done me a world of good. . . . Now, I advise you to have a drop of alcohol—come on, two brandies. I swear to you that I've rarely suffered the way I did back there, when that faker was playing games with you. . . . You answered this Oscar with such tenderness and such feeling. . . . It made me sick. . . . There are certain things that vulgarity cannot even touch, that nothing can soil. . . . And even in the midst of a crowd that snickers, and can't understand, there is always someone who, fortunately, can understand. . . . I don't live anywhere near here. . . . I was in the neighborhood by chance. . . . It was all because of fate. . . . Perhaps you will understand me better if I tell you that my first name is Oscar.

Cabiria is on her guard with Oscar D'Onofrio (and so is the viewer, who remembers that the magician with the horns on his head first spoke to the woman in the tones of "Oscar"), but he seems so sincere that she agrees to see him again.

In the following scenes, Cabiria meets Oscar in Rome's Terminal Station, walks with him in the sun on the city streets, and continues to listen with less and less skepticism to his steady outpourings. Oscar informs her that he has no family, that he was born in the provinces, and that—like her—he is extremely lonely. At first, Cabiria had lied about her profession. "I work in a store," she'd told the man at their first meeting. When she finally reveals the truth, however, Oscar is not deterred: "I love you, I want to marry you," he says. "I don't want to know about anything. I don't care about the past, about prejudice."

Cabiria goes to see an old friend, Father Giovanni, who practices charity rather than merely mouthing it, in order to make her confession. When told by one of the priests at the church that Father Giovanni has not the power to forgive sins, Cabiria waits to see him anyway. The simple priest is contrasted to the clergy present at the Madonna's shrine. Whereas the latter fail to relate in human terms to their flock, Father Giovanni —who, like Cabiria herself, remains partly comical, a true eccentric—sees people instead of souls. Since Father Giovanni had advised Cabiria to forsake her profession and to marry, the heroine feels confident that her prayers have been answered, that she has met the right man.

Therefore, Cabiria withdraws all her savings, sells her house, and says goodbye to Wanda. The sight of a large, poor family waiting to enter their new home momentarily unnerves the heroine. Cabiria "feels that they are invaders, mice and weasels to whom the house has been sold," Fellini explained to Charles Thomas Samuels. "She is like children who say yes and then change their minds." Fellini added that he also showed the family because they "are other wretches who will fill the house with their own misery and desperation." Yet Cabiria—resilient as always—soon begins smiling again and boards a bus for her rendezvous with Oscar.

Slow panning shot of a lake—the water reminiscent of the Tiber into which Cabiria was pushed by Giorgio—followed by a shot of the engaged couple sitting on a terrace of an inn among the Alban Mountains. With touching generosity, Cabiria takes out her money and offers it to Oscar, who raises his dark glasses to better observe the bills. Quietly, he remarks: "You'd better put that money back in your handbag." Then, gazing down at the lake, he suggests a walk in the woods: "I want to observe the sunset on the water . . . up close." Cabiria agrees. "But what about our suitcases?" she asks. "We'll pick them up later," Oscar shiftily replies. And the viewer's sense of uneasiness grows stronger.

Shot of Cabiria and Oscar walking in the woods, sunlight filtering through the branches of the trees and dappling the ground, the ecstatic young woman singing and plucking flowers. Presently the couple arrive at the edge of a cliff overlooking the lake. Believing that she stands poised on the brink of a new life, believing that she has attached herself to a saintly man who will prove to be her salvation, Cabiria says: "What I've been through —the men I've known. They'd do anything to a girl. Of course, you wouldn't know about such vileness. . . . But now, everything's different. Justice does exist. One suffers, but finally one does experience true joy." Suddenly Oscar begins to tremble. "What's the matter?" Cabiria asks. And he ominously replies: "Can you swim?" Cabiria stares at him in horror. Tight close-up of Oscar's eyes, which fill the entire screen. "You're going to kill me!" Cabiria shrieks. "Here, take the money. I don't want it—I don't want anything. Kill me!" In Fellini's world, not even an Oscar remains completely inhuman, or wholly beyond a possible future redemption, however, for the man now reveals a sudden inability to cast his victim into the water. With obvious self-loathing, he grabs Cabiria's handbag, which she had tossed at his feet, and rushes off into the woods. Fellini conveys a sense of Oscar's shame—as well as of his own revulsion at the theft and Cabiria's point of view—by keeping the camera low, so that only the lower part of the criminal's body can be seen as he disappears. It is as though the camera-eye itself did not wish to gaze upon the face of such a despicable man. Cabiria is left on the ground, sobbing and clawing at the earth. (One is again reminded of *La Strada*, in which both The Fool and Zampanò dig at the earth with their bare hands—the former when he dies, the latter when he realizes that Gelsomina is lost to him forever.)

After a while, Cabiria slowly rises and stumbles back into the woods, moonlight shining through the trees. When she reaches the main road a group of young people—who are singing and dancing to the music of harmonicas and guitars—appears. They begin to serenade the unhappy Cabiria. At first, she does not respond. When one grinning young man says: "Buona sera!" however, Cabiria manages a smile, even as her mascara continues to trickle down her cheeks. The last shot in the film is a close-up of the heroine's face, her gaze almost, but not quite, meeting that of the viewer, her brave smile a final affirmation of life.

The structure of *Nights of Cabiria*, then, is circular: it begins with a man deceiving Cabiria and with some young people saving her life, and it ends in the same way. The form is also episodic and vertical; that is, in place of a tight, causally joined progression of scenes, we are given a sense of life "just happening" in front of the camera (this is, of course, the art that conceals art), the emphasis on character and theme rather than plot. By structuring the action around Cabiria, Fellini provides an intense experience for the viewer, who identifies with his symbol of suffering humanity, unsurpassably portrayed by Giulietta Masina. Highly unified in terms of its conceptual design, *Nights of Cabiria* is also—in spite of its deceptively simple presentation of events—a complex film, in that Fellini stylistically combines the serious and the comic, the "realistic" and the "lyrical."

Nights of Cabiria is not a study of one who develops in a certain moral direction—toward either good or evil—but of one who, in spite of constant disillusionment, finds the strength to declare: "Yes—I will go on. For it is better to smile than to weep, better to live than to die." Far from being merely a picture featuring still another "whore with a heart of gold" (but is it not in the nature of genius to transform stereotypes into great art?), *Nights of Cabiria* has a theme of universal significance. Nonetheless, Fellini has been criticized for his conclusion, as though it were an afterthought, an attempt to provide a spurious happy ending to an otherwise gloomy and hopeless narrative. As I have tried to suggest, however, the ending is foreshadowed at the start. Furthermore, the "idea" behind *Nights of Cabiria* is thoroughly consistent with Fellini's philosophy as revealed in his other films; for the director has always believed in the regenerative powers of man, in the ultimate goodness of human existence, in hope for the future. Still, the ending of *Nights of Cabiria* remains "open." As Siegfried Kracauer points out in *Theory of Film*: "we don't know what will happen to [Cabiria]; we only learn from a change of facial expression that she will walk on and that there is no end to her story."

Fellini has never deviated from the position that the viewer, if properly moved by a film, should construct his own ending through personalizing the screen experience. And surely, one would have to be in an advanced state of rigor mortis *not* to be moved by Fellini's sympathetic depiction of the prostitute as symbol for aspiring, suffering humanity. *Nights of Cabiria* is surely one of the most powerful motion pictures ever made.

CHAPTER 9

La Dolce Vita

*In Italy, we are a confused lump of people of all
kinds, all mixed up, and our boat is sinking. It's
happening in other countries, too. There is this tragic
fascination of witnessing a boat going down, taking
an entire epoch with it. We've ended one part of
history and haven't yet begun the next. We are
living in a gray limbo. We have no great ties with
the past which hold or move us. . . . At the same
time, we're unaware of what lies ahead. We just feel
that something is coming—there are flashes and
signs, but no clear indication.*

—FEDERICO FELLINI

After completing *Nights of Cabiria*, Fellini had thought of taking
up Moraldo Rubini from *I Vitelloni* again and making a movie
about that character in Rome. However, the film-maker soon
decided that he was not interested in going back to 1939, nor
was he any longer concerned with Moraldo's inner life. Perhaps,
he thought, a story could be developed that would be loosely
based on the original character—who would be seen twenty
years later "already a little hardened, already on the edge of
shipwreck"—but who would be fused with other elements to

form a new creation. As Fellini traveled around Europe and America, accompanying his pictures to festivals, giving interviews, attending cocktail parties, he began to feel that the disquietude he found in his own particular milieu was not isolated but remained part of a more profound and widespread social illness. Hence, "modern man in search of a soul" (to borrow a title from Jung, one of the director's favorite authors) became the subject matter of the new project. Consciously or unconsciously, Fellini also worked into *La Dolce Vita* some of the themes dealt with in his previous films.

Although morally beyond reproach, *La Dolce Vita* was attacked when it first appeared for being "obscene." For example, the Vatican organ *L'Osservatore romano* called it "disgusting." In February, 1959, as Fellini left a Milanese theater where *La Dolce Vita* was having its première, a man spat in his face and snarled: "You're dragging Italy through the mud!" As late as 1964, Fellini's mother had still not recovered from the shock of the event: "*La Dolce Vita*—why did you make such a picture?" she asked her son. When Fellini visited Padua in the early sixties, he discovered a sign on the door of a church which read: "Pray for the salvation of the soul of public sinner Federico Fellini." Not surprisingly, when moviegoers learned that *La Dolce Vita* was "lewd" and "depraved," they flocked to see it; consequently, the picture became an international success (today it still stands high on *Variety's* list of "all-time box-office champs"). Not surprisingly either, when critics saw that *La Dolce Vita* was attracting the masses, many of them deserted Fellini in favor of Antonioni, whose masterpiece *L'Avventura* appeared in 1960, only to be booed at the Cannes Film Festival. Some critics are incapable of being catholic; if they praise one picture, they feel compelled to damn another. For snobs and certain types of neurotics, box-office success automatically spells inferior workmanship, whereas failure guarantees aesthetic values that the vulgar herd can never understand.

Without ceasing to be either cinematic or contemporary, *La Dolce Vita* (The Sweet Life) suggests, in both conception and execution, a medieval morality play. As Fellini sees it, the "greatest human quality" is "love of one's neighbor"; the "greatest defect" is "egoism." He adds: "There is a vertical line in spirituality that goes from the beast to the angel, and on which we oscillate. Every day, every minute, carries the possibility of losing ground, of falling down again toward the beast." This idea, as will be seen, is embodied in the thematic structure of *La Dolce Vita*. Though Fellini's form is episodic, each sequence remains strictly controlled by the major theme. Within the different episodes, a number of motifs contribute to the complexity of the picture. As the action develops, the motifs coalesce into patterns that support the main structure of meaning.

One unifying element in the film is the progressive deterioration of a journalist named Marcello Rubini (Marcello Mastroianni), whose job takes him to places in Roman society that offer "the sweet life" to those who want it and can afford it. Two other devices that aid coherence in the thematic structure might also be mentioned at this point: one, many of the sequences originate on the once glamorous Via Veneto; and two, throughout the film a group of news photographers (*paparazzi*) plague the lives of the rich and famous who move across Fellini's landscape. It is important to note that *La Dolce Vita* is not just about café society; the film also surveys the intelligentsia, the entertainment world, and even the common man (for example, the mob at the site of the "miracle," to be discussed in due course). By crowding his picture with people of various nationalities, Fellini likewise extends the thematic scope of his action. Some viewers have berated Fellini for presenting so many of the doomed in handsome poses amid elegant surroundings. Such jejune moralizing misses the point. Even a puritan would have to concede that sin, in order to attract, must be appealing, at least in some of its aspects. As I have previously quoted Fellini as saying: "I always like to show both sides of a thing."

In *La Dolce Vita*, Fellini presents an ordered appearance of disorder; the scenes seem fragmented because the lives of the characters are fragmented. Most of the sequences, as Gilbert

Salachas points out, follow "the same dynamic rhythm; the adventure begins in the evening, reaches its greatest frenzy in the heart of night, and ends in the imprecise haze of dawn. Each daybreak brings a provisory, gloomy conclusion that disperses the nocturnal spell." As in *La Strada*, Fellini structures his film on a two-beat rhythm: a night sequence followed by a day sequence. However, although both films begin in daylight, *La Strada* ends at night, *La Dolce Vita* at dawn. Similarly, whereas Zampanò moves from a "beast" to the possibility of becoming a human being, Marcello—finding no exit from the *inferno* in which he finds himself, or rather not yet able or willing to make use of the exit—gradually degenerates into a "beast." Also, just as Gelsomina represents what is positive in the world of *La Strada*, Paola stands at the opposite end of the spiritual spectrum from Marcello in *La Dolce Vita*. Paola is the "angel" of Fellini's morality tale.*

Let us, however, start at the beginning of the picture and examine the episodes in detail.

La Dolce Vita opens with one of the most celebrated shots in the modern cinema. A helicopter is seen flying over Rome carrying an enormous statue of Christ to St. Peter's Church. Marcello views this flight as a good publicity stunt for his paper; trailing in a second plane, the journalist and a photographer cover the reaction of people below. On a terrace some girls, who are sunbathing in bikinis, stare up at the "entertainment" in the sky. "Oh, look," remarks one girl, "there's Jesus!" As Marcello's helicopter passes over the terrace, he attempts to make a date with one of the girl's; but the sound of the plane's motor drowns out his voice.

Fellini has said that "the star of my film is Rome, the Babylon of my dreams." The opening scene establishes the "setting" for all that is to follow. Fellini is a master of juxtaposition. Here two worlds, or two Romes, are contrasted: the Christian and neo-

* Fellini spent months searching for a girl to play Paola, studying the faces of more than 5,000 teenagers. Even when shooting began on the film, the director had still not found his actress. Finally, at dinner in a friend's house, Fellini met thirteen-year-old Valeria Ciangottini, whom he hadn't seen in years. "Paola" was signed the next morning.

pagan, the spiritual and material. By opening in such a manner, the artist suggests a scheme of values by which the protagonist and the other personages can be measured. That the characters in *La Dolce Vita* possess an inherent dignity is clear. Equally apparent is Fellini's ambivalent attitude toward the church. It is not only that a religious statue suspended from an airplane is an incongruous sight in the modern world; the statue itself— like the God it represents—is "dead." The shadow of Christ falls over the great city; but only a few boys pursue the image, and those who bother to glance up do so in a curious, idle way only. Obviously this is not the world of the Old Testament where men lifted their eyes to heaven with awe, reverence, and wonder at the prospect of seeing signs of God's presence and majesty. The living God is gone now—only idols, of one kind or another, remain.

Fellini replaces the image of the gilt statue of Christ with a shot of two muscular—but sexually ambiguous looking—Siamese dancers in a nightclub. The statue is thus linked associationally with the entertainers; the sacred is rendered profane by a commercial industrial society that allows only "work" and "fun" (and not even work for the aristocratic class). With the disappearance of man's vital contact with spirit and nature, individuals lose their sense of identity. Behind the masks with which they confront society, men suffer from loneliness and the lack of a purpose in life. In the scene under examination, Marcello meets a bored rich woman, Maddalena (Anouk Aimée),* who takes the journalist for a drive in her white Cadillac convertible. Manifestly, the protagonist envies the woman's wealthy position; however, Maddalena wearily informs Marcello that "only love matters." Though Maddalena is experienced in the

---

* In his piece on Anouk Aimée, Fellini writes: "There is a great contradiction in Anouk that fascinates. She can be so absolutely shy and the next moment as tough as a shark, a dweller in the abyss. She can be quick as a bull in doing certain things and then suddenly resume a stuttering timidity. With me, Anouk always maintained her little-girl role, but I feel that behind the facade of *brava ragazzina*, the good little girl, there was in her at least a little of what I wanted her to show as Maddalena. . . . Her face suggests an almost metaphysical sensuality."

LA DOLCE VITA: *Christ juxtaposed to modern Rome, the celebrated opening sequence.*

mechanics of sex, she lacks firsthand knowledge of love—the reason being that, like so many moderns, she does not know how to love. To add novelty to her erotic pleasures, she entices Marcello to sleep with her on a prostitute's bed, while the professional whore waits on the staircase outside. Sex thus becomes a way of filling a void in life.

When Marcello arrives home the next morning, he discovers that his mistress, Emma (Yvonne Furneaux)—who rightly feels that she is losing her lover—has tried to kill herself. Marcello rushes the girl to the hospital in time to save her life. Fellini contrasts the darkness of the previous scene between Marcello and Maddalena in the prostitute's flat with the brightness inside the Roman Catholic hospital. Yet it is important to note that there is no neat symbolic balancing in the two episodes between the "bad" and the "good." Throughout the scene at the hospital, Fellini keeps Marcello and the single nun who remains on duty at a marked distance from one another. The viewer is made to feel that institutional religion is coldly impersonal, that man is alienated from the values of the past. But the action at the hospital, in order to be fully understood, must be grasped in relation to the rest of the picture—especially to the scene immediately following.

From the empty hospital dedicated to Christ, the action shifts to an airport where an immense crowd has gathered to greet Sylvia (Anita Ekberg), the latest sex goddess from Hollywood. The actress has come to Rome to star in a Biblical epic. On the ride from the airport to the producer's suite in Rome, Sylvia expresses delight at the sight of chickens along the rural roads. Her remark: "Oh, look, there's a chicken!" echoes the bikini-clad sunbather's previous observation: "Oh, look, there's Jesus!" God or chickens—it's all the same; nothing really matters.

While Marcello is present at the press conference for Sylvia, he receives a call from Emma, who pleads with him to see her at once. "I want you to make love to me," she says, hoping that her expression of sexual longing will interest Marcello. Emma even promises to cook ravioli for him. During this pathetic appeal, Fellini crosscuts between Emma alone in her cheap, quiet, cramped flat and Marcello in the producer's expensive, noisy, crowded suite. Having persuaded Emma that his job requires him to follow Sylvia's movements around Rome, Marcello turns back to the voluptuous actress. "What do I wear to bed? No, not a nightgown. Not pajamas," Sylvia is informing reporters. "Just two drops of French perfume!" At this point, Marcello has more than a professional interest in Sylvia's "movements." Echoing the perverted Maddalena, Sylvia sighs: "All I care about is love, love, love!" Like Maddalena, however, the fleshy actress knows nothing of love. The men howl lasciviously, for love to them is a three letter word. It remains one of the ironies of the picture that the celluloid sex goddess is also deficient in sexual drive.

In the next scene later in the day, Marcello takes Sylvia to visit St. Peter's dome. The woman arrives wearing clerical garb, complete with a "cardinal" hat. Whereas Marcello can barely manage to reach the dome, Sylvia, the apparently healthy animal, has no difficulty climbing to the top. Few, if any, men in *La Dolce Vita* are presented as convincingly "masculine." When the couple attain the summit of the church, they look out over Rome. Presently the sex goddess—who has "changed hats" with the cardinals of the Church, and who now supposedly reigns with authority over the cities of the earth—decides to bestow a kiss on Marcello. Before she can do so, however, her hat blows off and floats down the street below. Like the clergy, Sylvia has been stripped of her "hat." The action is symbolic, and foreshadows further frustrations for Marcello.

From the shot of Sylvia's hat floating downwards, Fellini match cuts to the parallel movements of a saxophone in the following scene. Marcello is dancing with Sylvia in an open-air nightclub fashioned from the ruins of the Baths of Caracalla. Soon a former acquaintance of the woman, a fellow actor, arrives and commences dancing wildly with her. Curiously enough, the man's bearded face, which suggests the visage of a satyr, also resembles the masked countenance of the sexually ambiguous Siamese dancers of the earlier scene. While the couple dance, Sylvia's present suitor, Robert (Lex Barker), watches jealously but impotently from a table. Here, the character identified in the popular mind with the movie Tarzan, the symbol of super-masculinity, is afraid to assert himself. Instead, he sketches a girl who is seated at his table, adding—as a "joke"— a beard to the portrait. In Fellini's world appearances are always deceiving.

Next Marcello and Sylvia are discovered riding in an automobile. When they stop, Marcello attempts to kiss the goddess, but she averts her face as she hears a dog barking. The sound delights Sylvia, who senses in the beast a kindred spirit. After a while, Marcello makes advances again, and again he is thwarted. Spying a kitten, Sylvia dispatches Marcello in search of milk. While he is gone, the woman lavishes affection on the cat and even places it on her head. Not surprisingly, the feline on Sylvia's head seems more appropriate than the "cardinal" hat she wore earlier.

Eventually, the couple find their way to the Trevi fountain. Sylvia wades into the water. "She's right," says Marcello, as he prepares to follow his idol into the water. "Morals aren't right." The satire that distinguishes *La Dolce Vita* is especially notable here. Looking at the actress with awe, the reporter allows himself to get carried away by his own journalistic eloquence. "You are the first woman on the first day of creation," he says. "You are the mother, the sister, the lover, the friend." Part of the comic irony lies in the fact that Sylvia, who is supposed to be four persons in one goddess, actually possesses none of the qualities for which Marcello praises her. Indeed she is not even a "real woman." Sylvia's maternal instinct is limited to kittens; she is too narcissistic to be an ideal sister; Marcello never does make physical contact with her; and she is too stupid to be a friend except to chickens, dogs, and cats. In a parody of baptism, Sylvia sprinkles water on Marcello's hair. When he tries for the last time to kiss her, the water in the fountain suddenly—and symbolically—ceases to flow. If the spirit has left the church of Rome, the waters of pagan Rome have dried up.

After Marcello leaves Sylvia at her apartment, Robert appears and knocks the journalist to the pavement. Robert was too

LA DOLCE VITA: *Marcello and Sylvia in the Trevi fountain.*

cowardly to attack the muscular actor who danced with Sylvia, but now he proves his "manhood" by beating up the weak Marcello. The sweet life is turning sour.

Next the journalist is discovered in church, listening to his intellectual friend, Steiner (Alain Cuny), playing the Toccata and Fugue in D Minor on an organ. The sounds of Bach appear to stir Marcello, who confesses doubts to Steiner about the kind of life he leads as a newspaperman and about the dim prospects for the serious novel he had hoped one day to write. Steiner tries to encourage Marcello. Throughout the scene, Fellini emphasizes the emptiness and stillness of the church surrounding the two men. At one point, a high shot of Marcello and Steiner makes both of them seem small and insignificant. The spectator recalls the earlier scene at the hospital. Since modern man is unable to love, he cannot find his way back to a meaningful relationship with God.

This point is made clear by the episode immediately following, which finds Marcello and Emma at the site of a supposed appearance of the Madonna. The place is jammed with people and television equipment. Just as the silent hospital scene was juxtaposed to the loud reception at the airport for Sylvia, and just as Emma's quiet flat was contrasted with the producer's noisy suite, the still church is played off against the clamorous scene of the "miracle." Two children claim to have held discourse with the Virgin. It is apparent to the viewer that the children are lying: but the latter are so terrified by the publicity that they have caused that they refuse to admit the truth. A priest scornfully informs Marcello that he does not believe in the visitation of the Virgin. "Miracles," he remarks, "take place only in quiet places of prayer." The viewer recollects, however, that Marcello experienced no miracle in church—unless the guilty conscience that troubled the hero there would pass muster as a miracle.

Suddenly rain begins to fall. The occurrence seems propitious; perhaps the fountain of faith, unlike the Trevi, has not dried up. The television lights are extinguished. In the darkness, Emma prays that Marcello will once again love her. Apparently others pray to receive blessings, too. The scene is now a quiet place of prayer. All the same, the children announce—after pretending to have another dialogue with the Madonna—that the heavenly personage is not coming back again. The result is a noisy, bloody, obscene riot. On the morning following, all is quiet again. Marcello, Emma, and a few others watch the priest pray over the body of a child who had come here for a cure—but who instead had been crushed to death.

Marcello and Emma next attend a gathering of intellectuals at Steiner's home. The protagonist appears to have deteriorated still further. He confesses that he no longer has any ambition, that he no longer wishes to write anything except trash, that his job is demoralizing him, but that he cannot find the will to arrest his downward plunge. Is Steiner happy? With his lovely wife and two children, with his cultivated friends, with his music, books, and art treasures, Steiner should be content. Yet, he is not. As the intellectual informs Marcello, he has attempted to make a womb out of the products of mind and art. At Steiner's party the guests listen to recordings of nature—bird calls, running water, the wind —all of which have been isolated from real life. Steiner is afraid of the irrational; he dreads events which cannot be calculated in advance; he is particularly concerned with the contingencies in the future of his children. A technological society of helicopters and tape recorders has superseded an older agrarian community that had been in tune with the creative mysteries. Sylvia has no more real authority than Mary in the modern world (which, as the author of *The Education of Henry Adams* saw, has replaced both Aphrodite and the Virgin with the Dynamo). Everywhere the synthetic—including ersatz, counterfeit sex—has been substituted for the real. Man has lost touch with nature, just as he has lost touch with God. Perhaps, Fellini suggests, "God" and "nature" are but two faces of a single coin.

As if to underline the point just made, Fellini next shows Marcello trying to write in a small café by the sea. It is morning. The preceding scene with Steiner, wherein the man's morbid fears were manifest, seems to have greatly depressed Marcello. Emma calls her lover on the telephone, begging him again to return to her; but the protagonist angrily refuses. Paola, a beautiful, innocent-looking young waitress in the cafe, plays "Patricia" on the jukebox. Marcello talks to the girl, whom he compares to an "angel" in one of Fra Angelico's paintings. Gradually, Paola's sweetness, natural spontaneity, and basic goodness work their spell on Marcello. Warmed and ennobled by the presence of the girl—who appears to be as much a child of nature as an emissary from another world—the reporter calls back Emma and apologizes for his bad temper.

From the scene by the sea—wherein the forces necessary for the renewal of life are to be found—Fellini makes another abrupt shift to an opposite milieu.

On the Via Veneto, Marcello, who continues to pursue his unworthy calling, meets his father (Annibale Ninchi), a traveling salesman from the provinces. Speaking of home, the father informs his son that his wife is not happy. "It's hard for a woman," he says of Marcello's mother, "to grow old gracefully." The father then expresses disapproval of Marcello's sinful ways with women. In the previous scene, Fellini provided the hero with a glimpse of the true "sweet life." If a person is to find his way back to God, the path would not seem to lie through a moribund church, but by way of love of human beings: Marcello must discover how to seize the possibilities latent in his encounter with Paola. Perhaps, through identification with his father, he can actualize the positive forces in his nature. Heretofore, however, Marcello has not had a close relationship with his father. After a few drinks, the hero agrees to show the older man around the city. The elder Rubini insists on paying the check; but when he does so, he complains about the high prices. Marcello's father has never been very good at giving.

Shot of a man with a large fake nose disguised as a clown. The abrupt juxtaposition resembles the one made earlier between the statue of Christ and the Siamese dancers. Marcello and his father are again discovered in a nightclub; behind their table— again reminiscent of the opening—is a huge, ugly, cheap gilt statue. On stage the clown has a whip in his hand; he is forcing several women with tiger masks to perform tricks. The significance of this "play-within-a-play" will be understood only at the end of the picture. Expressing admiration for the charms of one of the girls, the elder Rubini remembers having seen a striptease act once in which the "woman" turned out to be a man. (At this point, one remembers how Robert had added a beard to his sketch of a girl as a "joke.") During a conversation in which the father confesses to being bored with life except when selling —which activity, it is important to note, makes him feel "power-ful"—he admonishes his son for failing to write more often to his mother. "I've been too busy," Marcello replies lamely. Pre-viously the journalist had sought for the "mother" in Sylvia, while apparently neglecting to show love for his real mother. Now Marcello longs to establish a close relationship with his father, while the latter appears more interested in sexual rela-tions with one of the "tigers." Indeed, the father presently deserts his son and goes home with the performer.

Later, however, Marcello receives word to come to the woman's flat. The elder Rubini has suffered a mild "heart failure," making his hopes for sexual "fun" impossible. Like the mother, the father has not had the grace to grow old with dignity; like the son, the father has tried to fill the spiritual emptiness of his life with the opiate of sex. The father's earlier disapproval of his son's loose living was mere hypocrisy. If the gilt masks of the Siamese dancers represent a parody of the gilt statue of Christ, the scene with the woman wherein the father makes a "clown" of him-self (he is identified with the clown, even to the phallic nose, which prop turns out to be as ineffectual as Sylvia's inflated sexual image) represents a parody in profane terms of the sacred father image of the preceding scene. The polarities of sex are also inverted, so that male becomes female and female becomes male. Order has vanished from creation; chaos has come again.

During the scene in the woman's flat, the father sits with his back to his son; he stubbornly refuses to accept the younger man's invitation to stay on in Rome as his guest. As the dejected protagonist watches his father drive off in a taxi, the director shoots the farewell from a high angle, calling to mind the scene involving Marcello and Steiner in church. Love between father and son is paradigmatic of love between God and man; but in the contemporary world, even family relationships are rotten with selfishness. In a consumer society, man does not learn to give—he wants only to receive; hence he remains arrested at an infantile level.

If the elder Rubini's one cure for boredom is selling, the idle rich lack even this mode of escape. In the next episode, Marcello attends a party at the Castle of Bassano di Sutri near Rome. The hosts are a famous aristocratic family in Spenglerian decline. At the dreary gathering, Marcello meets the jaded Maddalena again. Together they wander aimlessly through the spacious, resounding castle. "These rooms are not all that's empty," remarks the histrionic Maddalena. Often Fellini's characters dramatize their sorry state, as if by doing so they could remove some of the sting from the situation and invest their lives with meaning. Impulsively, Maddalena assumes the initiative and proposes marriage to Marcello. By this time, the couple have drifted into separate rooms. As the two talk to one another, their voices ring hollow through the device of a symbolic echo chamber. Suddenly Maddalena says: "I'm nothing but a whore—I'll never be anything but a whore!" And she proceeds to retract her proposal. While Marcello protests, insisting upon his undying "love" for Maddalena, the latter is busy kissing another man.

Presently a group appears, and Marcello is off with them in search of the ghost of the pope who built the castle in the sixteenth century. During a séance presided over by a drunken woman, a female hand stretches out for that of the increasingly passive Marcello. The aristocratic owner of the hand looks like Elsa Lanchester in *The Bride of Frankenstein*,* but she nonetheless succeeds in getting the man to have sexual intercourse with her. Fellini conveys the impression that Marcello is committing necrophilia. Dawn, as usual, finds the group still searching for their ancestors—the dead in search of the dead.

Shot of Marcello and Emma seated in his car on a country

---

* Directed by James Whale, 1935.

road at night. Emma accuses Marcello of not being able to love. The man agrees; but he argues that he does not want to waste his whole life loving her. "I want more than a prison of bed and kitchen," he says. He then strikes the girl and shoves her out of the car. Emma cries: "You've lost the only thing of value in life—a woman who really loves you. One day you'll be old; there'll be no more women. And you'll die alone like a dog!" Angrily, Marcello drives off. When the sun rises, however, he comes back for the girl, who is still waiting where he left her on the road. Without a word, the couple drive off together. In modern society, Fellini suggests, man lacks the capacity not only to love but also to enjoy the simple pleasures of life. Having lost contact with the spiritual and natural worlds, having attempted to computerize and rationalize all experience, man has been left weighted with boredom—seeking always new experiences, fresh shocks to his jaded flesh and tired nerves, hoping to find in the accumulation of things what has been lost in human feelings.

This is perhaps why Steiner, in the next episode, kills his two children and then himself. The act seems senseless. Earlier, however, Steiner told Marcello: "It is peace that makes me afraid. . . . Perhaps because I distrust it above everything. . . . I feel that it's only an appearance, that it hides a danger. . . . They say that the world of the future will be wonderful. But what does that mean? It needs only the gesture of a madman to destroy everything." Steiner himself becomes a "madman" because the peace that he has imposed on his life is an unnatural one. Man has estranged himself from the positive and creative, as well as from the negative and destructive, in himself and in nature. Steiner was too much the rationalist to have really loved his children with natural feelings; behind his peaceful façade was a profound disquietude. During the episode involving Marcello's father, the latter quoted Dante: "*Disperto dolor che il cor mi prime.*" As John Simon points out, "this line about the desperate grief that clutches at his heart is spoken in the *Inferno* by Count Ugolino, the father who, to assuage his hunger, ate his son." The function of Marcello's father in the thematic structure of *La Dolce Vita* has already been sufficiently discussed. That Steiner destroys *his* children "to assuage *his* 'hunger'" seems plain.* As for Steiner's suicide, the act is merely the "logical" outcome of a consistent, self-destructive pattern of behavior. Most of the episode, which is relatively long, focuses on Marcello as he waits with police for Steiner's wife to inform her of what happened. The justification for this extended scene becomes clear at the conclusion.

The final episode reveals Marcello presiding over an orgy at the home of a movie producer. No longer a journalist, the hero is now a public relations agent for an actress. In his new role, Marcello is expected to keep the entourage of the performer amused with various forms of perverted sex. Present at the gathering are actors, chorus girls, loafers, whores, lesbians, and both effeminate and muscular homosexuals. The occasion for the party is the marriage annulment of a rich woman, who celebrates her "freedom" by performing a striptease to the tune of "Patricia," the song identified with the sweet and innocent Paola. Here, then, is another inversion of the sacred and profane. Although Marcello's assembly of specimen characters try desperately to have "fun," the party grows increasingly dull. "Nobody is leaving!" shouts Marcello. "We are all here to stay!" Which, alas, seems all too true—though, as we shall see, the future is not entirely without hope.

"Marcello," observes Salachas, "seems to take a strange pleasure from degrading himself." Salachas is right; for the hero, like Steiner, and like the modern world, seems bent on self-destruc-

---

* Simon also observes that "a young British gigolo" at Steiner's party "seems moved enough, as he plays back on a tape recorder some sounds Steiner recorded from nature, to recite a verse from . . . Shakespeare: 'Sounds and sweet airs, that give delight, and hurt not.' Lovely, but these words in *The Tempest* are spoken by Caliban, the monster." Like Fellini in *La Dolce Vita*, Shakespeare in *The Tempest*, as in all his plays, is concerned with the idea of order, with the great chain of being between beast and angel. Caliban, like Fellini's characters, is unable to appreciate moral and spiritual beauty, and thus he fails to become truly human.

tion; but the protagonist appears to have reached the point where he takes pleasure in degrading women, too. During the party, Marcello amuses the guests by having a drunken woman crawl about the floor on her hands and knees, while he sits astride her. Now we see how the clown, who cracked a whip over several girls disguised as tigers, was identified not only with the elder Rubini but also with Marcello. Like father, like son. At the beginning of the picture, the reporter was more interested in the half-naked girls on the terrace than in God. One's hunger for the divine, however, continues, even if repressed. If man makes an idol of woman (Sylvia, the sex goddess), he ends by hating the substitute, inasmuch as his spiritual needs remain unsatisfied. Technological society alienates man from nature ("Mother Nature"); and women are made to suffer for man's perversion of values. Marcello's father is bored with family life—he neglects his son and cheats on his wife; Marcello refuses to embrace a simple family existence—he even strikes the pathetic Emma. Steiner kills himself and his children— leaving his widow emotionally and spiritually ruined. Now we also understand how Fellini uses homosexual relations, which remain sterile, as a sign of man's rejection of woman, nature, and God.

The ending of the film emphasizes this last point. Dawn finds Marcello shredding a pillow and sprinkling the feathers on the heads of the creatures present in a mock baptism, similar to Sylvia's earlier parody of the Christian ritual. One is also reminded here of the previous association of Jesus and chickens. Dazedly, the revelers dance outside into the gray light of morning. "They say that the sun reveals flaws and shows you the truth," a homosexual with the grotesque face of a woman remarks to Marcello. "By the year 1980 the whole world will be depraved." With the waning of religious faith, man's penchant for ritual, as the sprinkling of feathers suggests, assumes different forms. Secular processions take the place of sacred ones. A long line of cars, containing devout worshippers of the flesh, followed Sylvia from the airport into Rome; later the sex goddess headed another profane procession as she danced in the Baths of Caracalla. Likewise, as Marcello and his friends drift down towards the Tyrrhenian Sea, they move in processional form.

Fishermen have just dragged to shore a huge monster of the deep. Marcello and the others stare at the fish, while a single eye in the head of the latter stares blankly back at them. The fish and the eye are both traditional symbols of Christ or God. Like Christ, who was buried for three days, the fish (according to one of the revelers) has been dead for three days. Whereas Christ rose from the dead (as reported in the Gospels), and appeared to his followers in a radiant, triumphant light, the monster remains dead. "It's been feeding on jellyfish," a spectator remarks of the catch—which would seem to be a reflection on the weak-willed decadents present. The film begins and ends, then, with a symbolic representation of God. For modern man, God is either a gilt statue—one idol among sundry competing, and more popular, idols—or merely a mirror of man's own ugly existence. Man defaces God, as he defaces nature, woman, and himself.

"The fish insists on looking at me!" Marcello cries. One other, however, is also looking at him. On the far side of a small stream, Paola appears; she waves to Marcello, who has collapsed exhaustedly to his knees. The girl—who stands for all that is pure and fine in the spiritual and natural world—beckons to the man. Slowly, painfully, Marcello crawls toward her on his knees. Observe the contrast with the previous scene at the party where Marcello rode the back of a prostitute. When values are healthy, man is humble before the mysteries incarnate in woman; when values are sick, man is arrogant, "queer," exploitative of the female. Paola speaks to Marcello; but he cannot hear her. Communication fails because the sound of wind and sea drowns out Paola's voice. Here is the final ironic inversion in the picture. At the beginning of the film, the drone of the helicopter prevented Marcello from communicating with the bikini-clad girls on the rooftop. Now the natural elements—which Steiner had tried to abstract from life and to insulate himself against—take their revenge, as they keep Marcello from hearing the saving words of Paola.* Shaking his head regretfully, the protagonist is drawn away by a party girl, back to that "sweet life" for which he has sold his soul. Paola looks after him. Fellini closes the film with the girl staring directly into the camera .... and into the face of the viewer.

In respect to viewpoint, Fellini told Gideon Bachmann that it "is not a question of *what* you show" but *"how* you show it." While *La Dolce Vita* faithfully reflects the deepest problems of the modern age, it is no exercise in mere documentary realism. Though every episode in the picture is said to have been suggested by an Italian scandal during the fifties, and though many of the characters in the piece play themselves, the film remains an artistic creation—a nightmare revealed through the camera of a master director. "Fellini's habitual selection of reality could hardly go further," John Russell Taylor has rightly observed; "here all is monstrous, misshapen, overgrown, the settings, the clothes of the characters, the faces, startlingly beautiful or shockingly grotesque, but never ordinary. . . . [T]his unrelenting concentration on the peculiar, the exceptional, the larger-than-life gives the film, within its superficially realistic coating, a feverish, expressionistic quality."

In the course of *La Dolce Vita*, Fellini occasionally uses a subjective camera. For example, when Marcello and Emma attend Steiner's party, the host and hostess open the door and look straight into the camera; when the girl who has taken Mr.

---

* Commencing with Plato's *Timaeus*, the concept of the chain of being involved the idea that the coarseness of the body prevents man from hearing the music of heaven, or word from the spiritual world. In *The Merchant of Venice*, Shakespeare—who like Dante, seems to have been on Fellini's mind while making *La Dolce Vita*—has Lorenzo say:

> . . . Look how the floor of heaven
> Is thick inlaid with patines of bright gold:
> There's not the smallest orb which thou behold'st
> But in his motion like an angel sings,
> Still quiring to the young-eyed cherubins;
> Such harmony is in immortal souls;
> But whilst this muddy vesture of decay
> Doth grossly close it in, we cannot hear it.
> (v.i. 58–65)

Rubini home comes for Marcello, she also gazes into the lens; and when the woman in the Castle of Bassano di Sutri seduces Marcello, she too is shot head-on from the central character's perspective. Naturally, the film-maker is aiming at more than variety here; he wants to force the viewer into a closer identification with Marcello. "I have no intention of playing the moralist," Fellini says, "but all the same I feel that a film is more moral when it does not offer the audience a solution, if such there be, for the problems of the protagonist. . . . My films . . . give the audience a very precise sense of responsibility." Thus, the final shot of the picture deliberately challenges the spectator into examining his own life and values: for Paola is not seen at last from Marcello's point of view, but from that of the audience.

Explaining the final scene to Charles Thomas Samuels, Fellini remarked that Marcello's reaction to Paola "is a result of the myth produced by a Catholic upbringing: a wish for some purity, something morally complete and angelic—stamped at the bottom of our minds and leaving us with a nostalgia for something rarefied." But he added that Marcello also "likes *la dolce vita*," and that his last gesture means: " 'I don't hear. I don't understand.' It could also be considered a bantering gesture: 'I don't hear you because I don't want to hear you'." Although Marcello doesn't "hear" Paola as yet, and although it remains impossible for him to recapture the innocence that once was, Fellini characteristically keeps the door open for "redemption" in the future—for Marcello can be reborn, even as Zampanò was reborn. Nicodemus asked: "How can a man be born when he is old? Can he enter a second time into his mother's womb and be born again?"; to which Christ replied: "That which is born of the flesh is flesh; and that which is born of the spirit is spirit. . . . The wind blows where it will, and thou hearest its sound but doest not know where it comes from or where it goes. So is everyone who is born of the spirit." At the end, it is not only Marcello who is left with a choice, with the possibility of turning his life around and becoming a new, and truer, man; the viewer is presented with the same option.

If *La Dolce Vita* resembles a morality play in structure, theme, and point of view, the same analogy can be drawn in terms of characterization. Marcello is a kind of everyman. He is not drawn in depth; he does not have a complex biography behind him; in short, he is rather "flat." The same observation can be made of the other characters, none of whom are fully developed. In a "realistic" film (narrowly defined) such an approach would be open to censure. Since the mode of imitation in Fellini's picture lies somewhere between realism and symbolism, however, the stylized characterization seems fitting within the overall construction. Three-dimensional character delineation is not an end in itself. More important than whether a specific character remains "flat" or "round" is the question whether the director has infused life into his creation. No one who has seen *La Dolce Vita* is ever likely to forget Marcello, Paola, Steiner, Sylvia, the elder Rubini, or the other characters who inhabit Fellini's Rome.

Visually, *La Dolce Vita* is a delight from beginning to end. If Fellini knows how to contrast scenes and sequences for maximum impact, he is also expert at alternating and varying close-ups, medium shots, and long shots. The cameraman for the picture, Otello Martelli, remarks:

> [Fellini] wanted to use perspective according to his fantasy, often completely in contradiction to the principles governing the use of certain lenses. . . . Federico wanted to use only long-range lenses: 75 mm, 100, and even 150. These lenses are supposed to be used for close-ups, for portraits; however, he wanted to use them while the camera was in motion. What mattered to him was really to focus upon the character, and he was hardly concerned at all about the effect this might have on the depth of the field. He almost never uses the 50 mm lens, which is the normal one for CinemaScope. With the 75, the panoramic shots and the broad movements risk becoming dull; you risk a kind of flickering. I immediately mentioned this to Fellini, but he replied: "What can that possibly matter?" And as is often the case, he was absolutely right. It gave a certain style to the film. A certain severity to the image. A concentration within the frame, a distortion of the characters and the setting.

Fellini's use of black and white—which some theorists would argue brings out spiritual values better than color—also contributes to the film's style, both visually and thematically. Formalization is perhaps easier to achieve in black and white; at the same time, the somber tones of the picture remain in keeping with its "medieval" or "Gothic" mood.

Finally, Nino Rota's musical score for the film is worthy of comment. During the scene in the last episode, wherein Marcello "blesses" the revelers with feathers as they dance outside into the dawn, the music is an excellent adjunct to the mood of mingled sadness, faded charm, fake gaiety, and moral opprobrium conveyed by the camera. Fellini's introduction of the song "Patricia" in contrasting situations is similarly telling. Sound effects in *La Dolce Vita*—such as the use of an echo chamber in the scene involving Marcello and Maddalena at the Castle of Bassano di Sutri, and the likewise thematically significant playing off of the helicopter motor against the roar of sea and wind— further show that Fellini is a master of the film medium in all its complexity.

An absorbing panorama, infused with love and disgust, with pity and humor, with reverence and mockery—and above all, projected with visual luster—of people caught in a moment of time, *La Dolce Vita* nonetheless transcends the fifties to portray man in his unending search for meaning and value.*

---

* "*La Dolce Vita* is only a substitute title," Fellini has said. "I wanted to call it *Babylon, 2000 Years after Jesus Christ* to bring out the element that is permanent, outside time and space, in a story that has been wrongly seen as controlled only by contemporary phenomena."

CHAPTER 10

$8\frac{1}{2}$

$8\frac{1}{2}$ is meant to be an attempt to reach an agreement
with life . . . an attempt and not a completed result.
I think for now it might indicate a solution: to make
friends with yourself completely, without hesitations,
without false modesty, without fears and
without hopes.

—FEDERICO FELLINI

The personal nature of $8\frac{1}{2}$ (1963) is suggested by its title. Allowing one unit for each of his previous seven pictures, with a half unit for *Variety Lights* (codirected with Alberto Lattuada) and for the sketches *A Matrimonial Agency* and *The Temptations of Doctor Antonio*, Fellini arrived at a total of eight and a half films. By drawing attention to his own career in the picture's title, Fellini aroused much speculation (most of it irrelevant and superficial) about the autobiographical significance of the events depicted on the screen.

As early as 1960, Fellini had considered the possibility of a movie about a man who goes to a bathing resort and contemplates the meaning—or meaninglessness—of his existence. A trip to Chianciano for a liver ailment subsequently provided Fellini with a specific setting for his new film. At first, he rejected the idea of portraying his central character as a film director; initially the man was to have been a lawyer or a doctor; later he was conceived as a screen writer. Creatively blocked so long as his protagonist was viewed from a distance, however, Fellini eventually decided to make the hero—Guido Anselmi (Marcello Mastroianni)—a film-maker like himself. Then, according to the director, "everything instantly fell into place."

Some critics, as I have suggested, evinced more concern with tracking down autobiographical leads in 8½ than in coming to terms with the objective meaning of the picture. Of course, Fellini has occasionally encouraged such a perverse approach by his offhand remarks; for example, he flatly declared to Charles Thomas Samuels: "I am Guido." Elsewhere Fellini has sought to point up the complex nature of his film, which exists as both personal statement, or autobiography, and autonomous art— that is, art that "speaks" its own truth in its own terms rather than referring for its significance to facts about the author's life. "I realize that 8½ is such a shameless and brazen confession, that it is futile to try and make people forget that it is about my own life," Angelo Solmi quotes Fellini as saying. "But I try to make a film that pleases me, first of all, and then the public. In 8½, the boundary line between what I did for myself and what I created for the public is very subtle." When he was in the United States to plug 8½, Fellini was quoted in *The New Yorker* (July 6, 1963) as follows: "I hope I can say [that 8½] is a picture about all men, and therefore about me. In any event, I could hardly say—could I?—that it was a picture about me, and therefore about all men." Similarly, Fellini told Deena Boyer: "[8½] is not so autobiographical as it would seem." Naturally, if one possesses certain facts about Fellini's life; and if one is familiar with the director's other films, one's experience of 8½ will be enhanced. However, one need not bring any prior knowledge of the film-maker's life and art to 8½ in order to enjoy what remains—visually and thematically— one of the most remarkable motion pictures ever made.

Indeed, 8½ is *so* remarkable that many critics refuse to believe that Fellini created the picture without help from other sources. Proust's *Remembrance of Things Past* has been cited as a model for *8½*; Fellini claims, however, never to have read the French author's masterpiece. More frequently, *Ulysses* has been called the "inspiration" for *8½*; yet, as pointed out in an earlier section of this book, Fellini has not read Joyce's novel either (although he doesn't rule out the possibility of indirect influence). Cocteau's *The Blood of a Poet* (1930) has been linked to *8½*; and so has Resnais's *Last Year at Marienbad*. Quite possibly, Fellini is familiar with the Cocteau; he denies having seen the Resnais, or even having read the script by Robbe-Grillet. Tracing influences on an artist's work remains a legitimate function of criticism. All the same, ascertaining the historical fact of influence, or even comparing two or more works in terms of that alleged influence, is not the whole task of criticism —it is not even the major task of criticism. The critic's first duty is to tell the reader *what* the artist is "saying" and to explain *how* he is "saying" it. "A truly humble critic would look at things from the inside, not from the outside. If the thing is vital and you look at it from your external point of view, you will never understand but will only project onto it what you think it should be," Fellini remarked to Samuels. "When a critic tells how the work should be according to his taste, which has been formed by a certain culture and certain artists, he is still judging by what is congenial to him." In short, citing influences can be the lazy critic's way of ignoring what is original in a film, and of avoiding the difficult job of explication and evaluation—the latter not on the basis of some prior model (valid up to a point), but in conformity with the work's own logic and consistency.

In *8½*, as noted, the focus is on Guido, a well-known director who is at a spa to prevent a nervous breakdown, and who is attempting to complete his scenario for a picture about the escape to outer space by the survivors of World War III. Guido is constantly besieged by his collaborators—the producers, the script writer, the actors—all of whom want him to discuss the picture. Unfortunately, the director cannot explain his thinking, because without fully realizing it he wants to make an autobiographical film. And when Guido finally comes to a recognition of this fact—when at last he realizes that it is impossible for him to turn out a simple picture with a message for mankind but must instead project a complicated story about his own confusions, uncertainties, and compromises—he abandons his original idea and can begin to conceive of a genuine artistic creation. What the viewer has watched for 135 minutes, then, *is* the movie that Guido intends to make . . . or *has* made.

Although 8½ is often classified as a stream-of-consciousness film, or an interior-monologue film, Fellini brilliantly manages complex shifts in viewpoint, alternating "objective" and "subjective" perspectives on the action. "Think what a bale of memories and associations and all we carry about with us," the director explained to Eugene Walter. "It's like seeing a dozen films simultaneously. There's memory, there's memory that's been sorted out and filed, what they call subconscious. There's a kind of idealized set of sketches of the dinner party we'll go to tomorrow night. And there's also what is happening around us, visible and invisible." In order to achieve the effect of "a dozen films simultaneously" unreeling, Fellini gives little help to the viewer in following the transitions from one perspective to another. For example, instead of proceeding from a shot of Guido in the present to a flashback or fantasy and then back to Guido in the original shot, Fellini often dispenses with such structural continuity and jumps forward from the flashback or fantasy to the next scene in the present. Some scenes are "objective"; that is, we see "what is happening around" Guido, what is "visible" to the camera-eye in external reality (or "daily reality," as Fellini puts it elsewhere in his interview with Walter). Other scenes are also set in the present, and also project recognizable elements of the phenomenal world; but these scenes are more or less touched with some degree of fantasy. Perhaps the best way of describing the latter viewpoint would be to label it as "objective-subjective." Three other narrative perspectives are wholly "subjective": in some scenes we are privy to Guido's daydreams in isolation from external events; elsewhere we are made to witness his memories through flashbacks; and sometimes we are plunged into Guido's nocturnal dream world. With great skill, Fellini integrates the different viewpoints, using the "objective" scenes to set off Guido's daydreams, flashbacks, and nightmares. Hence much of the action in the film proceeds via the "logic" of free association.

8½ opens on a city street with Guido caught in a traffic jam. Around him drivers and passengers in other cars either ignore him or stare back at him as though he did not exist. At first, the mode of imitation suggests "realism"; when we notice a woman with bare breasts in one of the cars, however, we begin to question our initial judgment. It soon becomes apparent that Guido is suffering a claustrophobic reaction. By using silence outside Guido's car (another element that arouses a suspicion in our minds as to the level of "reality" being depicted, inasmuch as we would normally expect drivers to be impatiently honking their horns), Fellini makes the sounds of the trapped movie director—his heavy breathing, his fingernails clawing frantically at the glass windows of his sealed car—almost unbearable for the viewer. Throughout this scene, as well as throughout the first half of the following scene, we are not shown Guido's face. Since Fellini keeps his camera in close to the man in the car, and since many of the shots of other cars are from his perspective, we tend to identify with the protagonist: the man whose face we do not see could be any man—his face could be any man's. Then, suddenly, Guido begins to rise out of the car and soar above the traffic—higher and higher into the clouds—an unequivocally surrealistic image framed in a long shot. The mood conveyed by the figure drifting over a sun-sparked body of water is one of unfettered joy, of transcendence. Unhappily, Guido soon discovers that his freedom remains illusory. Using a subjective camera from the protagonist's point of view, Fellini has Guido observe that his ankle is caught by a rope and that, far below, a man is pulling him down to earth . . . or more precisely, and less metaphorically, down into the sea.

The opening scene of 8½ is not just visually arresting. In retrospect, we see how skillfully Fellini prepares us for a number of developments, how he takes us immediately and pictorially to the heart of Guido's yearnings and myriad problems. Subsequently, we learn that Guido feels trapped because he cannot finish his scenario about the trip to outer space. The director is surrounded by people who do not really "see" him; they fail to comprehend his personal and creative difficulties. Guido would like to express his deepest concerns; he dreams of being released from the bondage of making a picture that merely engages his conscious mind, when it is the unconscious from which true inspiration springs. The man who prevents Guido from achieving complete artistic freedom is a symbol of the spectacular which the film-maker has contracted to make, and for which an expensive launching pad has already been erected. In structural terms, Guido's nightmare of being suffocated and then drowned is balanced by the ending in which the hero celebrates human existence in a waking fantasy by dancing with all the characters who have shared his life.

Abruptly, Guido wakes up from his nightmare of plunging into the sea and finds himself in his hotel room being examined by two doctors and a nurse. "Are you preparing another film for us?" one doctor inquires sarcastically. "Another film that offers no hope?" Guido does not reply. The critic-writer Daumier enters and, by his air of detachment, conveys disapproval of the director's unfinished scenario, which he has just finished reading. Ironically, the doctors prescribe mineral water and mud baths for what ails Guido.

In the next scene, Guido is discovered at a spa garden. An orchestra is playing a musical piece with nerve-racking loudness as the patients, most of whom are middle-aged and elderly, mill about the fountains. Again, Fellini's camera involves the viewer in the action of the film by its movements into and among the people present as they stare directly at the lens. Sometimes a subjective camera appears to be in use—that is, the patients are apparently gazing at the unseen Guido; sometimes, however, they seem to be gazing at us. In either case, the film-maker provides the audience with the vicarious experience of being at the spa with his hero. A satirical mood is conveyed by numerous long shots of the patients grouped ritualistically about the fountains, the orchestra performing solemnly in the background, the garden shown in a celestial white light (an effect that prefigures numerous other scenes in the picture). Behind the railing of the fountain girls duck for mineral water and arise with glasses brimming for the faithful. Guido, who is also standing in line, visualizes his ideal woman (Claudia Cardinale) materializing under the arches of the court. When Guido reaches the fountain, his ideal—dressed in white—smilingly offers him a glass of spa water. "She is the most disturbing sign of Guido's impotence," Fellini explained to Samuels, "and he projects through this figure all his own confusions, his desire for an ideal woman who would tell him, both as man and artist, what to do; she is his nostalgia, his childish desire for protection, his romanticism. These all are embodied in a figure who mocks him because she is only an abstraction." In an instant, the ideal woman disappears—her place taken by a real woman, who is impatiently extending a glass to the preoccupied Guido.

Daumier joins the hero in the garden and begins to criticize his film script: "Your story lacks ideas. It has no philosophical base. It's just a series of meaningless episodes. It has none of the merits of the avant-garde film and all the drawbacks." Guido suffers in silence. Next the director encounters his old friend Mezzabotta, who introduces him to Gloria, a girl he intends to wed as soon as his marriage of thirty-one years is annulled. As Mezzabotta himself shamefully recognizes, Gloria is young enough to be his daughter. Here Fellini touches again on the theme of aging. In the second scene of the picture, Guido informs the nurse that he is forty-three; like the majority of the patients at the spa, then, Guido is in the second half of his life. The artist's creative problems are tied to his personal problems. Not only is Guido unable to receive emotional support from Mezzabotta—since the latter is obviously infatuated with the physically attractive but emotionally shallow and intellectually pretentious Gloria (who is writing a thesis entitled "The Solitude of Modern Man in the Contemporary Theater")—but his friend's affair represents a vain attempt to meet the challenge of advancing years. No man can live his life over. Rebirth is possible only on the spiritual and emotional planes. Guido must learn to accept himself and the world as it is, must learn to move forward, not backward—must learn, in a word, to be honest.

In the following scene, Guido reads Daumier's comments on his script ("of all the symbols in which your work abounds, this girl in white is by far the worst"); reluctantly meets his mistress Carla (Sandra Milo) at the spa railroad station; takes her to a restaurant where she chatters about her husband (she wants Guido to help her mate find suitable employment); and then goes to bed with her (at Carla's hotel because, as Guido cautiously explains, too many people know him at his place). Guido does not seem to love Carla—indeed, as we are soon to learn, an inability to love is one of the hero's most serious failings. In large measure, Guido's relationship with Carla is a desperate stratagem for warding off the shadows. To reveal the adolescent regression involved in Guido's attitude towards his mistress, Fellini has the couple play a game in which the woman pretends to be a whore by entering the bedroom as though the director were a customer. (One is reminded of that scene in *La Dolce Vita* in which Marcello and Maddalena have intercourse on a prostitute's bed.) Unfortunately for the suffering Guido, Carla is too unimaginative to enter fully into her role: "I don't think I'd like being a prostitute," she remarks. "I'm really a homebody."

Afterward Carla reads a comic book while Guido sleeps . . . and dreams. An elderly woman enters the room. It is Guido's mother. She gestures for him to follow her. They visit a cemetery; and there, in one of the tombs, Guido meets his dead father (Annibale Ninchi, who also played Marcello's father in *La Dolce Vita*). The departed Anselmi complains that his tomb is cramped and unsatisfactory. Instead of the ecstasies of heaven or the torments of hell after death, Guido learns that the next world is just more of this world—nothing but petty annoyances and everlasting boredom. Pace, the producer, appears and begins to revile Guido for his inability to finish the scenario; the director's parents concur that their son always did have a tendency to be lazy. Guido would like to be a child again, but he realizes that there is no escape from the present. Not even death offers a satisfactory way out. Perhaps Carla's gloomy hotel room triggered Guido's dream of an equally gloomy cemetery; and perhaps Guido's sexual experience with his mistress unconsciously carried him back to an earlier relationship with another woman. In his dream, the hero chastely kisses his mother goodbye. Suddenly the old woman begins to embrace her son with sexual feeling; and just as suddenly, Mother is transformed into Luisa (Anouk Aimée), Guido's wife. . . . End of dream.

In the elevator of his hotel, Guido—awake now—watches an austere Roman Catholic cardinal reading his breviary. Throughout the remainder of 8½, Guido will recall unpleasant experiences with clerics, and he will seek in vain for spiritual nourishment from the church. As Fellini has pointed out, Guido "is a victim of medieval Catholicism, which tends to humiliate a man rather than restore him to his divine greatness" (quoted in Newsweek, June 24, 1963). In the hotel lobby, Guido examines four elderly men who hope to be cast in his picture. "How old are you?" he inquires of each; to which they reply: "Seventy-one," "Sixty-three," "Seventy-eight," and "Eighty-four." With a seeming nonchalance, Guido turns away from the men, announcing: "You're not old enough."

At the spa's nightclub, the magic team of Maurice and Maya perform their act. Maurice asks Guido to think of anything he wants, so that Maya can read his mind and write his thoughts on a blackboard. Guido agrees. The words "Asa, Nisi, Masa" appear in chalk and Guido nods approval at Maya's telepathic powers. When asked what the words mean, however, Guido refuses to reply.

Cut to a flashback in which Guido and other little boys are bathed in an enormous vat by his mother and numerous female relatives. This flashback represents not only a brief retreat for Guido from the difficulties of the present—since the boy receives both physical and emotional warmth from the ministering women —but also provides an explanation for the mysterious words introduced in the previous scene. The boys play a game in which, if "Asa, Nisi, Masa" is uttered, the eyes in a portrait on the wall are supposed to move. "Perhaps," the mature Guido seems to be reflecting, "my problems can be solved by recourse to magic —that magic I believed in as a child. For wasn't it by magic that Maya read my thoughts? And isn't it by a kind of 'magic' that I create my own world on film?" (When, earlier in the picture, Guido applies an eyebrow pencil to Carla's face in order to transform her into a prostitute, the woman exclaims: "I'll look just like one of your actresses!") However "magical" the world of artistic creativity remains, Guido's personal problems can only be solved—as opposed to being temporarily sublimated via art—in terms of the "real" world. Finally, this flashback foreshadows the harem scene, one of the most discussed episodes in the film. Although 8½ appears chaotic on the surface, then, the structure of the picture is consummately unified.

Back in the present, Guido is called to a telephone in the hotel lobby. Fellini again uses the camera subjectively, tracking in on the phone held out by an elderly porter until Guido steps into the frame and picks up the receiver; then, as the protagonist talks to his wife, the camera stays on the old man as he crosses the cold empty lobby—surely a visual trope intended as a comment on the Anselmi marriage. Except for a significant shot of Mezzabotta and Gloria also stepping across the lobby, Fellini keeps Guido in focus throughout the remainder of the scene, though we hear Luisa's voice on the other end. The couple are experiencing marital problems of a long-standing nature: Luisa is hurt by her husband's lack of love and by his numerous infidelities. When Luisa asks him if he wants her to come up to the spa, Guido replies in the affirmative . . . but not very convincingly. Nevertheless it seems clear Luisa will join Guido, and thus the viewer is prepared for an eventual crisis.

In the corridor outside the production office, Guido encounters his assistant director, Conocchia, who complains that he is being ignored by the film-maker. "You tell me nothing," Conocchia says. "And once we were friends." Guido remains insultingly quiet. "I've worked in pictures for thirty years," the elderly assistant goes on. "And in the old days we did stuff you fellows haven't the guts to try!" Suddenly angry, the vulnerable Guido

shouts: "Get away from me—you old fogy!" However, Conocchia takes a final thrust at Guido's sore spot: "You're not the
man you used to be!" Indeed, this is one of Guido's biggest
worries: that he is finished as an artist, that he has nothing
more to say nor command of the means to say it. Yet by the
end of 8½, Guido learns that there is still much he can com-
municate to the world through film—provided he does not attempt to substitute stale formulas for his deepest intuitions, or
mechanically designed architectonics for organic structure.

As he steps into his bedroom, Guido "sees" his ideal woman.
"What is your name?" he asks; and she answers: "Claudia."
After turning down the bed, Claudia gets under the sheets with
Guido and assures him that she will never leave him.

Next Guido appears in Carla's bedroom. As a result of drinking too much mineral water, the hero's mistress has developed
a fever. Guido carefully wipes the perspiration from her face and
bosom with a cloth, half listening sympathetically to her delirious
ravings, half fascinated by her ample breasts. . . . The following scene also takes place in the present, its viewpoint likewise
"objective." In the woods near the spa, Guido attempts to talk
with the Cardinal. Before he can explain what he wants to
discuss, however, the prelate asks him irrelevant questions—
"Are you married?"; "Do you have any children?"—and when
Guido confesses some doubts about his new film, the priest
commences a monologue on Diomedes. Frustrated, Guido gazes
off at the sight of a peasant woman descending a hill, her legs
and feet bare. This image—coming after the two scenes set in
the present—sets off another flashback . . .

Shot of little Guido running down to the beach with his schoolmates to watch La Saraghina—big-bosomed and bare-legged—
perform an "obscene" rhumba. (As noted in the first section of
this book, La Saraghina is a character out of Fellini's childhood.
Since around Rimini sardines are called *saraghine*, and since
the huge woman used to prostitute herself in return for the small
fish, she was dubbed La Saraghina.) Fellini informed Samuels
that the enormous prostitute represents "sex seen by a child.
Hence she is grotesque, but also seductive to one so innocent."

To the priests, however, La Saraghina is the devil. Consequently, two men of the cloth chase Guido across the sand—their slipping and sliding rendered all the more comic by being photographed in fast motion.

Solmi quotes Fellini as saying that "to a certain extent" La Saraghina "is and does represent the devil." Actually, Fellini's approach in this sequence is complex. After the beach scene, there is a traveling shot past portraits of dead clerics, until the camera stops before the face of a priest in the flesh. The juxtaposition of elements should require no commentary. Little Guido —dragged before a congregation of black-robed clerics as though he were a criminal—is punished by being shown the tears he has brought to his mother's eyes. Afterwards he kneels with deep respect before a statue of the Virgin (reminiscent of Giudizio's gazing at the angel in *I Vitelloni*). Still later, Guido returns to the shore and discovers La Saraghina facing out to the sea; when the prostitute smiles at him, the boy, almost reverently, tips his cap. La Saraghina serves as both a symbol of crude sexuality and innocent nature, both the devil and the powerful, awe-provoking incarnation of the life force. The priests are made to look absurd. And yet, the manner in which little Guido stares up at the Virgin suggests a sense of spiritual wonder no less real than the amazement inspired by La Saraghina. In part, Guido's image of Claudia, his ideal woman, is probably derived from his boyhood feelings about the mother of Jesus—and about his own mother. All three women represent the "clean" and the "orderly." In Freudian terms, Guido seems to have divided women into sexual creatures and ethereal Madonna figures. The dream in which Guido's mother kisses him in a carnal manner before changing into Luisa seems relevant here. It is worth remembering also that Guido, as he cared for the sick Carla in the scene just before his meeting with the Cardinal, was torn between tenderness and sexual curiosity. Women, however, fail to conform to Guido's simple classifications; Carla, for instance, pretends to be a whore but she would rather be a housewife. Even Guido experiences difficulty keeping the categories separate; for in one scene, as noted, Claudia goes to bed with him.

Possibly, Guido's marital problems are traceable to this basic confusion in his attitude toward women.

Back to the present. Guido, his entourage, and the other patients at the spa—all of them wrapped in sheets—are discovered at the baths, descending through hellish vapors of steam a seemingly endless flight of stairs. At the lowest level, the viewpoint shifts from "objective" to "subjective," as Guido imagines an interview with the Cardinal. "Guido!" sounds impersonally over a loudspeaker. "His Eminence will see you now!" It is a topsy-turvy Fellinian vision in which the representative of the Church is to be found at the center of the earth, where in Dante the devil himself is confined. (When questioned about influences, Fellini admits that he *is* familiar with Dante!) "Your Eminence," Guido laments, "I'm not happy." The decrepit Cardinal, his naked torso shrouded by mist, barely acknowledges the suppliant's existence as he drily replies: "And why should you be happy? That's not the purpose of your life." Before Guido can get another word in (the fantasy is obviously a parody of the previous "objective" interview), the prelate begins to pontificate in Latin: *"Extra ecclesiam, nullasalus . . .* Outside the church, there is no salvation. . . . *Extra ecclesiam, nullasalus . . ."* The fantasy ends with a shot of a tiny cellar window, through which Guido observes the Cardinal, slowly closing—thus separating the hero from the church, forever.

Using the romantic song "Blue Moon" as a sound transition (religion and women are associated in Fellini's vision), the action jumps forward in the present to an "objective" scene on the street wherein Guido meets Luisa, who has arrived in town with some friends. Although the couple smile at each other, there is an evident strain in their relationship. After an episode at the site of the launching pad involving Guido, Luisa, and others—an episode designed to further our comprehension of the artist's troubles ("Aren't you tired of films where nothing happens? Well, in my film everything happens. I put in everything," the director asserts. "I have nothing to say. But I want to say it, anyway.")—Fellini presents a scene in which the hero and his wife have a bitter quarrel in bed over his lack of

8½: *In the last scene, Guido has a fantasy in which he tells Luisa: "Accept me as I am . . . Let's try again."*

love and his repeated failure to change his habits. The alter-
cation ends with both partners turning away from each other,
their conflicts unresolved.

Next morning at breakfast in the garden, Luisa continues to
berate Guido for his inability to tell the truth, or indeed for his
inability to even know the difference between truth and false-
hood. Although one can sympathize with Luisa, one can also
understand how Guido's weakness as a man on the score of
"truth" nevertheless constitutes his imaginative strength as an
artist. When Carla arrives at the garden and takes a table in
view of the Anselmis, Luisa mutters: "Cow! . . . Whore!" Guido
insists that he ended his relationship with Carla three years
before; however, Luisa knows better. Occasionally in *8½*,
Fellini signals a fantasy by having Guido peer contemplatively
over the rim of his spectacles; this is what the hero does now.
. . . And suddenly we see what Guido wishes to "see": Luisa
and Carla embracing in front of the latter's table, smiling at each
other, complimenting each other, dancing together. . . . This
fantasy is followed by a much more elaborate one in which all
the women Guido has known reappear as slaves in his harem.

The setting for the fantasy is the country home where, earlier
in the picture during a flashback, little Guido was bathed and put
to bed by his young mother, the latter calling him "the sweetest
boy in the whole world." When the fantasy commences, Guido
appears in the doorway with fake snowflakes cascading about his
shoulders, his arms filled with gifts—thus projecting an image
of one who gives and gives and gives. In reality, of course,
Fellini's hero merely *takes, takes, takes.* As in the past, the
women bathe Guido in one of the vats, the large black hat on
his head not only functioning (as Suzanne Budgen has observed)
as an anti-erotic device by comically removing our sense of the
man's naked body underneath the water but also maintaining
the symbolism of the hero as an authority figure. (Later in the
film, Claudia makes fun of Guido's floppy hat and baggy suit
by saying: "You dress like an old man.") In the harem, one of
Guido's rules is that a woman who reaches the age of twenty-six
must be segregated from the younger ones and banished to the

8½ : *In the spa garden, Fellini signals a fantasy by having Guido peer over the rim of his glasses.*

Siberia of the second floor. When an aging dancer is informed of her fate, Guido's harem—stirred by Wagner's "Ride of the Valkyries"—revolts against their despotic ruler. Armed with a whip, the hero quells the disturbance and soon has matters in hand. However, the good mood has been irrevocably lost.

Shot of Guido standing at the head of a table, his slaves gazing up towards him expectantly: "What happened, my friends? he asks. "Why couldn't we have a pleasant time, such as we have every evening, tucked away here safe from the world?" Although Guido would like to see himself as a strong father figure—even as a brutal master of females when occasion warrants—he reveals in his fantasy a deeper longing to be taken care of by women as his mother took care of him as a boy. He is frightened of old age, of the loss of sexual and creative potency; but he knows that there can be no escape from reality, that one cannot elude one's fate by exiling all women over twenty-six, or by pretending that a man over eighty isn't really old. "Happiness," Guido remarks to the women, "is being able to tell the truth without hurting anyone." Is such "happiness" possible? The screen slowly fades to black. . . .

Return to an "objective" perspective in the present. The scene: the inside of a movie theater, where Guido sits alone, Daumier a few rows back, Luisa and friends a few rows down, the producer, Pace, and his lackeys in a row up front. The occasion: Guido is trying to select his cast from the screen tests, which are about to be shown to the group. As usual, Daumier is debunking the film and criticizing the hero. Weary of his intellectual associate, Guido has a fantasy in which, at a signal by him, two men appear, seize the carping writer, slip a black hood over his head —and hang him, right there in the theater. Shot of the corpse, swinging from a rope. . . . followed by a shot of Guido staring straight ahead, Daumier still seated a few rows behind him. . . . Images of actresses portraying Luisa, Carla, and La Saraghina appear on the screen. It is now clear that Guido has hopelessly mixed up the spectacular he had contracted to shoot with the autobiographical film he really wants to create. As though that confusion were not enough, Guido has not even honestly presented his relations with women. "What you give people is an idealized version of yourself," Luisa, at one point, says to her husband—the truth of which Guido acknowledges at the end of the film.

Since the screen tests bore Guido, he appears delighted when a press agent informs him that Claudia, an actress whom he once knew, is waiting to see him about a role in his new picture. As it turns out, Claudia is the real life model for the ideal Claudia of the hero's fantasies. "How big will my part be?" Claudia demands, seated behind the wheel of her car, Guido beside her, the night seeming to engulf them as "Blue Moon" again is heard on the sound track. Instead of answering, Guido tells her about his block, about his inability to exclude material Daumier would consider irrelevant. "Could you choose one thing and be faithful to it?" Guido asks. They stop on a dark, deserted street. In an upstairs window, we see what Guido now imagines: the ideal Claudia, resplendent in white, is shown holding a lighted candle; next she is seen downstairs, in the street, setting a table. Then the vision disappears. "There's no part for me in this picture," the real Claudia says, "Is there?" Guido concurs: "Because a woman can't change a man or save him. . . . Because there won't be a picture, because I refuse to film a lie." While Guido elaborates on his remarks, Claudia three times observes: "Because you don't know how to love. . . ." The scene ends with the sudden arrival of Pace, who has called a press conference for the next day at the site of the launching pad.

Lillian Ross quotes Fellini as saying: "The movie business is macabre. Grotesque. It is a combination of a football game and a brothel." Nowhere is this observation brought home with more force than in the scene of the press conference, which in viewpoint moves through "objective," "objective-subjective," and "subjective" modes in a bewildering fashion. A cold wind lifts the sand on the beach and, mercifully, drowns out some of the stupid questions asked of Guido by the newspapermen. "Leave me alone!" the director shouts; but to no avail. An American woman, half facing the camera, yells with vindictive glee: "He has nothing to say!" Guido is forced to sit at an enormous table,

crowded with strangers and waiters, where Pace waits for him
to inform the world about the new picture. ("You'd better come
up with something," the producer warns. "I'll destroy you. If
you ruin me, I'll ruin you. You'll never make another picture.")
Suddenly Guido finds a revolver thrust into his hand. With a sense
of relief, he dives under the table, crawls along on all fours,
stops, and—with his back facing the camera, with a sigh: "What
an incurable romantic!" and with a final memory-glimpse of his
aged mother ("Guido, you bad boy. Why are you doing this?")—
shoots himself in the temple. . . .

The press conference is over, the launching pad dismantled.
Guido—who only imagined his suicide, but who really called off
the picture—tells some technicians: "Maybe we'll work together
on the next film." Daumier joins Guido, and the two men sit in
the hero's car. As Daumier congratulates Guido on his decision
to abandon the movie ("Why offer the masses still another work
that says nothing? The world already abounds in superfluity;
much better to destroy than to create what's inessential. We
artists must dedicate ourselves to silence."—the latter from one
who never shuts up!), the hero stares fixedly ahead, gazes over
the rim of his glasses . . . and proceeds to fantasize the concluding
scene of $8\frac{1}{2}$.

"Wait a second!" Maurice grins, looking into the camera at
both Guido and the viewer. "We're ready to begin!" The magician
points with his wand—and Guido sees his parents, Claudia, and
all the other characters from his real and imaginary life. Everyone is dressed in white. "How right it is to accept you and love
you, and how simple it is," Guido says, in an interior monologue.
"I am what I am, not what I want to be. Life is a holiday to be
enjoyed. Let us enjoy it together." He gets out of the car, takes
a megaphone in his hand, and at last becomes a director by
arranging his cast as they dance on the rim of a circus ring.
When Carla appears, Guido tells her: "I'll call you tomorrow.
Now get in line." Next his wife comes to him. "Luisa, I have no
answers," he confesses. "All I can do is question and search.
Only with this in mind can I look at you without shame. Accept me as I am. . . . Let's try again." With some doubt as to

the rightness of Guido's attitude, Luisa nevertheless agrees to give their marriage another trial.

At first, the characters who will provide the material for Guido's future pictures move on the screen in processional form from right to left, whereas the hero's own movements in front of them are from left to right, the camera tracking with him. In order to dramatize Guido's complete acceptance of life-as-it-was, life-as-it-is, and life-as-it-will-be, Fellini reverses the hero's movement and has him join the procession and flow along with the other dancers in perfect harmony. Claudia alone has no part in the roundelay. The last time we see her, she is moving off toward the sea and waving goodbye. By embracing the real, Guido apparently relinquishes his need for the ideal.

Three musicians appear (reminiscent of the ones in *La Strada*), joined by little Guido dressed in his school uniform, but this time in a white one instead of a black one. Throughout 8½, Fellini juxtaposes light and darkness—one thinks of the gleaming walls of the childhood home and the shadows moving across them, of the white ceilings of the Catholic school and the black-robed priests below, of the ideal Claudia's white dress and the hero's black hat and suit. Here, at the end, Fellini clothes everyone in white to suggest that Guido has overcome the past, that there are no more dark places in his memories, and that reality itself can be more beautiful and worthy of veneration than the ideal. The tension between the real and the ideal, however, is never finally resolved in Fellini's work.

Gradually, the light vanishes from the screen, until only little Guido is visible. . . . And then, he too disappears, and the music dies.

"8½," Fellini has said, "is a film of liberation—nothing more." Now it seems perfectly true, as critics have pointed out, that Guido has not changed in some important respects at the conclusion of the film. For example, the hero will continue to deceive —or attempt to deceive—Luisa about his relations with Carla; thus one wonders how long the Anselmi marriage can endure, since it will prove easier for Guido to accept himself as he is than for Luisa to do so. When Samuels brought this problem

to Fellini's attention, the film-maker simply observed: "8½ is
. . . a comic film." Evidently, as Fellini sees it, Guido will never
change because he doesn't really want to change. He needs
Luisa, but he also needs Carla, and other women, too. At least
Guido has learned to be honest about himself, however one might
evaluate the nature of that honesty. Furthermore, the hero appears to have come to terms emotionally with his past. At the
end, he is able to move forward into the second half of his life,
sure of himself again as both man and artist. Granted, the truth
often hurts, life cannot always be a "holiday," and one does not
normally learn to love in reality with the suddenness that 8½
suggests. It could also be argued that Fellini raises more
questions in the course of his picture than he manages to answer,
though it should be added that such a situation probably is inevitable in any complex psychological film.

If Guido's awakening as a man perhaps leaves something to
be desired, his rebirth as an artist is totally satisfying. Like
Daumier, some critics equate what a film "says" with "ideas" in
the philosophical sense; they approach a work of art as though it
were a thesis to be demonstrated. For instance, John Simon has
questioned Fellini's "metaphysics": "Can one say Yea to life
without apprehending its quiddity?" One is almost embarrassed
to inform Simon: "Most of us do, every day of our lives—otherwise, we'd cut our throats." Pascal asks rhetorically: "Is it by
reason that you love yourself?" And is it by reason that the
artist says Yea to life? Guido's affirmation of human existence—
like the creative force itself—issues from a source beyond the
rational. By accepting himself, others, all the manifestations of
life, Guido is released from the strait jacket of conscious thought.
The world in which Guido really lives is the world of his imagination; and in that world, he loves everyone and everything.
Although he remains to some extent the active shaper of experience (the ringmaster), Guido is also passive, open to sug-
gestion, free to move where his heart and his imagination take
him, part of the mysterious, terrible yet joyful flow of life (the
roundelay). Has there ever been a movie about spiritual ex-
haustion rendered with such visual gusto? Isn't Fellini's hymn

to life consistent with the thematic approach taken in all his work? In short, what the film "says" or "means" *is* the film: form and content are indivisible.

Guido's artistic triumph—which is, of course, also Fellini's—remains 8½ itself.*

* 8½ won over sixty international awards, including an Academy Award for the best foreign film of the year and seven Silver Ribbons (Italy's equivalent of the Oscar).

CHAPTER 11

Juliet of the Spirits

*For 8½, I wanted to do a polydimensional portrait
of a man. For* Juliet of the Spirits, *I am getting
closer to what really interests me. The cinema is the
unique and perfect tool to explore with precision
the inner landscapes of the human being. I've always
wanted to do an extrasensorial tale, born entirely
of the imagination. This should be it.*

—FEDERICO FELLINI

When *Juliet of the Spirits* (1965) was released, it aroused much
the same controversy as had *8½*. "Is the film based on the Fellini
marriage?"—that, for some critics, became the burning question.
As usual, Fellini encouraged such speculation, at least in part.
Speaking of *Juliet of the Spirits* with Tullio Kezich, for example,
the film-maker said: "It was born as a film about Giulietta and
for Giulietta." When Tom Burke pressed him further on the
subject, Fellini replied evasively: "Ah, but everything the artist
does is somehow about himself, yes? The woman, Juliet, is not
precisely my wife, the marriage is not *precisely* my marriage." On
other occasions, the director vigorously denied that the film was
autobiographical, while at the same time making no secret of the
fact that Mrs. Fellini, like the title character in his picture,

experienced visions as a little girl, still believes in the existence of spirits, and is no stranger to mediums, astrologists, and fortune-tellers. For that matter, Fellini himself is strongly interested in mysticism and magic. Prior to making *Juliet of the Spirits*, the film-maker attended a séance in which he claims to have seen and spoken to the ghost of his dead father.

Juliet of the Spirits was the sixth—and up to this writing the last—film made by Fellini in which Giuletta Masina appeared. Because Fellini and his wife had battled constantly when he'd directed her in previous films, the actress had remained unwilling to take on the part of Juliet. "My wife is an aggressive, strong-minded woman," Thomas Meehan quotes Fellini as saying, "not a wistful, pastel figure as some writers have pictured her; and I am strong-minded, too, so we had our clashes." Although Giulietta Masina had been enormously successful in bringing Gelsomina and Cabiria to life on the screen, Fellini insisted that she not repeat those interpretations in the role of Juliet. "She found a thousand objections," Fellini remarks in the Meehan piece. "This or that did not 'feel' right to her. And I became angrier and angrier. 'But don't you understand?' I would say. 'I want you to play *yourself*. What I'm asking you to do is what you *always* do—what I'm asking you to feel is what you *always* feel.'" However, there were instances when Fellini listened to his wife. "A number of times, on the spur of the moment, I just asked Giulietta what she would say, what she would do," Fellini told Kezich, "and I accepted her solutions without the slightest change."

Like *8½*, *Juliet of the Spirits* is complex in viewpoint. Some shots depict "objective" reality. Other shots are variously "subjective": sometimes we see what Juliet recalls from her past as it actually happened; sometimes we see past events distorted by what Juliet wants, or needs, to remember; and sometimes we see Juliet's visions—projections into the phenomenal world of her fears and longings, and occasionally projections of future happenings—in the form of dreams or waking fantasy. Also, as in *8½*, there are entire scenes that can only be described as "objective-subjective," because the viewpoint oscillates continually between a faithful representation of external reality and a stylized presentation of what Juliet is thinking and feeling.

Unlike *8½*, however, *Juliet of the Spirits* is in color. "The apparitions in the film have the same substance as the real characters, and vice versa," Fellini informed Kezich. "Indeed, sometimes more than one character is presented suddenly with a completely unreal look, so much so that a stimulating ambiguity between fantasy and reality is created. The ambiguity is intentional and is one of the keys to the film. The thing that really made it effective was the color—it was a very important element." More will be said about point of view and color in the analysis that follows.

Juliet of the Spirits opens with a trucking shot: the camera inches forward through the foliage of a weeping-willow tree and discovers a white house illuminated against the night. The effect is as though the camera—and with it the viewer—were about to spy on the inhabitants of the house. Appropriately, Fellini will follow through on this initial technical stroke later by opening up Juliet's mind for the viewer's understanding. Cut to a shot of Juliet's maids, Elisabetta and Teresina, inside the house, where they are debating whether to light candles—followed by another cut to Juliet's dressing room. Throughout the film, Fellini uses quick cutting within scenes and between sequences to create a nervous tempo, to underline the disordered state of Juliet's mind and the restlessness of the people surrounding her.

As in *8½*, we do not see the face of the main character during the opening of the film. Half-concealed behind a partition, her back to the camera, Juliet cannot decide whether to wear a wig or even what dress to wear for the intimate dinner she has planned to celebrate her fifteenth wedding anniversary. In general terms, Juliet is going through a crisis—she seems unsure of her identity, indecisive about her role in life. When her husband, Giorgio* (Mario Pisu), is heard outside, the lights in the house are extinguished; illumination is then provided by candles.

---

* Fellini *will* have his little jokes. In *Nights of Cabiria*, the previous film in which Giulietta Masina appeared, the title character is robbed and almost drowned by a "lover" named Giorgio.

Fellini's camera does not show us the heroine's face until Giorgio steps into her presence. Symbolically—and this remains the chief "idea" in the film—the artist is "saying" that Juliet does not exist as a person except in terms of her husband. Speaking of *Juliet of the Spirits* to Lillian Ross, Fellini remarked: "I want to help Italian women to become free from a certain kind of conditioning produced by the middle-class marriage. They are so full of fear. They are so full of idealism. I want them to try to understand that they are alone, and that is not a bad thing. To be alone is to be *all of yourself*. Italian women have this myth of the husband. I want to show that it is sentimental, this myth." Juliet is disappointed to learn Giorgio has forgotten their anniversary; instead of the quiet dinner for two she had arranged, there will be a houseful of visitors, because Giorgio has invited home some of their friends. One of the friends, Valentina, has brought Juliet a present from America: wind-bells to ward off spirits.

Later in the evening Juliet, Valentina, and some others hold a séance in which they make contact with a spirit named Iris, whose message for the group is: "Love for everyone." A lawyer present interprets this message in sexual terms. When he stares at Juliet and kisses the back of his hand significantly, however, the heroine ignores him. Like the lawyer, the thoughts of the others at the session also turn to sex; but Juliet, who is not amused by their ribaldry, lowers her gaze. Then Iris raps out another message—a more specific one for Juliet: "Who do you think you are? You're no one to anybody. You don't count, you wretched thing." Juliet, stunned by these words from the spirit-world, faints. Employing a subjective camera from Juliet's point of view on the floor as she returns to consciousness, Fellini pans slowly around at the cold, unloving faces staring down at her. One of the faces is Giorgio's.

Cut to the following morning. Juliet upbraids Teresina for kissing the plumber behind the fence. . . . Other women indulge in casual sex—why not her? Alone, Juliet whispers to herself: "Love for everyone." Cut to the next scene, later in the morning, showing Juliet on the lawn at the same table used for the séance.

A rap is heard. "Iris?" inquires Juliet. Another rap. Juliet grins. A breeze wafts the wind-bells, causing them to tinkle. Juliet continues to grin enigmatically.

Cut to a scene on the beach. Juliet's doctor—overfed, suntanned, representative of the physical world and the scientific temper—pooh-poohs spirits: "Haven't you ever been in a plane, signora? Haven't you heard the radio up there? You should hear those voices . . . human voices. . . . These are the voices of the air—not spirits, not spirits." As Roger Ortmayer observes: "First seeing the materialist doctor against the background of brilliant orange chair and tent makes an aggressive complement to Juliet in white, in a white deck chair, against white sand and white sky. Such sensational use of color is one of the great moments in film art." Juliet insists that even as a child she was in touch with spirits. Closing her eyes for a moment, Juliet "sees" a beautiful woman in a circus swing; when she looks back at the doctor again, however, he laughs his mocking laugh. "That could simply be bad digestion," he tells her. "Once we are dead, we are but a handful of dust. . . . Go swimming, buy yourself a horse and take it jumping, but, above all, tell your husband to make love to you more often."

Cut to a shot of Susy (Sandra Milo), arriving at the beach on a canopied raft, surrounded by admirers and servants. Susy resembles the woman on the circus swing seen earlier from Juliet's subjective viewpoint (and indeed, both characters are played by the same actress). Fellini told Kezich that Susy emerges from the water because she is like Venus; but she is to be seen, he added, as a caricature of sex—for she is nothing but sex. All the same, simply because Susy represents an element in Juliet that has never been fully aroused, the sex symbol casts a spell over the heroine. After watching Susy for a while, Juliet grows drowsy. Here Fellini proceeds with imagination from the objective to the subjective: As Juliet's head slowly drops, her broad white hat fills the screen; then there is a cut to her dream—whiteness replaced by blackness, the afternoon scene at the beach converted into a vision of the beach at night.

Shot of a fat man, pulling on a heavy rope: "Juliet, will you

JULIET OF THE SPIRITS: *Susy as she appears in one of Juliet's apparitions.*

help me, please? I'm old, and besides, this really is your concern."
Juliet begins to pull on the rope. Later we discover that the man
is Lynx-eyes, a private detective whom Juliet hires to follow
Giorgio. Since at this point Juliet has never met Lynx-eyes, however, his appearance in her dream must be described as prophetic
or precognitive. No doubt, the rope Juliet is pulling stands
for the burden of her marriage and of her unlived life. A barge
with sick-looking, seminude men and women on it appears.
One recalls that Susy arrived by water. Is this unprepossessing
vision intended to represent Juliet's fear of sex? Or is it a form
of death imagery meant to be seen as Juliet's unconscious means
of correcting the overemphasis on sex that Susy's life symbolizes?
A raft floats by, carrying three horses; the animals also seem
half dead. The doctor had advised Juliet to go jumping on a
horse. In psychoanalytic theory the horse stands for the "power
of life"—generally sexual power—so that the emaciated condition of the animals in Juliet's dream again suggests either her
fear of sex or her deep understanding that sex is not enough, that
there must be more than sexual liberation to make life meaningful. Probably both ideas are present.

Frightened, Juliet wakes up. Around her everything is "normal"
—children romp, swimmers lay sunbathing, and Susy stretches
her full body before plunging voluptuously into the water. Juliet
continues to observe Susy.

Cut to the next scene in the pine woods. Juliet, her two little
nieces, and their nurse meet Adele, Juliet's sister and the girls's
mother. Adele is pregnant. Apparently, Juliet has never had
children of her own, so that she remains unfulfilled in the
maternal sense, too. Sylva, another sister, and Juliet's mother
also arrive. Beside them, Juliet seems dumpy, lacking in poise
and elegance; beside Juliet, however, Adele seems aggressive,
Sylva frivolous, and Mother cold as cold. When Sylva says goodbye to Adele and her mother, the three women "kiss" without
touching each other: their lips brush a veil—or merely the air.
Juliet has grown up unloved by her vain mother, overshadowed
by her more attractive sisters, made to feel like an ugly duck-

ling. . . . If the viewer did not experience sympathy for Juliet before, he certainly does now.

In the following scene, Juliet and Giorgio watch television together before retiring. Once in bed, Giorgio mumbles the name "Gabriella" in his sleep, which naturally disturbs Juliet. The next morning—in a kitchen flooded with sunlight, a sunlight so soft, so lovely that its beauty merely accents the heroine's pain—Juliet questions Giorgio about Gabriella. He, of course, denies knowing a woman by that name. Later in the morning, while Juliet sits at a lawn table stringing red peppers with her maids, Fellini projects her thoughts through the technique of an interior monologue. "Yes, yes, I heard correctly," Juliet reflects. "He said, 'Gabriella.' Yet he seemed so sincere when he denied. . . . It is true that he likes women. However, one time he said to me: 'I'll never lie to you, never.'" So much for the vows of lovers. . . . Valentina appears, ecstatic over the morning dew: "This *is* dew, isn't it?" Obviously, Valentina is alienated from nature. "I'd love to roll naked in the grass," she declares; but when Juliet says: "Why don't you?," she replies: "Oh, no, we've become too complicated, civilized." Later she observes: "Oh, a wreath of peppers! What a wonderful housewife you are! I can do absolutely nothing. . . . Why am I the way I am? I feel so lost, like I'm drifting. Peppers—they seem to be nothing, and yet, if I were able to prepare them, maybe I would be safe." Ironically, Juliet knows how to string peppers but she is not "safe," either. Valentina invites Juliet to meet Bhisma, the Eastern seer and oracle, who will be on view at the Plaza Hotel that evening. Perhaps the great man—or is "he" a woman?—will show Juliet the way out of her difficulties.

Cut to the lobby of the hotel. All the lights are out; illumination is provided by candles. Since this scene looks back to the opening of the film, in which Juliet and Giorgio meet in semi-darkness, the symbolism appears unpropitious: the heroine has come to Bhisma for help—but here, unfortunately, she will find no "light." On the way up to the seer's terrace, Juliet pauses before one of the rooms to watch a wedding party. A priest,

addressing a bride and groom, says: "Love your wife like yourself, because he who loves his wife loves himself. Love each
other for better or for worse, for richer or for poorer, in health
or in sickness." The priest's approach to the relationship between
a man and a woman underlines the *reciprocal* nature of sexual
love; at the same time, however, it takes cognizance of the
fact that true love includes more than sexual gratification, that
it may demand sacrifices and entail suffering. Such love, Fellini
suggests, has gone out of style. When Juliet calls Valentina's
attention to the wedding party, the latter observes condescend-
ingly: "How charming."

In Bhisma's suite, the seer speaks to Juliet of the *Kama Sutra*,
the Hindu ritual of love. He—or she—advises Juliet to cultivate
certain sounds (*put, pat, plat*) and bites (the dark bite, the
swollen bite, the wolf bite) to heighten the enjoyment of sexual
intercourse. Hence, the great "mystic" turns out to be no less
materialistic than the skeptical doctor who instructed Juliet to
make love more often. What Bhisma's message amounts to is
further subordination of the woman to the man ("Love is a
religion, Juliet. Your husband is your God," the oracle informs
her), even unto prostituting herself ("Women want to be treated
like sirens, but they don't even know their trade," he says).
Juliet's rejection of Bhisma's philosophy causes the latter to
fall into a fit of slobbering, moaning, choking, and retching.
Although repelled by the grotesque Bhisma, Juliet has a vision
of the trapeze artist revealed earlier in the film during the beach
scene: in the first vision, the woman swings above a bed; in the
second, she sits astride a circus horse. Juliet also "sees" Susy.
As she takes leave of the seer, Juliet is informed that tonight
some new and beautiful event will occur in her life. "Sangría
quenches all thirst for anyone who drinks it," Bhisma says, "—
even that thirst which is never confessed." To which another
voice—a quiet male voice—adds: "They call it the drink of
oblivion."

Driving home, Juliet tells Valentina that she saw Iris in
Bhisma's suite. Juliet believes that Iris may be the spirit of the
ballerina with whom her grandfather, a professor, once had an

affair. Cut to a subjective perspective as Juliet "sees" her grand-father, her mother, her sisters, and herself as a little girl. After the performance of Fanny, the trapeze artist with whom Grandfather also once had an affair, the old man takes Juliet backstage to meet the woman. "A beautiful woman," he says, "always makes me feel more religious." (As I pointed out in Chapter One, Fellini shares Grandfather's sentiments.) Shot of a circus biplane, with Juliet's voice over: "God knows why, I always thought that Grandfather and the dancer ran off in that plane." Shot of Grandfather, Fanny, and the others outlined against the sky as they dash across the brink of a hill; followed by a freeze frame, which suggests how the memory—or fantasy —has remained in the heroine's mind, impervious to the passage of time; then, after a moment, the figures begin to move again, as Grandfather flies away with Fanny. Apparently, Grandfather represents the spontaneous life as opposed to the repressed life. By running off with Fanny, the old man defied the headmaster at his school, lost his teaching position, and was denounced by the local bishop for being in league with Satan. Juliet needs to believe in Grandfather as a model for her own future behavior.

At home, Juliet meets José, a house guest from Spain. Mixing Juliet a sangría, José remarks: "They say it quenches all the thirsts of anyone who drinks it, even the thirst which is never confessed. They call it the drink of oblivion." Juliet not only remembers what Bhisma told her about sangría but also rec-ognizes José's quiet voice. Although the heroine is fascinated by the Spaniard, he does not seem quite real. If Susy represents sex without love, José represents romance without substance, or form without content. The man from Spain talks of killing bulls with "a pure heart and clear thought." "It is a matter of style and poetry," he remarks solemnly, and quotes some lush lines from García Lorca: "No one understands the obscure magnolia in your womb. No one knows who hides a charge of love behind the teeth." Later in the film, José waxes eloquent on the subject of water: "When I want something absolutely pure, trustworthy, I always ask for water. We have a great need for simple things, things which don't hide something else." José's search for simplicity, his fondness for ritual, smacks of spiritual deterioration. The last two times we see him, José appears in Juliet's hallucinations: on both occasions, he is literally "bored stiff"—thanks to stop-motion photography.

Following her first meeting with José, Juliet overhears Giorgio talking to Gabriella on the telephone. The next day, Juliet and Adele call upon Lynx-eyes, the private detective. Ironically, the man who Juliet goes to for help is disguised as a priest. "You will excuse my strange mode of dress," he says, meeting the two women in the hall. "My work often demands such transformations. We are at the service of our neighbors who need to know." As the three walk towards the detective's office, the sound of their heels echoes throughout the cold, empty building. During the interview, Lynx-eyes makes standardized inquiries in a standardized way: "You must forgive my deplorable indiscretion, but I am not finished with my questions. Have you ever found handkerchiefs stained with lipstick?" Lynx-eyes does not relate to Juliet as a person—she is merely a client, a case. Similarly, the psychologist who works for Lynx-eyes approaches Giorgio in a ludicrously external manner. Merely by gazing at some photographs of Giorgio, the psychologist "analyzes" the unfaithful husband: "I'd say he is a man from thirty-eight to forty-five years of age . . . of a nervous temperament, docile only on the surface. Successful with women. Cold angers. One must watch him because he is capable of sudden irresponsible actions. Repressed fears and a great need for his mother." Nevertheless, Juliet feels that she must hand over her privacy to these unfeeling professional snoopers. "I want to know," she says. "It's my right, because I don't know who he is any longer, what still belongs to me, what I mean to him. I must know what he is thinking, what he is doing. I must know everything, everything, everything!"

Juliet's real task, however, is not so much "to know everything" about Giorgio as *to know more about herself.*

A visit to Dolores, a sculptor, provides the heroine with some insight into her deepest problems. According to Dolores, her "art is profoundly spiritual"; yet she represents God "physically, corporeally, a hero of the perfect form who I can desire and even take as a lover." How is Juliet, surrounded by people like Dolores and Susy, to find the middle road between the extremes of spirituality and materiality? The viewpoint shifts as Juliet recalls an incident from her past. Whereas Dolores's studio is filled with statues of naked bodies, Juliet's daydream begins with a shot of a nun whose body—and even her face—are concealed by a black robe. Offscreen, we hear the adult voice of Juliet: "The play that year was about the life of a martyred saint. I was chosen to play her part." And ever since it would seem, Juliet has been playing the same part, at least unconsciously. Shot of nuns, all dressed in black, all hidden by their robes, fastening angel's wings to the white costumes of little girls. A saint "sees" God, one nun informs little Juliet, when she goes to heaven "among the flames of martyrdom." Unfortunately, the nun fails to add that there are also other ways to know—or "see"—God. In the play, little Juliet is tied to a burning grill; afterward a nun, offstage, hoists the martyr upward toward the ceiling. Suddenly Grandfather strides down the aisle, jumps on stage, and puts an end to the sadomasochistic proceedings. "Strapping a six-year-old girl to a grill!" he shouts. "Where are we—among cannibals?" Shot of Grandfather leading Juliet away from the camera; Fellini holds on this image for a moment—then trucks back to frame the old man and the little girl with two rows of nuns, their black figures seeming to engulf the loving couple. It is one of the most memorable shots in a film outstanding for its visual beauty.

Next, back in present objective reality, Juliet calls on Susy. The garden surrounding the latter's house, overrun as it is with strange vegetation, looks like something out of the Decadents; inside, the furnishings are luxurious but the plaster in many places is peeling off the walls. If Susy's habitat represents Eden, it remains an Eden after the Fall. As usual, Juliet's sensual neighbor is not wanting for male companionship. A handsome, muscular young man in a breechcloth waits on her; another man—a sorrowful Russian—begs the woman for one of her shoes. "I can't encourage your fetishism, Alyosha," Susy informs him;

nonetheless, she gives the poor wretch what he wants, and she even wiggles her rump for his additional gratification. "I'd like to love only one man," Susy tells Juliet, "but how is it possible?" Upstairs in her bedroom, Susy shows Juliet a mirror attached to the ceiling directly over her mattress; there is also a hole in one wall through which Susy slides down a board into a swimming pool after love-making. "I accept everything. I deny myself nothing," she says, childishly. Outside, Susy takes Juliet up into her treehouse, where the two women bask in the sun—Susy naked, Juliet fully clothed. Susy asks Juliet to tell her about Giorgio. "I always thought that marriage should be like this: I should be all for him, he all for me," Juliet explains. "I'm almost ashamed to admit it, but Giorgio was my first love. As soon as I saw him I fell in love and didn't want anything but to live with him, and when he asked me to marry him, I was so happy I couldn't believe it was true. He became my whole world—my husband, my love, my father, my friend, my house. I didn't need anything else. I thought I was happy." Susy, however, is paying no attention to Juliet's heartfelt outpourings; instead, the selfish hedonist is watching two young men below. "Oh! I dropped my shoe!" Susy announces, coyly, as the men scramble to retrieve it. By linking Susy with the perverted Alyosha, Fellini further casts suspicion on her as a viable alternative to a puritanical way of life.

Soon after the scene with Susy, Juliet is summoned to the office of Lynx-eyes, who now provides her with evidence of Giorgio's perfidy. In the darkened room, Juliet watches a film in which her husband and a young woman are seen together in compromising poses. "I always ask clients to regard everything we show them with a certain detachment," says the detective. "Ours is an objective point of view, and therefore limited. Reality at times may be quite different, more innocent." Juliet, however, knows the truth. Standing up, so that her figure is between the projector and the screen—her shadow obliterating a shot of Giorgio and Gabriella fondling each other—Juliet exits, her face set.

In spite of her doubts about Susy as a model for behavior, Juliet's anger and hurt lead her to attend a party at the villa of her erotic neighbor. Throughout most of the film, Fellini clothes Juliet in white in order to suggest her innocence and purity; however, in this scene the heroine is garbed in red, a color that symbolizes a mood of passion. Susy's party is typical of such gatherings in Fellini's pictures. There is the usual assortment of beautiful women and handsome men, complemented by freaks and grotesques of one kind or another—the international, multiracial cast trying hard to enjoy themselves but, unfortunately, not succeeding. Everyone looks bored. Susy's mother dozes in a chair. Momy, Susy's sixty-five-year-old fiancé, plays dice. One of the guests is being hypnotized by a man with a goatee. "I really want to enjoy myself tonight," Juliet announces, pathetically.

Susy suggests that they play a game in which the women pretend to be prostitutes in a brothel. (Similar games are played in *La Dolce Vita* and *8½*.) One of the women, dressed solely in a white sheet, stands before the man with the goatee:

MAN: Kneel down. What is your name?
WOMAN: Hildegarde.
MAN: No, your name is Sex. What is your name?
HILDEGARDE: Sex.
MAN: No, your name is Womb. What is your name?
HILDEGARDE: Womb.
MAN: No, your name is that of the divinity. You are no longer yourself. You are the door and the earth, the corolla, the crown of the goddess.

The woman, it would seem, remains everything but "Hildegarde," a human being, an individual with a distinct personality and a value in her own right. Once again, Fellini makes clear that Susy does not offer a solution to the problems facing Juliet. In his dialogue with Kezich, the director says "that husbands should not oppress their wives, consider them private property, place them in slavery without real love. . . . The intention of the film . . . is to restore the woman her true independence, her indisputable and inalienable dignity. . . . The wife must not be the Madonna, nor an instrument of pleasure; and least of all a servant." Susy merely offers Juliet more of the same depersonalization and dehumanization from which she is already suffering, both in her marriage and in society at large.

Nevertheless, Juliet attempts to take part in the prostitute game. Susy, holding a flashlight (which recalls the opening scene as well as the scene involving Bhisma), leads Juliet up an outside stairway to her bedroom. Inside, Susy's godson—a handsome but effeminate young man—arrives to service Juliet. Although part of the heroine wants to revenge herself on the unfaithful Giorgio, and although another part of her wants to experience promiscuous sex, her puritanical background stops her from such indiscriminate coupling. Hence, Juliet "sees" a young girl surrounded by flames, and "hears" the voice of a little girl: "Juliet! What are you doing?" Abruptly, Juliet exits.

In the next scene, Juliet and Giorgio give a lawn party. However, inside the house Juliet is alone, and very much disturbed. Her conscience is tormented by images of sex—naked breasts inside a closet, Susy's leering face, a woman in net tights. "Forgive me! I'll never do it again," Juliet cries. "Leave me in peace!" Outside, an American psychoanalyst, a woman named Dr. Miller, takes Juliet for a walk in the pine woods. Without doubt, Dr. Miller, like most psychoanalysts in movies, speaks with a nauseating glibness (here one also recalls the psychologist who works for Lynx-eyes); nonetheless, there remains much truth in her evaluation of Juliet's difficulties. Moreover, to a large extent she speaks for Fellini himself:

> I'm bold enough to state that I understand your trouble: You identify too closely with your problem. . . . These ancient trees are the most impressive symbol of this way of life. They are deeply, securely rooted. Up there their branches spread open in all directions. Yet they grow spontaneously. This is a great, simple secret to learn—to fulfill yourself spontaneously, yet without putting yourself in conflict with your desires, your passions. . . . You're afraid of being alone, of being abandoned. You're afraid that your

husband is going to leave you. And yet you want nothing more than to be left alone; you want your husband to go away. . . . Without Giorgio you'll start to breathe, to live, to become yourself. You think you're afraid. Actually, you fear only one thing— to be happy.

Juliet laughs derisively at Dr. Miller's interpretation. . . . And, as though endeavoring to refute the psychoanalyst—or to deny that in her deepest being she craves freedom to grow and to be truly happy—she visits Gabriella in an attempt at a confrontation. As it turns out, Giorgio's mistress is not at home, however, and Juliet leaves without seeing her.

Cut to the last sequence of the film. As Juliet returns home, two lovers are ironically shown on television. "Our happiness," the man and woman smile, "has only one name." Just then, Giorgio enters the room, carrying his suitcases: It is manifest that he is leaving Juliet and that he is going off to live with the younger Gabriella. As the couple stand awkwardly before one another, clowns appear on the television screen. In the course of this episode, Fellini juxtaposes shots in the objective present with brief shots seen from Juliet's subjective perspective on the past. For example, there are images showing Juliet introducing Giorgio to her mother and sisters for the first time, and images revealing the couple lovingly embracing each other in bed. At one point, Juliet even "sees" Giorgio and Gabriella kissing in a convertible. In present reality, Giorgio nibbles at some food, diplomatically allows the phone to ring without answering it, and finally takes leave of his wife. The entire scene is effectively underplayed . . . as a marriage of fifteen years ends with neither a bang nor a whimper.

Cut to a scene later in time, with Juliet alone in the house. Outside it is black. However, inside it is even blacker—for Juliet's dark night of the soul has now begun. Everywhere the heroine is pursued by visions, spirits. She "sees" Laura, a childhood friend, who at the age of fifteen committed suicide for love. "Come with me—a long sleep, with no more pain," Laura says . . . but Juliet refuses. Lynx-eyes, rows of nuns, José, Susy's godson, and numerous other characters appear before Juliet, frightening her. Dr. Miller says: "Without Giorgio you'll begin to breathe, to become yourself." Rushing into her bedroom, Juliet conjures up her mother, who refuses to comfort her. A small dark door glows across the room—a symbol of Juliet's unconscious. "Don't open it!" Mother shouts. "Obey me!" But Juliet, like her grandfather, has at last found the courage and strength to rebel. "You don't scare me any more," she says. Behind the door, Juliet discovers herself as a little girl, tied to the burning grill. Here Fellini alternates shots of Juliet untying herself—or overcoming the dark past—with shots of Juliet tossing and turning on her bed. As the woman finally succeeds in releasing herself from fear, the images of the characters who have been haunting her lose their substance and, through the technique of double-exposure, seemingly melt away. . . .

On the front lawn, Grandfather stands before his airplane. "Let's say good-bye to those boors," he tells little Juliet. Shot of an enormous wagon filled with the people who have appeared in Juliet's apparitions, together with their symbolic props: Laura's hearse, the basket Susy used to get up to her tree house, and the prow of the ship seen in the vision at the beach. The wagon slowly vanishes. Then Grandfather gets into his plane —Fanny sitting on the wing—and the old man tells little Juliet: "Don't hold on to me—you don't need me any longer. I, too, am an invention of yours; but you are full of life."

The adult Juliet steps out through the gate, leaving her white doll's house behind. Sunshine is brilliant all around her. Standing in an open road—Fellini's recurrent symbol of life—the heroine listens to the sound of voices: "Juliet . . . Juliet . . . Juliet." To her question: "Who are you?" the voices reply: "True friends, true friends, true friends. Now, if you want us to, we can stay, we can stay, we can stay. . . . Listen to us, listen closely. . . ." These voices would not seem to represent the Furies but rather the Eumenides. Whereas the spirits had previously signified the presence of a neurotic condition in Juliet, the final voices suggest the possibility of a healthy attitude toward the complexity of life, a true synthesis of the material and the spiritual.

Like Gelsomina, Juliet remains in tune with the primordial mysteries, for Fellini has always insisted on the reality of a world beyond that which can be verified by the senses.

Juliet of the Spirits ends with a shot of the title character walking towards the pine forest—the house at the left of the frame, the trees at the right—a beautiful long shot emphasizing the heroine's acceptance of her fate. Somehow, Juliet will learn to follow the example of the trees: she will be securely rooted to the earth—yet she will grow spontaneously, her arms reaching toward the heavens; she will come to love everyone . . . but in different ways.

It seems doubtful that any one who has seen *Juliet of the Spirits* will ever forget the images—the colors, the sets, the costumes. As Philip T. Hartung pointed out in his review: "At times, Fellini imaginatively uses the color for meaning; more often it is for the sheer beauty of the pictures, pictures which seem to stem occasionally from the masters—like the stunning tree-lined paths that are right out of Corot or that sun-splashed Renoir garden where Juliet's little nieces, even dressed like Renoir models, romp and listen to the fairy tales that Juliet is telling." Although the Freudian and Jungian symbolism in some places is too obvious—the tiny door that leads into Juliet's unconscious being the most egregious instance—the visuals for the most part deserve the superlatives they have often received.

In his interview with Ross, Fellini comments on *Juliet of the Spirits* as follows: "The story is nothing. There *is* no story. Actually, the picture can be described in ten different ways. Movies now have gone past the phase of prose narrative and are coming nearer and nearer to poetry. I am trying to free my work from certain constrictions—a story with a beginning, a development, an ending. It should be more like a poem, with metre and cadence." Now, in a strict sense there is no "story" in *Juliet of the Spirits*—if by "story" is meant the arrangement of events as they occur chronologically—because the point of view in the film shifts continually. And surely, there is no "plot" in the picture—if by "plot" is meant a series of actions moving from a beginning through a causally related sequence, to a logical outcome—because *Juliet of the Spirits* remains episodic in structure. However, in a loose manner of speaking there *is* a story in the film: the viewer wants to know what will happen to Juliet. And although the film's construction lacks unity according to Aristotelian standards, there is a "beginning" (Juliet's problem concerning Giorgio and her own unfulfilled existence), a "development" (Juliet's struggle with Giorgio and her spirits), and an "ending" (Juliet's liberation). To say that *Juliet of the Spirits* is episodic does not imply a pejorative evaluation; the film achieves unity largely through character, theme, and the visual approach, making the looseness of the architectonics for the most part irrelevant. Of course, Fellini is somewhat cavalier in his attitude toward "story." If cinema is not to be confused with either drama or fiction (a horror to contemplate for most film artists today, and rightly so), neither is it to be equated with poetry or music (a confusion that some film-makers, oddly enough, do not find similarly horrifying). Still, Fellini's description of the picture's design is in large measure an accurate one: *Juliet of the Spirits* tends to be more vertical than horizontal.

If there is a weakness in *Juliet of the Spirits*, it lies perhaps in the nature of the method that Fellini has chosen. Gelsomina and Cabiria make a stronger impression on us than Juliet—they make us *feel* more deeply—because in *La Strada* and *Nights of Cabiria* Giulietta Masina had an opportunity to act as well as to react. For the most part, Fellini's approach in the two earlier pictures was both objective and subjective. His characters moved in a real world of external relationships. Technically, a balance was struck between narrative art and the "lyric" mode. In *Juliet of the Spirits*, the emphasis is on the subjective. The title character reacts some, does little, fantasizes much. The technique, as Fellini himself acknowledges, is "more like a poem." However, 137 minutes may just be a bit too long for a "poem," even for one so delightful to look at as *Juliet of the Spirits*.

Aside from the problem of stasis—a threat that arises whenever stream-of-consciousness subject matter is used (whether in film or literature)—there remains another related difficulty. In spite of the fact that Fellini attempts to reveal Juliet's psyche in depth, the viewer never really seems to get close to her. There is a certain abstractness, something of an illustrated lecture, about Juliet's interior landscape as projected on the screen. To some extent, 8½ suffered from the same "intellectualization" of affective states. Nonetheless, in the previous film, Fellini stayed close to Guido's problem of making a film in the present, so that the subjective portions of the action still retained the "feel" of a concrete, individually realized character. In *Juliet of the Spirits* a slight disjunction is felt between the middle-class housewife and the bizarre daydreams, nightmares, and visions that upset her throughout the picture. Not that middle-class housewives are barred from having a rich fantasy life. But it is the responsibility of the artist to make us feel the oneness of the character, to credibly relate the dreams to the dreamer —a task that Fellini, unhappily, does not consistently accomplish. All the same, the weakness is a relative one. Although Giulietta Masina's performance in her last picture is not quite so memorable as her renditions of either Gelsomina or Cabiria—and chiefly, as noted, this is because *Juliet of the Spirits* is a different *kind* of film than either *La Strada* or *Nights of Cabiria*—she still manages to project a moving image of a middle-aged wife who must face the fact that her marriage is dead and who must find a new, more self-fulfilling purpose in life.

Thematically, however, *Juliet of the Spirits* is not limited in its scope to the troubles confronting modern Italian women. Nor is its theme sectarian in approach. Fellini told Eileen Hughes: "*Juliet of the Spirits* exposed the problems of a Catholic woman which I think are universal." It seems doubtful that Fellini intends "universal" in the theological sense—namely, that the Catholic church is "universal" because all its members profess the same faith, practice the same form of worship, and are joined under the Pope. Rather, Fellini would seem to be saying that the problems facing Juliet are the problems of all women living not only in the second half of the twentieth century—the age of "women's liberation"—but also of all women in all times. As Simone de Beauvoir points out in *The Second Sex*: "If her functioning as a female is not enough to define woman, if we decline also to explain her through 'the eternal feminine,' and if never-theless we admit, provisionally, that women do exist, then we must face the question: what is a woman?" It is this "question," as de Beauvoir puts it, that is treated so memorably by Fellini in *Juliet of the Spirits*.

CHAPTER 12

Fellini Satyricon

When watching Fellini Satyricon, *the audience must fight as never before their . . . preconception about movies having to tell them a story with a start, a development, an end; preconceptions about historical pictures; preconceptions about myself, personally, because they know that before, Fellini always tells them some story. This is not an historical picture, a Cecil B. DeMille picture. It is not even a Fellini picture, in the sense of* La Strada *or* Nights of Cabiria *or even* La Dolce Vita. *They ask me why I make it. How do I know? Because, as a little boy, in Rimini, my papa took me to my first film, and it had Roman gladiators in it? Because for thirty years I have enjoyed Petronius, and now the moment comes right? I cannot answer.*

—FEDERICO FELLINI

Fellini Satyricon (1969) was Fellini's first full-length picture in four years. He had planned for about ten months to shoot a movie entitled *The Voyage of G. Mastorna*, with Marcello Mastroianni, but illness and bickering with the producer put an end to the project. According to reports, the bill for *Fellini*

Satyricon came to $4,000,000.00, which made it the costliest movie Fellini had directed up to that time. It was also his first costume picture, requiring five thousand wigs, eighty-nine sets, and an enormous cast.

So far, *Fellini Satyricon* is also the first feature-length film that Fellini has based on another artist's work. *Based*, not adapted. Numerous critics have attacked Fellini for not being "faithful" to Petronius; but it was never the director's intention to bring *The Satyricon* to the screen the way Laurence Olivier brought *Hamlet* to the screen, say, or Tony Richardson brought *Tom Jones* before the camera. A first-rate film-maker like Fellini knows that a masterpiece can't be adapted, anyway; and besides, Fellini is interested in *his* vision, not Petronius's. True, *Fellini Satyricon* owes something to the original; even the director admits that the picture is twenty per cent Petronius and eighty per cent Fellini. Nonetheless, Fellini has also rightly pointed out: "I didn't illustrate a book; the book was simply a pretext." *Had* Fellini intended to adapt a classic for the screen, comparison with the original would not be invidious; however, it is patently silly for critics to pommel Fellini for having failed to accomplish a task that formed no part of his conception.

This is not to say that Fellini's conception on other counts was entirely clear, or that he chose the right method for "getting at" his subject. He told Tom Burke: "I know that I want no help from books, from archeology, and I feel better. A voyage into total obscurity! An unknown planet for me to populate!" Yet according to Dario Zanelli, who edited the screenplay for publication, Fellini read not only Petronius but also *The Detectives of Archeology* by C. W. Ceram, *Daily Life in Rome* by Jerome Carcopino, *The Decline of Rome* by Joseph Vogt, *The Petronian Question* by Enzo V. Marmorale, *Les Peuples de L'Antiquité* by René Menard and Claude Sauvageat, and other books. Why all the research, if the plan was to populate "an unknown planet"? Although *Fellini Satyricon*, as its creator points out, is not an "historical film," it obviously bears *some* correspondence to historical reality, at least in Fellini's mind, otherwise how explain the rationale behind his preparative scholarly labors?

On the one hand, Fellini declares: "I've tried first of all to eliminate what is generally called history. That is to say, really, the idea that the ancient world 'actually' existed. Thus the atmosphere [of the film] is not historical but that of a dream world." On the other hand, he argues: "we find disconcerting analogies betwen Roman society before the final arrival of Christianity—a cynical society, impassive, corrupt, and frenzied —and society today, more blurred in its external characteristics only because it is internally more confused." Such remarks would seem to posit the idea of a link, historically and spiritually, betwen ancient Rome and the modern world. Zanelli quotes Fellini as saying: "Have you grasped the analogies? From a pre-Christian period to a post-Christian one: Christ has disappeared and we've got to get along without him. This is the relevance of the film to today." Yet Fellini told Mark Shivas: "I am not looking for [an] analogy between today and ancient Rome, though it may be present. That is a very vulgar type of operation" (*New York Times*, October 13, 1968). Similarly, he informed Eileen Hughes that there was no analogy intended between past and present; but later, he told her there *was* such an analogy. When he was in the United States to promote his picture, he announced that *Fellini Satyricon* was more autobiographical than *8½* (quoted in *Variety*, January 21, 1970); however, he also told Hughes that there was nothing autobiographical about *Fellini Satyricon*.

So *Fellini Satyricon*, according to the film-maker, bears a relationship to historical reality and, being pure dream, bears no relationship to historical reality; bears an analogy to the modern world and bears no analogy to the modern world; is and is not autobiographical. . . . Perhaps Fellini really meant it when he confessed: "Actually, I don't know why I'm doing this film."

Structurally, *Fellini Satyricon* comprises nine sequences, with over sixty scenes and something like 1200 shots. The action is extremely fragmentary. Encolpius (Martin Potter), Ascyltus (Hiram Keller), and Giton (Max Born) are the chief personages in the film, and Fellini offers up for our inspection discontinuous events from their lives. The film opens with Encolpius's lament ("speaking," according to the screenplay, "who knows to whom, maybe only to the public"); occasionally, in the course of the picture, Encolpius returns to a narrative posture. However, the point of view is never really in the first person or subjective mode; often Encolpius is not even present (nor are Ascyltus or Giton). Even when characters stare directly into the camera, they are never looking at anyone in the picture; instead their gaze meets that of the viewer, who is made to feel as though he were intruding where he had no right. The action, such as it is, remains impossible to adequately summarize. Suffice it to say that we witness the adventures of Encolpius and Ascyltus, and their sexual rivalry for the effeminate Giton; we watch a man's hand being chopped off in a play for the entertainment of the audience; we peek into a whorehouse; we are present at Trimalchio's Feast; we observe Encolpius's suicide; we are there as Ascyltus services a nyphomaniac; we watch as Encolpius and Ascyltus kidnap a hermaphrodite; we see Encolpius struggle with the Minotaur; we witness Encolpius losing his potency, then regaining it; we observe a group of heirs eating the corpse of what was once a man because otherwise they will receive no benefits from his will. . . . We witness, we watch, we peek, we are present, we observe, we see—but we are never involved. At the end, Ascyltus is killed in a fight; and Encolpius—who was too busy enjoying his returned potency to help his friend—sets off for more adventures with new companions. Encolpius does not weep for Ascyltus, and neither do we.

Like some other Fellini films, *Fellini Satyricon* has a circular form in that the picture opens with a shot of Encolpius standing before a reddish wall defaced by graffiti and concludes with the same character and others transformed into figures on a wall painting. (Also, like some other Fellini films, *Fellini Satyricon* ends by the sea.) However, it seems doubtful whether one can point to any other type of patterning in the picture. There is no plot, no narrative, nothing that could be described as resembling a story; there is not even an increment of tension. The sequences could be reversed, for the most part, without damage to the structure. Other Fellini films are open-ended; but *Fellini*

Fellini Satyricon: *Trimalchio's Feast.*

Satyricon doesn't end in any meaningful sense—it just stops. Fellini has said: "I have made no panoramas, no topography, only frescoes, and so the cutting is very fast. It has no real time. It is like riffling through an album. There is no psychological movement in the characters. Things in front of you are like frescoes. The rhythm is slow but also very fast." Elsewhere he has asserted: "The meaning should become apparent only at the end: as it happens to whoever looks at a bas-relief carving, starting from any given point, at random. Only after looking at the whole sequence does he succeed in giving a meaning to the actions he saw sculptured in stone." Such theoretical musings sound better in print than when translated into filmic images; for there remains little meaning in *Fellini Satyricon*, and that little is conveyed to the viewer at the beginning of the picture. What follows is just more of the same.

Fellini's approach to his material in *Fellini Satyricon* is faulty in both conception and execution. Throughout the planning and shooting of the movie, Fellini constantly remarked on his "objective" point of view: "The film demands a detached, cold, and impassive approach." . . . "Nothing wears me out more than this detachment I've imposed on myself. My temperament always tends towards identification with the characters. Here there's only a secret identification, an aesthetic one. This side-stepping I'm obliged to do all the time is an unhealthy operation, at least for the spirit." . . . "This [film] is really a cold-blooded operation." . . . "To be detached from your work is unnatural, like a mother who does not recognize her son." . . . "To create is to be in love, to be involved. Detachment is to become cold and uninvolved." *Fellini Satyricon* is the only cold, unloving, humorless, "objective" picture Fellini has made; and a Fellini picture without warmth, love, humor, and emotion, or "subjectivity," has little to recommend it. Fellini's various remarks on the undertaking, quoted above, suggest that he entertained some doubts about the propriety of his approach, that he suspected negative reactions to the picture would have less to do with audience "preconceptions" as a barrier to understanding and evaluation than with an error on his part in shaping the material of his film in such a way as to preclude audience identification with, or even interest in, any of his characters.

Even if complete objectivity in art were possible, it would remain aesthetically undesirable. Back in 1959, Fellini correctly pointed out to Gideon Bachmann that "always the important thing is to know *who* sees the reality. . . . [W]hy should people go to the movies, if films show reality only through a very cold, objective eye?" Why indeed? Some critics have argued that *La Dolce Vita* and *Fellini Satyricon* both have a fresco structure, and that therefore both films are identical in form. This is far from being the case. Although some similarities exist between the two films, the differences between them are crucial. In *La Dolce Vita*, for example, Fellini positions Marcello at the center of the action; the journalist's steady disintegration, morally and emotionally, provides the picture with a concentration and development in terms of structure, character, and theme that is not present in *Fellini Satyricon*. Needless to add, there is nothing intrinsically wrong with an episodic, thematic form. After all, Fellini's films prior to *Fellini Satyricon* are scarcely cinematic equivalents of Sophoclean, much less Scribean, architectonics, yet a number of them are masterpieces of screen artistry. A film-maker can scrap plot, story, character—whatever he chooses—provided he supplies some compensatory qualities in the revised work. . . . But this, in my judgment, is exactly what Fellini fails to do here.

"*Fellini Satyricon* is a film which should ultimately be based on bad acting," Fellini once remarked; "you understand in what sense, do you?" The acting in the picture, however, is not so much "bad" as nonexistent. Although Encolpius, Ascyltus, and Giton are faintly distinguishable as discrete entities, many of the other characters are not. Fellini told Rino Carboni, the chief make-up man for the film, that "every character must have a hallucinatory aspect or a spectral look because all of them are seen as through the smoke of a drug." In the past, Fellini regarded the face as a "*human* landscape"; in *Fellini Satyricon*, the face represents an *inhuman* landscape. And not because all the faces are grotesque, either. Even the blank, sexless features of the two handsome leads, Encolpius and Ascyltus, tend to be in-human, because neither of them has any real presence, much less a mind or a heart or a soul. All the personages in the picture are flat and static; that is to say, they remain two-dimensional: things happen to them without things happening inside them. And the fact that Fellini intended such a method of "character-ization" does not confer success upon the enterprise.

Eileen Hughes quotes Fellini as saying of *Fellini Satyricon*: "It's not a film of ideas but of images. Its dimension is purely visual. It must be contemplated." Again, contemplation suggests detachment. "I want to create a suggestive, mysterious fable," Fellini observed during the shooting of his picture. "A film made up of static shots—no tracks, no camera movements whatsoever. A wholly contemplatory film, like a dream: and you'll emerge from it hypnotized." Instead of being "hypnotized," the viewer will probably emerge from *Fellini Satyricon* bored by the monotony of the cinematic—or rather noncinematic—proceed-ings. Obviously, much directorial care was lavished on the individual shots, the make-up (which Fellini calls "the most important thing" in the film—a bad sign), the color, the sets, and the costumes. Faces are painted yellow, green, red, blue, gold, orange, and white to match costumes or décor, and to augment the dreamlike mode of imitation; ships and buildings are constructed to appear both real and unreal; in Trimalchio's bath the guests jump up and down in order to create a human wavelike effect; the sky in one scene is colored blood red; another scene is shot through a mist, with a soft focus lens, to suggest the remoteness of time and an hallucinatory quality, and so forth. Yet the end result of all this ingenuity and toil is an aesthetic zero. The film is dead.

At times, one gets the impression that one is watching a photo-graphed stage play, thanks to Fellini's stationary camera and the aloof distance he maintains between himself (or his camera-eye) and his subject. At other times, one seems to be observing portraits arranged in a picture gallery, thanks to Fellini's "static shots" and "contemplatory" purposes. The effect is often not much more rewarding as an artistic experience than a screening of Andy Warhol's *Empire*, which is a perverse attempt to "prove" that motion isn't necessary in motion pictures. As Pauline Kael points out in her review of *Fellini Satyricon*: "Afterwards, one recalls astonishingly little; there are many episodes and anecdotes, but, for a work that is visual if it is anything, it leaves disappointingly few visual impressions." No picture that runs for 120 minutes can afford to be "purely visual," not even a silent picture. Fellini did not intend to make a "film of ideas," but the plain fact is that *Fellini Satyricon* could use a few ideas. To express the point differently: Pictures—even when they are arresting and beautiful and capable of lingering on in the viewer's consciousness—are not enough. *Fellini Satyricon* lacks a depth to match its length.

In his preface to the screenplay of *Fellini Satyricon*, Fellini draws certain parallels between ancient Rome and the modern world:

> Then as now we find ourselves confronting a society at the height of its splendor but revealing already the signs of a progressive dissolution; a society in which politics is only the sordid, routine administration of a common affluence and an end in itself; where big business intrudes at all levels in the brutality of its instruments and the vulgarity of its ends; a society in which all beliefs—religious, philosophical, ideological, and social—have crumbled, and been displaced by a sick, wild, and impotent eclecticism; where science is reduced to a frivolous and meaningless bundle of notions or to a gloomy and fanatical elitism.

Unfortunately, *Fellini Satyricon* fails to embody the complex analogies between the two worlds asserted in the foregoing remarks; instead, Fellini presents a fantasy about the sex habits and social behavior of a pre-Christian people. On the whole, *Fellini Satyricon* is neither a convincing satire of the present nor an accurate recreation of the past. Even if Fellini did not intend to satirize the contemporary period (although, in one of his moods, he has said that the picture is "a satire of the world we live in today"), or to recreate the age of Petronius (although, by insisting on making concrete analogies between the ancient and modern world, he ipso facto opts for at least some historicity), his film remains unsatisfactory at the conceptual level.

Why did Rome fall? According to St. Augustine, sex and the wrath of God was the explanation; Gibbon blamed Christianity and barbarism; Spengler argued that all civilizations perish as a result of natural decay; most historians have attributed Rome's demise to the interplay of economic, political, social, and moral factors. By focusing mainly on the sex life of his "characters," however, Fellini gives the impression that Rome was done in simply by concupiscence. Up to a point, of course, this view is a valid one. As Morton Hunt writes in *The Natural History of Love*: "Roman love flourished in the context of the disintegration of family life, and even accelerated it; in that circumstance it produced a problem of utmost seriousness—the voluntary infertility of the native Roman stock. For it was when sex moved outside of marriage and called itself love, while marriage itself lost its values, that the long decline of population began"; and that "decline" helped bring about the end of Roman society. Of course, overpopulation is the problem in the twentieth century; however, the inability of so many people in our time to love, to form durable relationships, to find an answer to human existence in endless sexual experimentation remains a key problem—one that Fellini has dealt with in a direct and complex way in *La Dolce Vita*, and in an indirect and superficial way in *Fellini Satyricon*.

Behind Fellini's "objective" and "detached" approach in *Fellini Satyricon*, I believe, lies his unwillingness to be honest about how he feels on the issue of pre-Christian and post-Christian sexual mores. For the most part, the images on the screen reveal a society that has no respect for the person. Like the Catholic he still is in the depth of his being, Fellini sees the "characters" in his film as corrupt monsters, as pitiable freaks or selfish narcissists in a world without God. In *La Dolce Vita*, unlike *Fellini Satyricon*, there is not only thematic complication but also love and compassion and affection. None of these virtues is present in *Fellini Satyricon*. There is a monstrous side to mankind—but this is only one side; part of Fellini's genius in his earlier pictures was to show that "vertical line in spirituality that goes from the beast to the angel, and on which we oscillate." There is no oscillation in *Fellini Satyricon*. Except for the papier-mâché couple who kill themselves in their villa, man is simplistically presented as a beast. On the one hand, Fellini says that Encolpius, Ascyltus, and the others "behave differently because they *are* different"; on the other hand, he says: "Man never changes, and today we can recognize all the principal characters of the drama." If the "characters" *are* different, then why speak of analogies between past and present? If mankind stays the same, then why leave out the love and pity and joy that the ancient Roman no less than modern man was also capable of experiencing? Fellini has said of ancient Rome: "What escapes us is the mentality of a world in which you went to the box office of a theater and bought a ticket which entitled you to entertain yourself with the agony of a fellow human being killed by the sword or devoured by a wild beast. . . . People watched men die as today Spaniards watch bulls die: joking, laughing, having a drink, eating nuts." But not all Romans enjoyed watching men die, any more than all Spaniards today enjoy watching bulls die; and though modern man can be brutal, he does not generally entertain himself with spectacles in which other human beings are mutilated and killed. There is no way of escaping the conclusion that Fellini had an insufficient grasp of what he was about in *Fellini Satyricon*.

Yet Fellini has uttered some grand remarks in defense of the "characters" in his film. "Why are there so many monsters in this picture?" Hughes asked; to which the director replied: "But they are not monsters. They are innocent. You are less innocent." In his preface to the screenplay, Fellini compares Encolpius and Ascyltus to "two hippy students . . . moving on from adventure to adventure, even the most gruesome, without the least remorse, with all the natural innocence and splendid vitality of two young animals." And he adds: "They are totally insensible to conventional ties like the family (usually built less on affection than on blackmail); they don't even practice the cult of friendship, which they consider a precarious and contradictory sentiment, and so are willing to betray or disown each other any time. They have no illusions precisely because they believe in nothing, but, in a completely new and original way, their cynicism stays this side of a peaceful self-fulfillment, of a solid, healthy, and unique good sense." It is difficult to believe in Fellini's veracity here. In his interview with Burke, the director praises today's young people because they have rejected a moribund society, and because "they just love, and feel." However one may evaluate Fellini's syrupy comments on contemporary youth, the fact remains that his heroes in *Fellini Satyricon* neither "love" nor "feel."

Encolpius speaks of his "love" for Giton, but his use of the word is semantically meaningless. Ascyltus, who "has rented himself out like a woman," says "Friendship lasts as long as it is useful." Giton, who has a severe identity crisis, would rather be female than male. Encolpius and Ascyltus find the two suicides outside the villa, and are struck with fear; they soon recover, however, and inside the villa, the two men—like the splendid and innocent animals they are—stuff themselves with veal, laugh, and have an orgy with a slave girl. Encolpius, Ascyltus, and Giton never rise one millimeter above the rest of their unlovely society. "This is a film which in spite of showing moral decay gives a viewer a feeling of being set free," Fellini told Hughes, "free from the myths of our time, for the man of tomorrow must be a man without myths." But the director informed Burke, apropos of *Fellini Satyricon*: "I do not mean to scorn religion; perhaps all I say is: 'We have always needed religion, we have not the strength to do without it.'" And in his preface to the screenplay, Fellini observes of his "characters" that "they embody the eternal myth; man standing alone before the fascinating mystery of life, all its terror, its beauty, and its passion." Aside from the contradictions apparent in such remarks, one should point out that the picture does *not* give the "viewer a feeling of being set free"—quite the opposite effect is conveyed (*Fellini Satyricon* must be one of the most oppressive films ever made); nor does the movie suggest life's "mystery" or "beauty" —everything shown remains all too obvious and unrelievedly ugly.

Fellini Satyricon presents a vision of the world in which there are only Zampanòs, no Gelsominas. If Fellini really approves of his "innocents," he has undergone a radical transformation—a transformation which, frankly, I doubt. I would prefer to regard *Fellini Satyricon* as a momentary aberration in the career of a great director, as an exercise in confusion and pessimisim and futility: the confusion traceable to the detached, "objective" approach; the pessimism responsible for Fellini's embarrassing comments on the "positive" attributes of Encolpius, Ascyltus, and Giton; and the futility apparent in nearly every static, noncinematic frame.

Both artistically and humanistically, *Fellini Satyricon* remains, in my opinion, Fellini's single out-and-out failure.

CHAPTER 13

The Clowns

Clowns are ambassadors of my vocation, of my work,
of my life, what I've done: I am a man of show.
              —FEDERICO FELLINI

The Clowns (1970) was originally made for RAI-TV (Radio-televisione Italiana), and only later released as a film for theater showing. Although Fellini is reported to have been paid over a million dollars by RAI-TV for his special, the director's experience with the tube was not a happy one. Shot in color, *The Clowns* appeared on the home screen Christmas night in black and white. "TV is not for me," Fellini observes. "It is a medium that sacrifices light, and light is vital to create images in all their nuances. Black and white programming practically decimated the substance and shape of my film" (quoted in *Variety,* January 20, 1971). As Fellini sees it, television is best equipped for recording news events on the spot. Contrary to what some theorists contend, the small screen does not provide a greater sense of intimacy than film: "it is really too broad, too distracted. When you think of all those people watching while they argue or eat or put the children to bed, it's very upsetting. TV people told me I would have to repeat things to get them across. That's like telling a writer to say the same thing every third page, because his reader is not paying attention. . . . The conversation with the viewer becomes more obvious, more banal. It cannot be

an expression of the private world of an artist" (quoted in the
New York Times, July 19, 1970). In sum, Fellini the film-maker
would not like to be Fellini the television director. "I am not
adapted to it," he says of the tube. "Just not adapted."

For anyone who has followed Fellini's career, there is nothing
surprising in his making a film about clowns. *Variety Lights*
deals with a troupe of comedians and much of *La Strada* takes
place in a circus. In *The White Sheik*, Cabiria begs a passing
entertainer to amuse Ivan by making an enormous fire blaze
from his mouth. Theatrical performances also occur in *I Vitelloni*,
Nights of Cabiria, *La Dolce Vita*, *8½*, *Juliet of the Spirits*, and
Fellini Satyricon. As noted earlier in this book, clowns have had
a life-long fascination for the film-maker. "The circus is congenial to me," Fellini remarks in some notes written to promote
The Clowns. "A traumatizing, total adhesion to that noise, that
music, those monstrous apparitions, those threats of death . . .
based on miracle, fantasy, jest, nonsense, fable, the lack of coldly
intellectual meanings—is precisely the kind of show that pleases
me." Throughout his career, Fellini has repeatedly drawn analogies between the cinema and the circus. Both types of entertainment, according to the director, involve a combination of
strict planning and improvisation; and both remain complex art
forms with varied sources of appeal. (Or as Fellini put it once
in a conversation with Eugene Walter: "Cinema is an old whore
like circus and variety who knows how to give many kinds of
pleasure.") What is even more interesting, however, are the
analogies Fellini draws between clowns and everyday people—
in other words, between clowns and *us*.

Fellini divides clowns into two classes: one is the "white
clown," who acts haughty in his white-faced makeup; the second
is the "*augusto*," the clumsy, down-at-the-heel character in baggy
pants, who is forever challenging his partner. The "white clown"
represents man's idealized image of himself—his drive towards
perfection; the "*augusto*" symbolizes man's impulse to mock his
own lofty aspirations. According to Fellini, the "*augusto*" would
be impressed with the ideal if the "white clown" were not so
overbearing and pretentious, if he did not make perfection

seem so remote, so unreachable. The conflict between the "white clown" and the "*augusto*," then, stands for an immemorial conflict in man between two sides of his nature. "The clown," Fellini told Doris Hamblin, "mirrors the confusions, the mysteries of life. He is funny and sad, naïve, frustrated. Things are always too much for him." Although Fellini favors the "*augusto*" (even unto consciously identifying with him), and although he would prefer to restrict the word "clown" to describe his favorite, the co-existence of the "white clown" and the "*augusto*" makes not only for a richer, more complex art but also for a truer, more complete vision of man.

Structurally, *The Clowns* is divided into three parts: an autobiographical memory-sequence of the first circus Fellini saw and of certain grotesque characters in his home town; a documentary-like search by Fellini for the clowns of his boyhood, which in epistemological terms develops into a critique of the documentary mode itself; and a concluding extravaganza, wherein Fellini enacts a clown funeral under the big top, brings off a resurrection scene, and presents his dual view of man in a coda not easily forgotten.

The first part of *The Clowns* opens with a child—Fellini himself—waking up in a dark room because of loud noises. Slipping out of bed, the boy pads to the window—and discovers a circus tent being erected by the light of a fire just across the road. We sense the boy's excitement, even his fear, for the experience is new and strange to him. . . . Next the boy appears at the circus. Throughout this scene, we do not glimpse young Fellini's face. His figure remains in shadow, the performance occasionally photographed from a subjective angle (the camera situated just behind the boy's head, which remains visible on the screen), or sometimes shot with a subjective camera (the boy, the audience, and the lens all "see" the identical happening). By concealing the boy's face, and by showing much of the action from his point of view, Fellini forces us to identify with his younger self (a strategy which the director also employs, but for a much shorter duration, at the start of both *8½* and *Juliet of the Spirits*). During the evening, the boy witnesses a number of acts that seem to have as their common denominator some form of violence. For example, a man throws knives dangerously close to the face and body of an attractive woman. An Amazon (resembling La Saraghina from 8½) defeats a burly male wrestler in combat; then the gigantic woman takes on another Amazon, the queer struggle underlined by the music of Wagner's "Ride of the Valkyries" (the theme also used during the revolt of the harem in 8½). A swami is buried alive in a glass coffin. A mermaid swallows live fish. What appears to be most frightening to the boy, however, is the sight of Siamese twins pickled in a bottle of lye: "You see them, little boy," the circus master grins. "Aren't they nice?" The blood-red noses, squirting flowers, chairs pulled out from under people, hammers and hatchets smashed against skulls, men disguised as animals—these and other staples of the circus world disturb the child. The adult Fellini's voice is heard offscreen: "That night ended badly. The circus people, with their twisted and crazy faces, scared me. I was reminded of other clowns." In the film, young Fellini recognizes the link between real life and the circus imitation of life, but he lacks the maturity and sophistication to laugh on cue. As yet, he cannot see that stylized enactment represents a form of exorcism, that the exaggerations of violence tend to act cathartically on a knowing audience, that laughter remains one of the ways for man to preserve his sanity in the face of "reality." Instead, the boy reacts to the conventions of the circus by whimpering, and his angry mother is obliged to take him home.

In his role as narrator, the middle-aged Fellini proceeds to introduce some "clowns" from Rimini (or from his imaginative re-creation of his home town). We see a dwarf nun, a veteran of World War I who sits by the sea with a woman who can recite all of Mussolini's speeches by heart, and a pompous little railway stationmaster. The latter character seems to represent the arrogant "white clown" who tries exceedingly hard to achieve perfection and to maintain his dignity. When schoolboys, cast in the role of the "*augusto*," direct vulgar-lip noises at the martinet, he is obliged to intimidate the youths and salvage his sense of dignity.

In watching *The Clowns*, viewers knowledgeable about Fellini not only grasp the relationship between the artist's early experiences and his later fondness for freakish imagery, but also renew their acquaintance with characters from previous films. (This is not to say, however, that a lack of such background will in any way diminish one's enjoyment of the picture.) Giudizio, who had a small but significant part in *I Vitelloni*, reappears in *The Clowns*, where he makes "*augusto*"-like obscene signs at a woman, who in turn threatens to "cut it off"—a gesture also reminiscent of the circus, where phallic ties are routinely severed by scissors. During a scene in a poolroom, the *vitelloni* (played by different actors of course than those in the 1953 film) also show up again. Two visitors to Rimini—a glamorous blonde in white fur and her dashing escort dressed in a driving coat, gloves, and goggles—enter the poolroom with "Fascination" playing on the sound track, and the local good-for-nothings stare at them. One of the *vitelloni* has slicked-down black hair, a pencil-thin mustache underneath a sharp nose with passionately flaring nostrils, and a silk scarf knotted rakishly about his throat. He could be a parody of Fausto, as he gives the blonde a look calculated to make her think of the white sheik, though he more nearly suggests the "white clown." Afterward Giudizio, wearing a veteran's cap, reminds the viewer of past wars (the crippled soldier from World War I) and future wars (the Fascist officer and the woman who knows Il Duce's speeches in toto)* by playing an infantryman in the street. When the supercilious *vitelloni* throw snowballs at the "*augusto*"-like Giudizio, he takes out an imaginary trumpet and blows "Taps." This gesture presages the ending of the film, when another familiar tune is played by two sad clowns, and Fellini again attempts to express the dichotomous spiritual condition of man.

In the second part of *The Clowns*, the action begins in Fellini's office, where the film-maker introduces himself and his crew to the audience. Occasionally, in this section and the final one,

---

* Elsewhere in *The Clowns* reference is made to an Italian lion tamer who trains his beasts in German, because "it's the one human language that they understand."

Fellini appears on the screen but his presence never becomes obtrusive. We see much more of Fellini's coworkers than of Fellini himself. Often, the camera provides us with reaction shots of the crew, while offscreen we hear the sound of the director's voice. When Hamblin asked Fellini why he put himself in *The Clowns,* he replied: "Because I am very narcissistic, I like to employ myself." However, he added: "To make it more documentary, to put into the film the inquirer himself—me—and to make fun of him a little bit. I made a joke of me and my crew and of the inquiry itself." On the screen, Fellini appears a bit stiff and self-conscious; yet, none of that narcissism frequently attributed to him—even by himself—is in evidence. Fellini projects an image of a large, earthy, amusing, compassionate man; and without doubt, his brief appearances in his own film are relevant to the design of the work. "In the middle of *The Clowns,*" the director informed Hamblin, "I realized I am not really doing a documentary. I am doing the world inside my mind."

What the viewer is presented with, then, is a documentary-like dramatization about the making of a documentary. By structuring the action in this informal-formal manner, Fellini remains free to juggle subjective and objective, tragic and comic, approaches to his material. The form also proves to be an economical method of narration. As Fellini and his crew set out to find the clowns of yesterday, the script girl faces the camera and explains to us where the search will begin, who we will encounter, and what we can expect to find. Sometimes Fellini, off-camera, will jokingly inform the girl that she is repeating herself, or making a mistake; or he will tell her to hurry up, so that they can get on with the action. This Brechtian "estrangement-effect" prevents *The Clowns* from drifting into sentimentality, for the thought that Fellini engenders in the viewer acts as a brake on the strong emotion inherent in the situation.

As the second part of the film progresses, Fellini is at pains to make the viewer see that a link exists not only between clowns and certain odd characters from Rimini—a situation that allows the audience to feel just a bit too smug and superior—but also between clowns and everyone else. Even here, however, Fellini offers his analogy gently or obliquely by making himself and his crew the butt of the joke. For example, in one scene as the director and his numerous associates emerge from their small car the audience laughs, because it is reminded of those tiny automobiles at the circus from which an army of clowns similarly emerge. Another instance strikes closer to home. In one scene, Fellini and his coworkers each stand before a portrait of a clown; then each member of the crew turns away from the image of a clown to face the camera, thus producing an unmistakable association of ideas. However, since the viewer is also staring at a "clown" now, the implication is that we are all more or less grotesque.

Fellini journeys to Paris. There he visits the comic and film-maker Pierre Etaix, married to the daughter of a Fratellini, who shares the Italian director's love for the circus. (Etaix's best film, made in 1965, is generally considered to be *Yoyo*, the study of a clown.) When Etaix promises to show Fellini a rare documentary about old clowns, the travelers from Rome are delighted. However, Etaix's projector fails to operate properly, and the ancient footage burns. So much for the documentary approach. A visit with clown expert Tristan Remy is also not a very happy event, since Fellini is informed that the clown no longer exists. Later, in a taxi, Fellini asks the driver what he knows about the circus. "The circus!" replies the indignant hack. "Whose got time for such nonsense? The circus! Indeed!" A close up reveals an expression of dismay and disgust on Fellini's face. Has modern man forgotten how to laugh? At a Paris studio, which resembles a mortuary, Fellini receives permission to view the only extant film showing the legendary clown Rhum. The projectionist, however, is ignorant of both Fellini (whom he calls "Mr. Bellini") and Rhum; and the performance on film remains brief, sketchy, wooden. One is forced to conclude that the celluloid Rhum could scarcely resemble Rhum as he was in the flesh. Hence the past for which Fellini has been searching appears to have vanished—the clowns of his childhood seem irretrievably lost.

Or are they? Next Fellini interviews some old clowns, hoping in this way to approach his subject not through unsatisfactory filmic records but through the living memories of those who actually performed in the past. Bario and Loriot are the only two clowns who ever retired from the circus ring with enough money to be considered rich; however, neither of them is happy— which appears ironic, considering that their profession was making people laugh. Bario does not care to discuss the past: "I spent sixty years with the circus. It was my whole life." Later, in reference to Bario, one of Fellini's coworkers remarks (touching on a theme that recurs again and again in later Fellini films): "Old age is horrible." As for Loriot, he feels the necessity to work at his act now and then, but the performance fails to yield its previous satisfaction. "In Rome," he sadly observes, "nobody laughed." Whereas Bario has a wife to console him, Loriot remains a widower. "Let us drink to the memory of my dear wife," the venerable comic says, in a touching scene. "We were together for fifty-three years. . . . That's not just a day."

Fellini and his crew become increasingly disenchanted. Perhaps Remy was correct—perhaps the spirit of clowning has indeed died.

In a Bavarian brewery, where what remains of Hiver's Circus is located, Fellini watches a performance by Baptiste, a psychiatrist turned clown, who developed his routine in a mental institution. Although Baptiste reveres the circus, and although he yearns to bring about a renaissance of clowning, his act remains flat, uninspired. Again, the point is made that the greatness of clowning remains in the past.*

As the second part of *The Clowns* draws to its close, Fellini suggests that by an act of the creative imagination he can make the circus live again on the screen for the contemporary viewer. During a visit to the home of the Fratellini family, a photograph of the three brothers is transformed into a shot of them enacting

_____

* It seems worth noting that Baptiste's assistant is Victoria Chaplin, daughter of Charlie Chaplin. By inserting the girl into his film, Fellini explained to Charles Thomas Samuels, he was attempting to pay "homage to her father." Anita Ekberg also puts in a brief appearance during *The Clowns*. "I met her one day, and I like Anita," Fellini told Samuels. "Besides, she has a circus personality."

THE CLOWNS: *The Fratellini brothers entertaining the patients at a mental hospital.*

a charitable performance at a mental hospital. In this reconstruction of a bygone event, music is heard but nobody speaks; it is as though the viewer were observing a silent film, an effect that seems suitable for a past episode nostalgically recreated in the present. Equipped with wings (one recalls "The Fool" in *La Strada*), the famous clowns play on their instruments as they float overhead, patently suspended from wires. Thus does Fellini mock "realism," substituting poetic vision for *cinema vérité*. As the inmates of the hospital imitate their psychiatrists, one remembers that Baptiste was a doctor who became interested in clowning while working in an asylum. Once more, Fellini erases the distinction between the grotesque and the so-called normal individual, between the clown and the nonclown. As the director put it to Hamblin: "We are all freaks."

Part two of *The Clowns* ends with a story about Guillon, a former *"augusto"* of enormous reputation. When Guillon, who is ill, learns that a circus has arrived in town, he leaves his hospital bed, slips past a dozing nun with a mustache (a nun with a mustache also shows up in *The White Sheik* when Ivan visits Wanda at the mental hospital), and goes to the circus. Here, Fellini reenacts the antics of two other well-known clowns: Footit, the "white clown," and Chocolat, the *"augusto."* Throughout this scene, Fellini crosscuts between the performers and Guillon, who reacts with enthusiasm to the work of his peers. After the performance, it is discovered that Guillon has died— an event that provides Fellini with his inspiration for the concluding section of his film.

The focus in part three is on the funeral of a clown. In symbolic terms, Fellini suggests that clowning itself has died. However, before the picture ends, the film-maker has made clear—through the inventive energy with which he has created the action*—that the spirit of the circus can never really die. As can be imagined, the funeral is presented in nonillusionistic

* During this scene, a Daumierlike critic (8½) asks the director: "What message are you trying to give us here?" Before Fellini can attempt to put his meaning into words, however, a bucket falls over his head, preventing him from speaking.

terms: the hearse is drawn not by real circus horses but by men in horse costumes; the "widow" is a clown with huge artificial breasts; as nails are hammered into the coffin, it collapses; inside, no body is discovered—only the empty garments of the corpse. A "white clown" delivers the "eulogy." Observing that the deceased expired prematurely at the age of two hundred (suffocated by an ostrich egg), the speaker adds: "We all mourn that he died now . . . instead of the moment he was born. He no longer lives . . . fortunately we still do." The oration, however, is not without pathos: "He made children everywhere laugh . . . but he made his own children cry."

Suddenly the dead clown is reborn. Projected out of a gigantic champagne bottle, he floats overhead—joyous and triumphant—while down below there is riotous merrymaking. Everyone literally gets into the act. Fellini's crew dance with the clowns as members of the circus audience also join in the fun. The air is filled with streamers and confetti; cannons and fireworks explode, and colored lights play on the big top. That circus music so closely identified with Fellini's vision of life is almost deafening. (As usual, Nino Rota's score can only be described as outstanding.) All at once, however, the gaiety ceases. And then the lone sound heard is that of the reborn comic, swinging among the colored ribbons, high above the sawdust.

"I liked it very much," says a clown to Fellini; to which the latter abruptly replies: "It's over. Turn it off."

Nevertheless, the picture is not yet finished. Although Fellini has already suggested the resiliency of the clown—for if the audience laughs at his beautiful, affectionate, comic film there can be no doubt about the clown's immortality—he adds a final scene to represent the two sides of man's nature. An old clown recalls the act he used to perform involving his search for a dead partner named Fru Fru. Unable, or unwilling, to acquiesce in the passing of his associate, the old clown would lament: "Where can I find Fru Fru? Perhaps if I call him. . . ." Then Fellini dissolves to a shot of the narrator, attired in the garments of the "white clown," as he stands on one side of an empty circus tent, facing an "*augusto*" on the opposite side. Each clown alternately plays "Ebb Tide"* on a trumpet—the camera panning back and forth with a spotlight from one to the other —as he moves toward the center ring. When they meet, the "white clown" and the "*augusto*" continue to play . . . two lonely figures in a cone of light surrounded by darkness. Then there is another dissolve, and the clowns vanish, leaving the viewer with an image of the spotlight gleaming on the sawdust in the barren circus tent.

The last shot of *The Clowns* remains a haunting one, characteristic of Fellini's art in that it is open-ended: a challenge for the viewer to find his own answer to the problem of human existence.

* Even when the sea does not appear in a picture, Fellini manages to suggest its existence through music.

CHAPTER 14

Fellini's Roma

What do I think of when I hear the name Rome?
More or less, I know. I think of a ruddy face, brown,
muddy ground; of a vast tattered sky, like an opera
backdrop, with tones of violet, black, and silver.
Funereal colors, but all things considered it is a
comforting sight. Comforting because Rome, a
horizontal city, stretched out, is the ideal platform
for fantastic vertical flights. The intellectuals, the
artists, who always live in a state of friction between
two different dimensions—reality and fantasy—find
in Rome the right liberating thrust for their mental
activity, with the comfort of an umbilical cord that
keeps them solidly anchored.

—FEDERICO FELLINI

La Dolce Vita and *Fellini Satyricon* both deal, in large measure, with Roman society—the first in contemporary, the second in ancient terms. It was inevitable that Fellini would eventually make a movie in which Rome itself would be the subject. During the filming of *Fellini's Roma* (1972), the director explained that the picture would be "an informal chat about one of the most fascinating cities in the world—a visual conglomerate of the new and old that people in all countries will understand. Nearly everyone in every country—consciously or unconsciously—has a personal relationship with a particular city" (quoted in *Variety*, August 25, 1971). In 1965, Fellini told Lillian Ross that, for him, living in Rome was not like inhabiting a city but like lounging about in his own private apartment; he compared the city's streets to the corridors of a building in which one has rooms. "Rome is still the mother," he added. Fellini made much the same point in an essay he wrote for the *New York Times* (June 3, 1973). In his article, the film-maker—viewing Roman society as one big family—describes the cemeteries of the city as a huge apartment. (One recalls *8½*, in which Guido's dead father complains that his tomb is not roomy enough for him, as though he were being forced to put up with cheap lodgings.) Again, Fellini compares the city to a mother—one, however, with too many children.

The *Times* essay underlines the ambivalence Fellini feels toward Rome. On the one hand, he argues that Mother Rome is "the best mother one could wish," because "hers is a warm in-difference"; she does not make her children feel dependent. On the other hand, he contends that Mother Rome, though she prevents neurosis with her "placentary belly," thwarts genuine adulthood; she produces children who are a "little deformed." Rome is a city of "mama's boys." Fellini's love-hate relationship with Rome accounts, in part, for the tepid reviews his picture received in the Italian press; although people flocked to see the movie, they insisted that what they saw on the screen was more a product of Fellini's imagination than a realistic portrayal of their capital. Now, it is true that *Fellini's Roma* is a mixture of memory, documentary, and fantasy. (Although some of the picture was shot in the studios of Cinecittà, even the outdoor scenes reflect the artist's manipulation of "reality," or make clear his expressionistic treatment of the *mise en scène*. Stylistically, much in *Fellini's Roma* has that grotesque, theatrical, carnival-like, phantasmagorical quality that has become increasingly evi-dent in Fellini's cinema.) It is also true that every city has its good and bad side, which could be revealed by any diligent *cinéma vérité* photographer; but only Fellini with his unique gifts and eccentric personality—including his ambiguous response to Rome—could have fashioned such a picture.

But let us examine *Fellini's Roma* in detail.

As the credits are being shown on the screen, we hear Fellini's voice on the sound track. He informs us—in quiet, measured tones—that his film has no story or even characters. And, of course, he's right. *Fellini's Roma* is sprawling in structure; beside it, *Fellini Satyricon,* in its architectonics, looks like a well-made play about the bourgeoisie. The film begins in the past with Fellini's boyhood introduction to Rome through teachers and movies; then it leaps ahead to show Fellini as a young man (played by an American named Peter Gonzales) arriving in the Eternal City to live; next it jumps to the present; then there are flashbacks to the Second World War period; followed by a return to our own day. In no sense can the character intended to represent Fellini as a young man be considered central to the design, inasmuch as that character remains absent most of the time; even when he does appear, we never get close to him, we never know what he is thinking or feeling. There is no character in *Fellini's Roma* who appears regularly on screen—no character with whom the viewer can identify, except fleetingly in a scene. The subject, as noted, is Rome . . . or rather, Fellini's response to, and imaginative reconstruction of, "Rome."

At the beginning of *Fellini's Roma*, the boy Fellini is shown with his classmates crossing the Rubicon—in the film, a shallow brook near Rimini. The students are also dragged to see a hammy play involving Julius Caesar and other wellknown personages connected with Rome's history. A priest's slide lecture on the great city is interrupted when a photograph of a seminaked woman appears on screen (a true incident, as reported earlier in this book, from Fellini's past). "Don't look! Don't look!" the priest begs the children, his arms outstretched in front of the screen, as he ineffectually attempts to shield the woman's body from the boys—all of whom are laughing and whistling and stamping their feet . . . and leering. There is a scene at the Fellini dinner table in which the Pope addresses the faithful on radio from Rome. Mother and children drop to their knees and pray, while Father—the traditional anticlericalist—picks up the pot of spaghetti and storms into the kitchen to eat. Later, the family goes to the movies; and there on the screen they watch a silent, romantic film about ancient Rome wherein Christians are slaughtered by Pagans. ("How do I know [why I'm making *Fellini Satyricon*]?" the director once said. "Because, as a little boy, in Rimini, my papa took me to my first film, and it had Roman gladiators in it.") Juxtaposed to the Cecil B. DeMille-type spectacle about the past is a newsreel concerning the present: shots of Mussolini's regime in Rome during the twenties. Thus, illusion is played off against reality . . . a recurrent theme in Fellini's work.

Next we observe Fellini as a young man arriving in Rome from Rimini by train. Throughout *Fellini's Roma*, the film-maker uses a moving camera (even more than he usually does) in order to convey a sense of life flowing ceaselessly in every direction. He also employs a zoom lens (a technique not generally part of his repertoire) for suggesting the confusion, the hurly-burly of Rome. At the railroad station, however, Fellini outdoes himself by offering up repeated tracking shots, sometimes using a subjective camera (we see what young Federico sees), sometimes using merely a subjective angle (we see young Federico, but the lens is just behind him as he saunters along, so that we identify with his viewpoint). Hence the fictional Fellini's initial entry into Rome—the "real" Rome, that is—is made to seem an overwhelming experience—for both him and the viewer—thanks to the technical approach used by the director.

The boarding house where young Federico goes to live makes the Maison Vauquer in Balzac's *Père Goriot* seem like a palace. Crude, earthy, freakish types abound. For example, the woman who runs the place must be the fattest human being in Italy, perhaps in the whole world. Her son—a grown man who sports a hair net—lies in the same bed with her. "Want to meet my tiny Granny?" asks a little girl. And young Federico is led up a flight of stairs, where, behind a door, sits a near-midget of an old lady. The *pensione* is a continuous side show.

FELLINI'S ROMA: *Lower-class Romans at dinner in an outdoor restaurant on a piazza.*

Afterward there is a nighttime scene in an open-air restaurant on a piazza. Here, young Fellini eats with his Roman neighbors, all of whom are lower-class, gross in appetite, and vulgar in language. There is much shouting, laughter, good-natured joking. . . . Cut to later at night, the piazza empty, rain falling in straight lines. One feels that humanity has been washed away, leaving behind scarcely a trace on the streets of Rome. . . . Cut to a field outside the city, the same night. On the ground lie scattered remnants of monuments—broken heads and torsos— suffering the downpour. Enter a prostitute. She is gazing toward the city expectantly . . . waiting for the end.

Now Fellini jumps ahead from the thirties to the present. In this scene, the real Fellini makes his first appearance on screen, as we see him get out of a car and issue orders to his camera crew. The viewer is taken for a ride on the Raccordo Anulare, a superhighway skirting Rome. It is twilight, during the rush hour; and before long, a storm breaks (the rain links this scene to the previous one), almost flooding the motorway leading into the city. In the course of this scene, we get sundry viewpoints on the action: we look out from numerous vehicles; we get an overview from the perspective of a crane; we see the crane itself, as it ducks for a close shot of a truck or bus, then snaps up again for a long shot of the road, its spotlights illuminated against the gathering darkness, its plastic, salmon-colored rainshield glistening wet. A riderless horse trots past the camera, showing the viewer its backside, and calling to mind that famous and equally hallucinatory scene in *La Strada*. A truck overturns, leaving the highway strewn with dead animals. Finally, the mechanized insanity, the uncivilized congestion, comes to a silent, dead halt in the rain in front of the Roman Colosseum. Again, past and present are juxtaposed; again, a doomsday note is conveyed as the scene fades out. . . .

Shot of Fellini standing in an open field, the sun bright overhead, student-types talking to him as his crew prepare to shoot another scene. On the sound track, the director tells us that the young people are critical of the film he is making, because it lacks "social consciousness." (Ironically, when *Fellini's*

Roma was released, the Communist press in Italy panned it on the grounds that its maker was unconcerned with socioeconomic values; they dismissed it as a mere invention of a defeatist imagination. As in *8½*, through the negative comments of Daumier on Guido's scenario, Fellini anticipated his critics in *Fellini's Roma*.) Since there is no dialogue in the scene, Fellini tells us that he informs the youths: "I haven't solved the problems in my own life. How, then, can I solve the problems of society?"

As if to underline the personal nature of *Fellini's Roma*, the director then goes back in time thirty years to a vaudeville house to show us the entertainment that molded him and the audiences of which he was a part. The acts are uniformly bad: a sexy dance by a well-shaped young woman; a poor imitation of Fred Astaire; three Italians—at least one about fifty—posing as The Andrews Sisters; three singers made up to resemble Oliver Hardy, Charlie Chaplin, and Ben Turpin, but not doing very well at it; and so forth. The spectators—especially the *vitelloni* —jeer at the entertainers, hurl spitballs and even a dead cat at the stage, and otherwise comport themselves in a manner worthy of their ancestors who watched lions devour human beings in the arena. The scene concludes on a grim note, as an air raid alert sounds throughout the city. Underground, an old man grumbles about the war and a patriotic Fascist upbraids him. A German woman smiles at a man, shows him a picture of her son, and tells him her husband is fighting on the Russian front. When the alert ends, the woman goes off with the stranger, arm-in-arm.

Back to the present. Fellini takes the viewer to Metro-Roma, the subway under construction in the city. According to an elderly bystander, the excavation began a hundred years ago; nobody has any idea when the job will be completed. As drills bore into the substrata, Fellini commences a seemingly interminable subterranean journey into darkness. The monstrous machines, as the film-maker humorously shows, create an earthquake effect. There is a shot of a horrified, middle-aged couple bouncing around their flat, with pictures dropping off the walls and a floor lamp performing a pirouette. It is like a scene from the climax of *San Francisco*.* Finally, the machines come to a stop when an engineer discovers a buried archeological monument: an ancient Roman home with wall paintings and another fresco—a face—at the bottom of a shallow pool of water. Although the workmen try to preserve their find, the air disintegrates the paintings. The unhappy Romans watch their link with the past fade before their eyes. (Naturally, Fellini created this discovery and loss for symbolic purposes.)

Shots of young people kissing each other and lying together on the Spanish Steps. Narrating offscreen, Fellini observes that today sex is out in the open. In the past, however, sex was sold in whorehouses: it was furtive, dirty, sinful. There follows another flashback in which we are taken to two brothels—one for the poor, the other for the well-to-do—both representative of the places men frequented in Fellini's youth. In the cheaper bordello, women parade around in front of the customers like prize cattle on display, promising a good time, their bare breasts flapping up and down unerotically. Most of the whores are overweight and overage. In the more expensive brothel, the customers wait on a velvet settee instead of standing; there is a quiet, church-like atmosphere instead of the air of a noisy auction. Here, the women are younger (when they get older, of course, they will end up in the less fashionable whorehouse); here, the prostitute descends in an elevator, the customer steps inside, and back up they go. Essentially, there is little real difference between the quality of the experience in either house. The relationship between the sexes in both places remains impersonal and commercialized. Both are flesh markets. Both leave the more sensitive, intelligent males longing for something more. Thus, the character standing in for young Fellini asks the prostitute who services him if, one day, he can take her out to lunch. He wants not only to romanticize the transaction with the whore but also to establish a human relationship with her, to bring sex and companionship together. Tactfully, Fellini fades out rather than showing us the young man's inevitable disillusionment.

* Directed by W. S. Van Dyke, 1936.

Next Fellini presents his vision of an Ecclesiastical Fashion Show, as an aging Roman princess recalls the days when the Church and the aristocracy enjoyed what Veblen called "conspicuous consumption." She introduces us to a pasty-faced cardinal wearing dark glasses, who presides over a specimen collection of nobility, all of whom look like candidates for a waxworks; as they sit motionless and speak in whispers to one another, their decadence, their death-in-life, is conveyed by repeated close shots of their mummified countenances. Pairs of priests, nuns, bishops, and cardinals enter, displaying habits and vestments of dazzling silk and gold and silver. This scene remains one of the most exquisitely satiric in all of Fellini's work. Two priest-models come on with roller skates because, that way, "they move faster to Paradise." By focusing on the Church's ostentatious love of finery, Fellini shows us how far the clergy have traveled from the simplicity of Christ's own life and teaching and how irrelevant religion has become for the masses in modern Rome. Fittingly enough, the baroque show concludes with a float constructed of human skeletons.

Fellini's Roma moves towards its close with a visit to the Festa de Noantri in Trastevere, the ancient section of Rome, where artists and intellectuals and gourmets enjoy food and drink in an open-air *trattoria.* Here we meet that distinguished author Gore Vidal, who informs us with a smirk that Rome "is as good a place as any to wait for the end of the world." The late Anna Magnani—who Fellini touchingly refers to as "a Roman countess" —also makes a brief appearance. Moving his camera freely about the festival, the film-maker juxtaposes a boxing match and dancing girls with a police attack on young radicals. The sound of laughter mingles with the sickening thud of clubs bouncing off human skulls.

. . . Later that night. Silence finally descends like a benediction over the Eternal City. . . . Suddenly, however, the roar of motorcycles commences as a platoon of young men in black burst into view. At three o'clock in the morning, the toughs seem to possess the city. The cavalcade (which resembles the messengers of death in Cocteau's *Orphée*) wind through the

Piazza di Spagna, the Navona, the Colosseum Circle, the Piazza del Popolo, and across the Tiber bridges. Around and around the cyclists tool, casting shadows over the facades and arches and monuments of Rome. Are these youths the new barbarians? Is Rome again ready for another fall? The director's voice is absent from the sound track. *Fellini's Roma* fades out on the motorcycle horde . . . fades out in ominous silence.

There is humor, *brio*, energy, and inventiveness in *Fellini's Roma*. In many ways, the film is an absorbing study of a great city seen from the perspective of one of the giants in motion-picture history. Visually, the movie has its impressive moments —such as in the scene when the Fellini surrogate arrives in Rome by train, the scene on the Raccordo Anulare, and the scene depicting the Ecclesiastical Fashion Show. Furthermore, the humane qualities that distinguish Fellini's best work are now and then manifest here, most notably in the music hall and bordello scenes. Nevertheless, *Fellini's Roma* is not first-rate Fellini. Every scene goes on much too long—a structural fault not evident in *La Strada, Nights of Cabiria, La Dolce Vita, 8½, Juliet of the Spirits,* or *The Clowns.* Thematically, *Fellini's Roma* is broad but not deep; it surveys many characters but not one in depth. Since Rome is the subject of the picture, this criticism would not be a serious one—were it not for the fact that the characteristics one finds in *Fellini's Roma* also appear in *Fellini Satyricon* and, as we shall now see, in *Amarcord*.

CHAPTER 15

Amarcord

*Sometimes I'm tired, and I say yes [Amacord is]
really my autobiography. It's a picture about a
little town, and I was born in a little town. And, true,
it was near the sea [just as the town in the film]. But
this kind of autobiography, in a sense, means nothing
because everything is autobiographical. It is not
important that it is something that happened to me.
The important thing is that the audience feels that it
happened to them. It's my life and also what I've
invented.*

—FEDERICO FELLINI

Amarcord (1974), which was one year in the making and cost
$3,500,000 (a large sum by contemporary standards), is Fellini's
most recent film as of this writing. During production, the
director explained that the picture would present one man's
attempt to overcome the alienation of today by creating another
reality out of his past joyful experiences. The film would be
"a sort of anthology . . . told with fantasy and tenderness, sometimes in a grotesque way," Fellini informed Hank Werber of
Variety (March 7, 1973). "It won't be an optimistic film . . . but
it might stimulate reflection on the gradual extinction of so
many simple and less simple pleasures . . . once a sum of hap-

piness that even provided a meaning to life if not fulfillment. I will certainly be accused of looking to the past when all I want to do is rummage and salvage before it all disappears."

Originally, Fellini planned to call the film *Borgo*, which means "village" or "suburb," generally one surrounded by walls in the hills. Since the period recreated in the film is the Thirties, the director wanted to suggest the isolation from reality that Italians experienced under Mussolini's Fascism. *Borgo*, however, seemed too serious as a title, whereas *Viva Italia*—another possibility—appeared too frivolous. Then, during lunch with a friend one day, Fellini scribbled "*amarcord*" on a napkin. "That word looks like publicity for an aperitif," the friend, who was not Italian, remarked. "You know, something like 'Drink Amarcord and your liver will be strong'" (quoted in the New York *Sunday News*, October 13, 1974). Thus, Fellini discovered the title for his film. *Amarcord* translates into *I remember*, which seems apt for a movie wherein reality and dream, actuality and memory continually merge.

Although *Amarcord* is intended as a kind of *comédie humaine*, one family remains at the core of the film. Most important is Titta (Bruno Zanin), who presumably represents, at least in part, the pubescent film-maker himself. Titta's father (Armanda Brancia) is a construction boss in a brickyard; Titta's mother (Pupella Maggio) is the boss in the home, although her husband turns purple with histrionic fury whenever they argue, especially over Titta. There is also a grandfather (Giuseppe Lanigro), who constantly reminds everyone of his former sexual potency. And, finally, there are two uncles—one, Pataca (Nandino Orfei), who is fond of eating and wearing a hairnet; the other, Teo (Ciccio Ingrassia), who is an inmate of an insane asylum. Aside from the family, the most prominent character is Gradisca (Magall Noel), the local hairdresser, whose name means "please do." Although Gradisca bears a resemblance to Sophia Loren—she is almost always seen on the street with two other young ladies on either side of her as though they were bodyguards to keep off the town Lotharios—the woman, aged twenty-eight, worries about becoming an old maid.

Amarcord is Fellini's remembrance of things past—if "remembrance" can mean fantasy as well as fact. For example, Fellini's father was really a traveling salesman, not a foreman in a brickyard. Yet, the Fulgor Theater appears on the screen, and that palace of dreams was part of the film-maker's landscape in Rimini. Even though he has a young surrogate for himself in *Amarcord*, Fellini does not narrate any portion of the film offscreen, nor does he appear directly within the picture. Furthermore, Titta is by no means the central character, for the simple reason that no one personage really enjoys a premier status. *Amarcord* is not a return to neorealism; it is not "objective" in point of view. Suffused with Fellini's unique vision of the world, grounded in his powerful subjectivity, the picture nevertheless has a number of visible narrators at the more obvious structural level.

The most important narrator is The Lawyer (Luigi Rossi), a middle-aged scholar with a taste for local and national history. Since the modern period is one in which man feels estranged from society, The Lawyer repeatedly attempts to suggest continuity beween the present and the past. Not satisfied with tracing the recorded history of the locale back to 268 B.C., he pedantically remarks at one point: "We had a record snowfall this year—excluding the Ice Age." Like the other narrators, The Lawyer gazes directly into the camera and addresses the viewer. However, the *vitelloni* of the town constantly heckle him, emit loud raspberries, and even bombard the loquacious bore with rotten vegetables and tin cans.

From time to time, other narrators appear on screen, occasionally just to say a few words, now and then to relate an anecdote. No set pattern is followed. Sometimes the narrator formally introduces himself, sometimes he steps out of a crowd scene to utter a few remarks—and then becomes an "extra" again. An old peanut vendor, for example, reminisces about the time he was called upon to have sexual relations with twenty-eight women in the harem of an Eastern potentate. The account is presented in a flashback, from the viewpoint of the narrator. During a Fascist rally, however, a woman in uniform suddenly—

and briefly—tells us her feelings about the proceedings, before vanishing . . . never to be seen or heard from again.

Although the flashbacks are patently colored by a specific narrator's subjectivity, one can nonetheless distinguish between the more conventional representations of past actions where a speaker is telling either the audience or another character a story and interior monologues in the stream-of-consciousness manner. Not surprisingly, inasmuch as this is a Fellini picture (recall *8½* and *Juliet of the Spirits*), there are a number of gradations or intermediate narrative strategies between these two categories. In one scene, when the young boys go to confession, we see what they see as they tell the priest of their masturbation fantasies—shots of women's behinds in the market place, for instance, or shots of their math teacher's breasts straining against a tight white sweater. Titta's confession of impure thoughts is mixed wtih the shame attendant upon rejection by a mature woman. As he makes his confession, we see Gradisca sitting alone in the Fulgor, cigarette smoke curling back past her head and illuminated in the rays of the projector—a fitting symbol for the dream-like movie world the attractive hairdresser inhabits. While she is lost in her vision of a uniformed Gary Cooper striding heroically across the screen in *Beau Geste* (William Wellman, 1939), Titta keeps changing his seat until he is next to her. Then, tentatively, he touches the woman's leg. At first Gradisca feels nothing; but as Titta grows bolder, she gazes at him slowly and coolly asks: "Looking for something?"*

Later in the film, a narrator tells us about Gradisca's rendezvous with a prince in his hotel suite. Perhaps the incident occurred, perhaps not. If it did happen, it may or may not have happened as presented. In any event, nothing the viewer is shown seems out of keeping with the character or personality of Gradisca

---

* Although Titta is devastated by Gradisca's response to his fumbling advances, and although he is humiliated by his recounting of it, the priest remains insensitive and preoccupied. During the confession, the priest interrupts Titta to lecture an old sexton on the proper way to arrange flowers on an altar. Fellini makes clear that the man of God is more concerned with aesthetics than with morality or human feelings.

as seen in the more "objective" (relatively speaking) portions of the picture. For instance, as Gradisca stares at the prince, who manifestly appears to the frustrated woman as a Gary Cooper in the flesh, Fellini reveals her in a series of quick cuts striking "cheesecake" poses in various stages of undress. What we are presented with, then, is Gradisca's fantasy life; she is acting out her dreams of celluloid adventures. Throughout *Amarcord*, the hairdresser generally sports a red beret at a jaunty angle. She wears the same hat in bed as she awaits her Prince Charming—a style of attire that taxes credibility and thus underscores the strong nonillusionistic mode of imitation evident in much of the movie.

As there is no central character in *Amarcord*, so is there no distinct idea or single story, much less plot, in the picture. "Life" seems to be Fellini's subject. Structurally, the film is patterned externally on the changing seasons, the "action" commencing with spring and coming to a term one year later. Fellini has always been fond of circular form. In earlier films however, the cyclical nature of his architectonics has been presented in a subtle manner. *Amarcord* begins and ends with the arrival of *"manine"* ("fluff puffs") or thistledown, symbolic of annual rebirth. Throughout *Amarcord* (which, like Chekhov's *Uncle Vanya*, could be subtitled *Scenes From Country Life in Four Acts*), Fellini attempts to buttress his thematic structure, such as it is, with mythological significance.

Amarcord opens with a shot of wash flapping in an early spring breeze . . . followed by a shot of a church, while on the sound track can be heard the ringing of bells. People leap into the air to seize the fluff puffs . . . At night, in the piazza, the townsfolk parade with a rag doll Witch of Winter, which they then place on a pyre. Undoubtedly, this scene represents a ritual going back centuries into primitive times. In order to emphasize the archetypal nature of the scene, Fellini introduces the village idiot Giudizio, who also appears in *I Vitelloni* and *The Clowns*. Trapped by the crowd on top of the pyre, Giudizio is afraid that he will be burned to death—much to the amusement of the onlookers. Although the idiot is in no real danger, and although his neighbors are guilty of nothing more than "harmless" sadism, Fellini seems to be suggesting here more than the symbolic death of winter. Arrested at a juvenile level, Giudizio stands for the adolescent; in ancient rites of an initiatory character, the ceremony showed the boy dying as a child and being reborn as a man. As already indicated, much of *Amarcord* focuses on the problems of adolescence.

Next Fellini reveals the world of school. Or rather, the "worlds" of school, since the teachers live in one world and the students in another. One teacher discourses on the ancient Romans but appears more concerned with the lengthening ash on his cigarette; when a malicious boy slams the teacher's desk, the ash falls off and the offender is severely reprimanded. Another teacher attempts to instruct a student in how to speak Greek; however, every time the boy places his tongue on a certain area of his palate, he only succeeds in presenting authority with a disrespectful raspberry. Another student, to be "funny," urinates on the floor, much to the consternation of his teacher. And so it goes. . . .

We meet Titta's father at the local brickyard, where the workers are bored and alienated. "My grandfather laid bricks, my father laid bricks, and I lay bricks," says one laborer. "But I've got no house." The town slut appears, a crazy nymphomaniac called Volpina (Josiane Tanzilli). First the young woman runs across the beach, her flimsy dress blowing in the sea breeze. Then she stretches out longingly towards the sky and the water. Finally, she squats in an obscene manner on the sand, her back to the camera, lost in autoeroticism. Afterward she appears at the brickyard, her famished gaze sweeping over the men, her tongue licking at her lips, her breasts heaving, her insatiable body writhing. Titta's father sends Volpina away, while the laborers stare after her with mingled lust and genuine sorrow. In modern society work has lost its meaning and eros, which should rejuvenate man, instead merely leaves him unsatisfied. Volpina—symbol of sexual libido—has been reduced to a misfit.

AMARCORD: *The dinner table in Titta's home.*

In Titta's home a quarrel erupts at dinner when the father learns that his son, as a "joke," urinated on the bishop's hat. Since the mother takes Titta's side, believing as she does that her husband is too severe, the titular head of the family uses the occasion to unburden himself of the resentments he feels for everyone present. As before, Titta's mother sets herself in opposition to her husband—which only succeeds in goading him into greater displays of melodramatic rage (at one point he threatens to commit suicide), even as he ridicules the others for what he conceives to be their "overreacting." Throughout it all, Fellini shows Pataca eating with a serene good appetite while everyone else is screaming and pounding the table. On the sound track, Nino Rota obligingly plays "Stormy Weather."

When a new prostitute enters town, the men standing on the street follow her progress to the bordello with keen interest. The scene fades out with a shot of religious paintings in a store window, in front of which stands The Lawyer, who smiles at the audience in a knowing manner. In previous films, such as La Strada and La Dolce Vita, Fellini presented similar juxtapositions but without underlining.

Subsequently, when a fascist general makes a visit, the bored populace also respond with pent-up enthusiasm. So much so, in fact, that the Brown Shirts are almost concealed by the dust rising from the railroad station, their pompous speeches nearly drowned out by the roar of the crowd. That night all the lights in the town suddenly go out. Then, from atop the church belfry, comes the sound of a violin playing a socialist anthem. The troops fire away, until finally the music stops. What the fascists have destroyed, however, is a phonograph. Titta's father, who made the pathetic but courageous protest, is arrested. Under interrogation, he not only confesses but also obsequiously recants. In order to "teach him a lesson," the fascist bullies force the "ex-socialist" to drink castor oil, an ordeal that in reality often killed prisoners of Il Duce's thugs. "They say that I have made a political movie," Fellini has been quoted as remarking. "Actually, Amarcord conveys mostly the emotive, psychological part of being fascist—fascism as mental sluggishness, as a loss of imagination" (*Time*, October 7, 1974).* At home, the wretched foreman sits naked and humiliated in a tub, his wife solicitously attending him. Titta ridicules his father for the stench rising out of the water, while the old man threatens not only his son but also the perfidious member of the family who informed on him—presumably Pataca.

As the seasons pass, the townspeople search for new amusements in order to alleviate their boredom. On one occasion, everyone stays up all night to glimpse an ocean liner named "The Rex" pass on its maiden voyage. Out they go in a flotilla of dinghies, canoes, and yachts, with much drinking and laughter, ribaldry and expectation. Finally, the ship appears, slicing through the foam, its myriad lights sparking against the mist. No matter that "The Rex" is obviously a miniature or small-scale model shot. "What does it look like?" asks a blind accordionist, who shows up repeatedly in *Amarcord*, much like the blind beggar in Joyce's *Ulysses*. In truth, however, the sightless man can "see" the ship as well as anyone. For what each character in the film witnesses is not the journey of a real vessel but the projection of his own romantic fantasy.

The line between sanity and insanity is a thin one in *Amarcord*. One day Titta's family is permitted to take Uncle Teo out of the mental institution for a visit home. As they proceed along the country road in their carriage, Teo shocks the others by showing them some rocks he carries in his pockets; but we are also informed that the deranged one was always smarter than Titta's father at school. Perhaps madness is the only intelligent response to a world such as ours. Soon, Uncle Teo feels the need to urinate. As he stands up to leave the carriage, Fellini shoots him from an extreme low angle, the man's head against the sky, the composition off-center, so that Teo appears on the extreme right hand side of the frame—all the rest of the screen merely empty space. The shot is, of course, a visual equivalent

---

* During a daydream of a schoolboy, the latter stands with his "bride" before an enormous portrait of Mussolini, who, like a god, confers his blessings upon the union. In this case, at least, the young fascist suffers no "loss of imagination."

of the man's bizarre mental state, a psychotic tableau. Pre-occupied with his fantasies, or perhaps mesmerized by the gorgeous scenery, Uncle Teo urinates without opening his fly. "I thought they said he was normal," Titta's father remarks. When they arrive at the farm, the madman climbs a tree and refuses to come down, using the stones in his pockets to good advantage by bouncing them off the heads of those who seek to retrieve him. "I want a woman!" he keeps shouting. Since Teo is intended to represent one of Fellini's "holy fools," and since "woman" in the director's imagination has often been a means for the redemption of man, the mad creature's longing transcends sexuality. Teo is finally "brought down to earth" by a midget nun—a sad commentary not only on "woman" but also on the diminished role of institutional religion today. As a male nurse takes Teo back to the asylum, he informs the disconsolate family: "One day he's normal, the next he isn't. The way it is with all of us."

Amarcord ends with the marriage of Gradisca to a local policeman, a plain-looking fellow whose only resemblance to the Gary Cooper of *Beau Geste* is his uniform. The scene takes place out of doors, the party seated at a long table, music supplied by the blind accordian player. Presently it begins to rain. Everyone scurries under an awning—everyone, that is, except the musician, who is shoved back in his chair by a celebrant and instructed to keep playing in spite of the rain. At last, the fluff puffs fall again, and the wedding party excitedly jump into the air to snatch them. Slowly, the scene disintegrates, as Gradisca and her husband exit, then more and more of the guests, until only a few scattered individuals remain. . . .

Compared to *Fellini Satyricon, Amarcord* is a masterpiece. Compared to *La Strada, Nights of Cabiria, La Dolce Vita, 8½, Juliet of the Spirits,* and *The Clowns,* however, *Amarcord* must be judged a disappointment. It would be pleasant to conclude this survey of Fellini's cinema by praising his most recent offering, but critical honesty forbids such a stance. *Amarcord,* thanks to the inconstancy and insecurity of reviewers, has been very much overrated. Critics who have been wagging their heads and stroking their beards over Fellini ever since *La Dolce Vita*, or in some cases, ever since *8½*, have suddenly decided that the old master is again the equal of Bergman. Most reviewers dread being out of step; since to laud Fellini is now chic, everyone——or almost everyone—wants to jump on the bandwagon.*

By structuring his action in *Amarcord* on the changing seasons, Fellini has merely provided a mechanical, external scaffolding; he has not fashioned an organic, internal structure. The freeform style is *too* free. There is no development, no tension, no coherence. *Amarcord* lacks proportion. For example, the death of Titta's mother near the end of the film is presented in an almost offhand manner, as though Fellini had suddenly decided in the course of shooting that the picture needed a bit of "pathos"; the event takes up less screen time than some of the inconsequential buffoonery.

In conception, "life" is an impossible subject for a film; in execution, *Amarcord* is barren of too much that is good, true, and beautiful in human experience. At the beginning of this chapter, I referred to Fellini's interview with Hank Werber of *Variety*. Now, whatever his intentions might have been, Fellini's achievement resulted in a good deal of "fantasy" but little "tenderness." We never develop an interest in any of the characters in *Amarcord* because we never get time to know any of them. The sequence involving Titta's father and the fascists remains one of the few moments in the movie when we are made to care about a character, one of the rare instances when the artist elicits compassion from us. Myth is not enough to lend a motion picture significance; myth needs to be individuated, archetypes

---

* Consider Vincent Canby. When he saw *Amarcord* at Cannes, Canby reported: "*Amarcord* looks as if Fellini were spending his time extravagantly doodling while awaiting an idea for his next real movie" (*New York Times*, May 26, 1974). Four months later in New York, however, Canby saw *Amarcord* as a "film of exhilarating beauty" (*New York Times*, September 20, 1974), and concluded that in *Amarcord* Fellini "is in the top of his form" (*New York Times*, September 29, 1974). John Simon, of course, panned *Amarcord*; but then, Simon hasn't liked any Fellini film in the past fifteen years (*New York Times*, November 24, 1974). The New York Film Critics Circle cited *Amarcord* as the "best film of 1974." Without doubt, the last few years have been lean ones for the art of the film.

require specificity; in art the universal becomes concretized. Before *Amarcord*, for the most part, a Fellini film was rich with a balanced sense of life, nourished by love, noteworthy for its celebration of existence. Unhappily, that is not the case here. There is not much in *Amarcord* to lift one's spirits; not much warmth; not much of value in Fellini's vision of the Thirties that one can look back on with regret at its passing.

If we compare Teo to Gelsomina, the "holy fool" of *La Strada*, we can see how little Fellini has engaged our sympathies in *Amarcord*. If we compare Gradisca's wedding with the wedding scene in *La Strada*, we can comprehend the difference between ersatz and genuine art, between volitional form and form born of true inspiration. Gelsomina is a person before she is a symbol; Teo is merely a stick. Although a theme of romance-versus-reality appears in *Amarcord*, it is not sufficiently elaborated, with the result that it possesses no affective meaning for the viewer. Consequently, Gradisca's wedding seems thematically irrelevant, apparently suggesting no more than the banal observation that aging beauties had better accept less than their "dream man" if they don't want to be spinsters. The wedding scene in *La Strada* is integral to the entire film; both emotionally and intellectually, it contains the essence of what Fellini is "saying" about human solitude in that powerful, unsurpassable masterpiece.

The "pleasures" depicted in *Amarcord* are not so much "simple" (as Fellini intended) as simple-minded, vulgar, obscene. Heretofore, the great director has given us an incomparable cast of memorable faces. In *Amarcord*, however, there are no countenances that haunt the mind, not even negatively as in *Fellini Satyricon*. The film-maker appears to have his own mind on other matters. Instead of faces, we get posteriors; instead of ecstasy, we get excremental humor. Aside from the bottoms of peasant women shown on bicycle seats (already mentioned), there are close-ups of Gradisca's rump being pelted with snowballs and the enormous rear end of the local tobacconist, whose anatomy severely tests the dimensions of Panavision. There is a particularly gross scene in which the elephantine woman shoves her breasts, which resemble two basketballs, into Titta's mouth, nearly suffocating him, and brutally instructs him in how to please her. Her grotesque aggression against the inexperienced boy is shot in a protracted close-up; and in spite of the following pseudotender scene in which the upset youth is ministered to by his mother, the crude behavior of the tobacconist and Titta's discomfit are both played for laughs, though only one with the psyche of a Brown Shirt, in my opinion, would find such sadism funny.

In *Amarcord*, Fellini also includes much breaking of wind and passing of water. He seems to have forgotten that there is a difference between "childish" and "childlike." When we are children, we find scatological tomfoolery amusing; when we grow up, we put away the fecal-urinary humor of children. Fellini, however, is still laughing. To be "childlike" is to preserve, as an adult, a sense of wonder, to be open to experience, to retain (as F. Scott Fitzgerald says of Gatsby) a "heightened sensitivity to the promises of life." Ordinarily, Fellini's vision is eminently "childlike." Yet in *Amarcord*, the director's attempts to balance vulgarity and obscenity with images of romance and beauty fail. Young men who masturbate together in a car might also enjoy sensitive romantic dreams; nevertheless, when Fellini shows us his young men dancing separately in front of the local hotel, each one with his arms extended to an imaginary partner, the camera floating dreamily away from the group to match the lyrical score, the whole business looks phony. Perhaps a connection between the two incidents exists in Fellini's mind; no connection, however, exists on the screen. We are being asked to do the work that the artist should rightly perform.

Similarly, when the youths stop hurling snowballs at Gradisca's buttocks in order to stare at a peacock who lands on the town fountain and spreads its bright plumage, we are supposed to see in the event a symbol of beauty in the midst of the mundane. Instead, we get the unfortunate impression that Fellini is perfunctorily reaching for "significance," that the bird, after perching briefly in a Technicolor lab, has somehow just flown in from Eisenstein's *October*. In short, the film-maker has not created the effects he obviously intends. As a result, we never feel that anything on the screen really happened to us, that anything really belongs to us.

Fellini revisited his past in *Amarcord*; however, he forgot to take along with him that complex vision of the mature artist which, as a rule, he possesses to a degree second to none in film history.

CHAPTER 16

Fellini's Casanova, Orchestra Rehearsal, City of Women, And the Ship Sails On

*You see, [art] is always a confession. For example, take
Kafka. He is completely autobiographical. He has
never been a vermin, he has never been processed and
killed. He has never been a criminal, a vampire. But
he was! A real artist is also a medium; he is possessed
by many different personalities. To write, to paint,
to make a movie is therapy. It is to psychoanalyze yourself. It's with reason that the artist can be, in a
certain sense, protected by a real neurosis. Because he
has the possibility to make a process with the phantoms,
the complexes, the tragedies, the insecurities. Making
order from an aesthetic point of view becomes thera-
peutic order from a psychological point of view.*

—FEDERICO FELLINI

In 1976 *Fellini's Casanova* appeared. It was preceded by the bally-
hoo a major undertaking of the famous film-maker normally gener-
ates. It was Fellini's most ambitious film since the abortive *Fellini
Satyricon* in 1969. With a production bill of $10,000,000, Fellini's

new film more than doubled the expense involved in shooting *Satyricon*, making *Casanova* the costliest Fellini venture to date. Reports varied as to the number of people in the film. Some articles claimed *Fellini's Casanova* had a cast of thousands, others a mere six hundred. On display would be three thousand costumes and four hundred wigs. Danilo Donati, the designer, had been instructed by Fellini to build fifty-four sets. Everything, we were told, would be on a big, *big* scale—as if bigness equaled greatness.

Like *Fellini Satyricon*, *Fellini's Casanova* is an adaptation. Giovanni Jacopo Casanova (1725–1798) was a Venetian writer, gambler, police informer, speculator, and adventurer. For a time he was imprisoned in the notorious Palace of the Doges in Venice, from which he eventually escaped. In his travels Casanova met Voltaire, Rousseau, Louis XV, Frederick the Great, and Catherine II of Russia. The *Memoirs* were not published until thirty years after Casanova's death. Because he apparently bedded hundreds of women, the name "Casanova" has become synonymous with "stud."

In 1974 the producer Dino De Laurentiis got the idea for making a sex film based on Casanova's autobiography, and he talked Fellini into signing a contract. Eventually Laurentiis pulled out, but Alberto Grimaldi jumped in. Because Grimaldi represented Universal Pictures, *Fellini's Casanova* became the film-maker's first movie in English.

When he signed the contract to film the *Memoirs*, Fellini had heard of Casanova but he had never read him. After reading him, Fellini regretted having contracted to make the adaptation. He found the *Memoirs* empty. Repelled by Casanova, Fellini almost despaired of making a movie about him.

As Fellini saw the *Memoirs*, the world of Casanova remained devoid of nature, children, animals, philosophy, aesthetics, sentiment, and human feeling of any kind. Casanova was a *stronzo*—a "turd"—who cared only for sex. Since there was no feeling or emotion in either Casanova or his *Memoirs*, Fellini concluded, there would be none in his film. Like *Fellini Satyricon*, *Fellini's Casanova* would be "objective"—that is, a cold film.

Some critics—as they did when *Fellini Satyricon* was screened —accused Fellini of not being faithful to the original, of twisting Casanova's work, as he had earlier twisted Petronius's, to square with his own outlook on life. But it's no accident that Fellini's name appears in both titles, for neither film is an adaptation in the ordinary sense. What we have is Fellini's view of Casanova as earlier we had Fellini's conception of Roman life in Petronius's novel. Why criticize an artist for not doing what he never set out to do? In both cases the original work was only a springboard for Fellini's own cinematic vision. If we want to know what Casanova thought of himself, we should read the *Memoirs*. If we want to know what Fellini thinks of him, we should see *Fellini's Casanova*.

For the part of Casanova, Fellini chose Donald Sutherland, who has not only acted in films but who has also performed on the stage in English productions of Shakespeare. Like any diligent actor, Sutherland did his homework for the part. He read Casanova thoroughly—all twelve volumes—plus numerous critiques of the work. Certainly, he thought, Fellini would wish to discuss "motivation" with him. Not so. Instead, Fellini told Sutherland to forget everything he had learned about Casanova and to leave himself open—totally open—to Fellini's interpretation.

Fellini chose Sutherland, he has said, because the actor has a forgettable face. And since, according to Fellini, Casanova possessed no individuality—remained no more than a personified phallus—the actor seemed made for the part.

With portraits of the real Casanova in mind as a starting point, Fellini set out to remake Sutherland to conform with his own conception of the character. Most of Sutherland's hair was removed, along with his eyebrows, and he was fitted with a prominent nose and a false chin. Even Sutherland's eyes were given an Asian slant, lending his immobile face an almost narcotized expression. In the popular mind Casanova was a dark magnetic seducer of women. In Fellini's mind Casanova was a cipher—alienated from nature, from others, and even from himself. Perhaps because the standard psychoanalytic interpretation of the Casanova-type is that he is a latent homosexual assiduously seeking to prove his masculinity, Fellini has Sutherland mince through the film like an effeminate fop.

FELLINI'S CASANOVA: *Actor Donald Sutherland is transformed to embody Fellini's conception of Casanova.*

Fellini's Casanova opens with striking cinematic effectiveness on a carnival scene in Venice. Overhead the sky is filled with fireworks. From the Grand Canal an enormous wooden bust of Venus —the Goddess of Love—is hoisted. Before the sculpted head is halfway out of the water, however, the supporting ropes break and the idol sinks back into the deep.

The sexual instinct is basic—it springs from the water, the source of all life. But sex is more than epidermal contact. Fellini's symbolism suggests the ancient link between sexual rapture and worship, between fertility and the mystery of creation. Casanova, however, knows none of this.

On the island of San Bartolo, Casanova has sex—he never makes love—with a nun while the impotent French Ambassador peeps at them through a hole in the wall of the castle. The hole is in the eye of a fish—another symbol derived from the water—that decorates the room. Before Casanova commences with the nun, he takes out a mechanical bird and winds it up. Throughout the film the bird—a Freudian symbol of the penis—accompanies Casanova on his fornications; it moves up and down, mimicking its owner. The fish is universally the symbol of fecundity and life, and in Catholicism it is also a symbol of Christ. Fellini used the same fish imagery before at the end of *La Dolce Vita*. As in the earlier film, Fellini again shows how man has defaced both nature and God.

Instead of being natural man, Casanova is rational man, therefore mechanical man, for he has been cut off from the wellspring of his own deeper being. To make this point clear, Fellini frequently shoots Casanova from a low angle during intercourse, showing him joyously pumping up and down like a piston. In *Fellini's Casanova* sex is hard work.

Shortly after his rendezvous with the nun, Casanova is thrown into prison. While there, he remembers, "the good old days"—and Fellini flashes us back to the past with voice-over narration.

In subsequent scenes Casanova—his eyes bulging, his body straining—pumps away on top of a woman who keeps fainting and being bled by a physician, pumps away on top of his brother's mistress, pumps away on top of an elderly woman while a younger woman nearby helps him along by shaking her behind, pumps away in a contest with a peasant coachman to see which one is the "better man"—of course Casanova is—pumps away on top of a hunchbacked woman, and pumps away on top of a lifesize mechanical doll.

Repeatedly in the film Casanova attempts to win the respect of people with his mind, his writing, and his oratory. But, like the comedian Rodney Dangerfield, he doesn't get any respect. Casanova remains a sex symbol—a joke. Like the real Casanova, Fellini's Casanova ends his days as a librarian to Count Waldstein in Bohemia. In the latrine of the castle someone draws a portrait of Casanova—and then covers it with excrement. Fellini's Casanova is indeed a *stronzo*.

The film concludes with Casanova escaping into fantasy. Fellini takes us back to the beginning of the film and shows us the Grand Canal again—this time, significantly, it's frozen over. Again we see the head of Venus; this time, also significantly, she's watching Casanova through the ice. Some of the hero's former sexual partners appear and disappear. Finally the mechanical doll shows up, and Casanova dances with her across the frozen canal. The scene is brilliantly photographed by Giuseppe Rotunno.

Fellini's Casanova leaves us with the thought that a mechanical doll is the right mate for a mechanical man with a mechanical bird —just as ice remains the right metaphor to suggest Casanova's inability to love, his substitution of sexual performance for human contact. Sex, Fellini is saying, should add up to more than just tabulating coital experiences and quantifying orgasms. Men and women need each other for more than just the satisfaction of physical desire. They need each other to grow in love, to develop emotionally and spiritually, to become whole.

In some ways Fellini hasn't changed much since he made *La Strada*, which he describes as "the complete catalog of my mythical world." Zampanò still needs Gelsomina; the sea still represents the woman, love, life, the unconscious, the transcendent. Fellini's sense of the holy, which he perversely often tries to conceal, is really outraged by Casanova's unholy pumpings. But, by his own admission, Fellini identifies with Zampanò. Does he also identify with Casanova? In any case, *Fellini's Casanova* is a world without a Gelsomina.

Is *Fellini's Casanova* a good film? The answer to that question, unfortunately, is no. At times *Casanova* is impressive visually, but we have a right to expect that—and much more—from a director of Fellini's stature. Nor can we speak of great acting in *Casanova*. How can we? Fellini hasn't created any real characters.

Part of the trouble with *Fellini's Casanova* lies in the subject itself. Even though the film represents Fellini's approach to Casanova, enough of the autobiography comes through to give the viewer a fairly accurate picture of the kind of person who wrote the *Memoirs*. To those who believe Fellini is too harsh on Casanova, one can only reply that the film-maker left out much that would have made him appear even more odious to an audience. For example, in reality—or at least according to the *Memoirs*—Casanova once fornicated with a former mistress while his illegitimate daughter looked on; later he fornicated three times with his daughter, finally impregnating her. By the time he had reached his forties, Casanova had become a prematurely dirty old man. He started collecting pornographic pictures, and on at least one occasion found sexual pleasure by caressing a girl of nine. Casanova was not a very nice person. Except as a sexual athlete—or freak—he has little claim on our attention. But as *Fellini's Casanova* makes obvious, being a sexual athlete isn't enough to justify a film that runs for nearly three hours.

Questions about whether *Fellini's Casanova* is or is not faithful to the original aside—and aesthetically such questions remain largely irrelevant—a good part of the trouble with the film lies in its inert structure. From beginning to end, *Fellini's Casanova* boringly repeats the same point about the protagonist. There is no development, no conflict, no contrast. Like *Fellini Satyricon*, *Fellini's Casanova* has no love in it, no warmth, no compassion. And a Fellini film that lacks these ingredients does not show him at his best. Instead of the big work of art everyone had hoped *Fellini's*

Casanova would be, the director's fourteenth film remains, to use the slang expression, a big bust.

Orchestra Rehearsal, made originally to be shown on Italian state television in 1979, was triggered by the shocking kidnapping and murder of the former Prime Minister Aldo Moro. In Italy Fellini's film aroused much controversy—over 150 reviews and articles were published—with conservatives, liberals, and communists focusing in on it according to their own special ideologies. If Italian critics seemed to complicate overly the political meaning of *Orchestra Rehearsal*, critics outside of Italy, especially in the United States, seemed to interpret the film in overly simple social terms, perhaps even in reductionist terms.

Subtitled *The Decline of the West in C# Major*,* Fellini's film is, on its most obvious level, about social and political chaos. The setting of the film remains a thirteenth-century church oratory, now deconsecrated, where because of its excellent acoustics, modern orchestra rehearsals are carried on. Into this burial place of three popes and seven bishops comes a television camera crew to shoot a documentary of the rehearsal. The viewer is prepared for this by an elderly copyist who explains the historical significance of the oratory as he gets the music stands ready for the artists. Off camera the voice of Fellini himself is heard playing the television documentarist who interviews the members of the orchestra.

The only professional actor in the film is Baldwin Bass, who plays a German conductor fond of shouting *Achtung*. For the rest, the musicians—all from Naples, according to Fellini—play themselves. As they wander into the oratory the individual members of the orchestra are questioned by Fellini about their instruments. Each musician egotistically asserts the superiority of his own instrument, and even identifies himself with it. For example, one

---

*The subtitle is, of course, a reference to Oswald Spengler's famous *Der Untergang des Abendlandes* (1918–22). In *The Decline of the West*, Spengler argues that our civilization is in decay, that democracy is a pretense, and that universal peace remains an illusion. The West is headed for dictatorships of one kind or another, and wars without end. To some extent Spengler's ideas prepared the way for Hitler and the Nazi party.

musician tells us that his violin is the brain and heart of the orchestra, whereas another claims that his clarinet is its penis. The trombonist views his instrument as "the voice of a solitary being"; the pianist refers to her piano as her "king." And so it goes. The musicians berate and ridicule each other. While the string section plays, the brass section prattles. After finishing a few notes, one musician listens to a transistor radio. There is no sense of an artistic whole, of various talents working towards a common end.

Enter the maestro—a new conductor. Furiously he attacks the company for its sloppy attention and poor playing. The musicians grow increasingly hostile. "What is this? A soccer field?" the conductor asks contemptuously, to which the musicians respond by flinging off their suit jackets and becoming more and more violent in their resistance. Finally the union representatives call for a break.

During the break the musicians congregate in a small bar. One says he feels as if they work in a Fiat plant; all express lack of feeling and respect for the conductor. Inside a tiny dirty room, the conductor describes the musicians as "wild dogs." He laments the passing of a time when musicians showed regard for the conductor. Sipping champagne, he says: "I own the world—I'm king." But it's obvious he owns nothing so long as anarchy rules in the orchestra.

When the break is finished, the conductor goes back into the auditorium. There he discovers the musicians in full revolt. "Down with assembly-line music!" they scream. "No conductors allowed in here!" They scrawl graffiti over the walls with spray paint: "Death to the conductor!," "All who play for the conductor are traitors!," and "Down with live music—up with records!" A man and woman in the orchestra fornicate under a piano. Balls of mud or excrement are thrown at portraits of Beethoven and Mozart. The musicians begin smashing everything in the oratory to pieces. "All power to the players!" they chant. Some want to replace the conductor with an enormous metronome.

Suddenly cracks appear in the old walls of the church. Then a giant wrecking ball pounds through the plaster, showering the

ORCHESTRA REHEARSAL: *The string section of the orchestra rehearses.*

room with dust. Frightened, disheveled, the musicians emerge from the fragments of the building, cowed at last. They await orders from the conductor. "From the beginning!" he commands. "And this time hang on to the notes!" The orchestra rehearsal begins again—this time with correct behavior on the part of the orchestra.

But the German conductor refuses to be satisfied with the playing of his docile orchestra. He begins screaming, finally switching to his native language in order to express with more symbolic force, no doubt, his now totalitarian attitude. The screen fades to black.

Orchestra Rehearsal appears straightforward enough in its sociopolitical symbolism. By setting the film in an ancient church building, Fellini juxtaposes a stable ordered past with a violent disordered present, much the way T.S. Eliot does in "The Waste Land." The orchestra represents our narcissistic society in which, as Fellini apparently sees it, each member thinks only of himself, only of expressing his own personality, with no thought for the welfare of the group. Fellini seems to yearn for a time when each person knew his place in society, when everything was arranged in a fixed system of hierarchies. It would be wrong to assume, however, that the film-maker looks toward some totalitarian model as his ideal. On the contrary, Fellini's stance is humanistic. The conductor wants the musicians to think of art, which enriches human life, instead of selfishly expressing their own egos. Art and society both demand form, subordination of one kind or another in order to achieve harmony. A balance must be achieved between freedom and order.

The childish anarchy of the orchestra members makes art—that is, social life—impossible. The type of men who murdered Aldo Moro represent in an extreme form tendencies that are destroying the West, undermining its cultural heritage. When there is no respect for art, morality, tradition—for everything that renders civilized existence bearable—the end, indeed, is near. Anarchy paves the way for dictatorship: after the wrecking ball comes the *Fuehrer*.

Interpreted in social terms, Fellini's symbols appear trite. And who would argue with the proposition that no society can function where esteem for law is absent? If *Orchestra Rehearsal* is approached solely as sociopolitical allegory, then, it seems both stale and superficial.

There is, however, another approach the viewer might take to *Orchestra Rehearsal*, another level of meaning in the film. In part, Fellini—who sees all art as autobiographical—is telling us something about himself. Not surprisingly, Italians and others often refer to Fellini as the "maestro." As a film-maker, Fellini is in much the same position as an orchestra conductor. The film-maker coordinates the various elements of film art—camera, music, sound effects, acting, scenery, editing, and the like—just as a conductor pulls together his stringed and wind instruments for a unified aesthetic effect.

"My job," the conductor says at one point in the film, "is to turn wine into blood, bread into flesh." In short, the artist's job is to play god. The concept of "transubstantiation" in Catholic theology asserts that bread and wine can be changed into the body and blood of Christ. In Fellini's analogy the film-maker transforms the world "out there" into a new world on celluloid. But he can do this only if the people he works with lend him their talents in the service of his cinematic vision. If they do so willingly, harmony results; if they oppose him, disharmony results. When there is disharmony the film-maker is forced to become a dictator. Instead of a benevolent leader, he changes into a despotic *Fuehrer*. People who have watched Fellini on a movie set know he can play both roles.

This "deeper" interpretation still does not make *Orchestra Rehearsal* one of Fellini's best films, although it does provide it with more complexity than it is generally given credit for. Shorter than *Fellini's Casanova* (it runs seventy-two minutes) and not as pretentious, *Orchestra Rehearsal* is less of a disappointment . . . but it is still a disappointment.*

Orchestra Rehearsal is dedicated to Nino Rota, who died after the picture was completed. Rota had scored all of Fellini's films from *The White Sheik* to *Orchestra Rehearsal*.

City of Women (1981) is another of Fellini's "big" films. Like *Fellini's Casanova*, *City of Women* has a large cast, a long running time (140 minutes, although it seems easily twice that length in psychological time, or in how long the film *feels*), an international star—Marcello Mastroianni—in the lead, and sex—with the focus on feminism—as its theme.

The film opens on a train where the sleepy Snaporaz* watches a tall, sexually attractive woman—played by Bernice Stegers—in a smart fur hat and striped suit who sits in the compartment opposite him. When she gets up to go to the toilet, Snaporaz follows her and at once begins having intercourse with her. Before this classy seduction can reach its orgasmic conclusion, however, the train stops at the woman's station. Snaporaz, unsatisfied, follows her, murmuring "Smick-smack" repeatedly as the woman's buttocks sway.

Fellini switches to a lovely forest—photographed by the sensitive Giuseppe Rotunno (whose camerawork deserves a better fate than *City of Women*)—and shows us the middle-aged, out-of-shape Snaporaz trying to keep up with the more vigorous strides of the woman. At one point he stands with her by a tree, ready to receive her passionate kiss; but when he opens his eyes—she's gone. Throughout this scene, Snaporaz acts like a slavering idiot.

Next we find Snaporaz inside a hotel, where he has pursued the woman, and where a noisy convention of feminists is being held. All kinds of women are represented: some beautiful, some ugly; some white, some black; some heterosexual, some lesbian. Snaporaz seems overwhelmed by the variety of activities: lectures, films, angry discussions—all intended to raise consciousness. A woman called Mrs. Small has six meek husbands, each of whom appears thankful when he receives the slightest attention from his wife.

---

*"Now the name Snaporaz—that's a joke between me and Mastroianni," Fellini has said. "We are like kids; we have nicknames. He calls me Culligan. We Italians were influenced by American names. We saw movies, and names like Culligan and Sullivan sounded very important. Snaporaz was Marcello's nickname. And when, midway in the picture, he asks me 'What's my name?' I say 'Snaporaz.' And that's good, because for the infantile side of this character—all these stories and dreams about women—Snaporaz is the right name." Sometimes in the film Snaporaz is called "Marcello."

When the woman on the train speaks out against Snaporaz—the sexist—the feminists begin threatening him.

Before Snaporaz can be castrated, and possibly killed, a woman named Donatella, plump and strong, leads him off to what he thinks is safety. But when he goes through a door she takes him to, he tumbles down a staircase. At the bottom another woman—another strong woman—grabs him and installs him on her motorcycle. Instead of driving him back to the railroad station, though, she goes to the farm she lives on and, in a greenhouse, tries to rape him. Snaporaz is saved by the appearance of the woman's mother—ancient, feisty, her consciousness unraised—who puts the would-be rapist to flight.

When the old woman directs her granddaughter to take Snaporaz to the station, the protagonist is relieved. However, the girl pushes him into a car filled with punk rockers—all female, of course—who smoke pot and act bored. Obviously afraid of them, Snaporaz jumps out of the car and, pursued by the girls, runs off. He is saved again, this time by a middle-aged, macho-type lech named Doctor Xavier Züberkock (one can gauge the juvenile level of Fellini's humor in *City of Women* by the name here). Züberkock stands in front of his mansion, which looks like an old Roman temple, with a gun and attack dogs. Firing blanks, he frightens off the girls.

Inside the mansion Züberkock informs Snaporaz that he is about to celebrate his ten-thousandth sexual conquest. Here everything is at a polar extreme from the feminist convention. There's a floor lamp that resembles an enormous penis, and women are viewed simply as objects to be used for man's gratification. Long corridors show off a gallery of Züberkock's nine thousand nine hundred and ninety-nine previously bedded women, all in full color transparencies. By pressing a button Züberkock can light up any portrait and listen to the woman on a recording moan again in orgasm.

Enter Snaporaz's wife, Elena (Anna Prucnal), who has been invited to Züberkock's party. She criticizes Snaporaz for being a bad husband. But later on, when he's in bed, she drunkenly sits astride him as if he were a horse (Fellini did this much better in *La Dolce Vita*), insisting on sexual satisfaction. Elena is wearing curlers and face cream. When Snaporaz is unable to perform, she slides off him and falls asleep, looking like a frustrated hog in heat.

At Züberkock's party his ten-thousandth—and, in all likelihood, last—conquest is introduced. The woman entertains the guests by standing on two stools, legs apart, and sucking up into her vagina— much like a Hoover vacuum cleaner—change tossed at her feet. As for Züberkock, he is putting out the ten-thousandth candle on his cake by either pouring champagne on it or urinating on it— this vital point is never made clear in the film. The party ends with Züberkock admitting that he's tired out from years of prodigious fornicating (in sheer numbers he makes Casanova seem like a celibate monk), whereupon he starts praying before, and kissing, a marble bust of his late mother. The psychoanalytic symbolism here is so crudely obvious as to make an admirer of Fellini wince with embarrassment for him.

After this point in the film the editing pace quickens. We see Snaporaz—wearing a top hat and sporting a cane—imitating Fred Astaire to the tune of "Let's Face the Music and Dance." Then he's on a gigantic roller coaster that goes back in time in order to review his sex life. It all started for Snaporaz—with a sense of style that has remained unchanged down through the years—on the floor under a kitchen table with a maid. In one Proustian remembrance of things better left in the past, we are treated to a view of twenty boys masturbating in a wall-to-wall bed under a sheet that moves rhythmically up and down as images of female movie stars light up a screen. (We have seen a scene like this one before in *Amarcord*, a film that, in comparison to *City of Women*, now seems like a masterpiece).

Finally Snaporaz ends up in a kangaroo court of feminists where he is found guilty of being a man. Then he is sent out into a Roman-style arena, probably to be killed, even though the court dismisses him as insignificant. Searching for the ideal woman, Snaporaz goes up in a hot-air balloon shaped like Donatella. On terra firma, however, the real Donatella, dressed as a terrorist, ends his celestial search with a submachine gun. Snaporaz falls to earth.

City of Women has a circular structure in that it goes back to

CITY OF WOMEN: *The woman is Züberkock's ten-thousandth conquest, and she is entertaining the guests in front of a cake with ten thousand symbolic candles.*

where it began, that is, to the train. Fellini resorts to that hack-
neyed device of . . . yes, the whole film has been a dream. Snaporaz
wakes up in the compartment we found him in. With our hero, besides the woman in the fur hat, are his wife and the really real
Donatella, the latter now seen to be a mere schoolgirl. Outside it
had been raining, but all at once the sun breaks through Fellini's
dark clouds. The film ends with a shot of the train entering a tunnel. At the end of the tunnel—are you ready for this?—a light
glows in the darkness. There's hope for Snaporaz, you see.

City of Women, Fellini has said, is a film about feminism and
sexual relations between men and women in contemporary society.

"My feminist critics are even now saying that in the whole film
there isn't one real woman," Fellini told Gideon Bachmann (*Film
Quarterly*, Winter 1980–81). "Of course there isn't. There wasn't
meant to be. Because if there was a real woman, it would have
been useless to make the film."

No matter, according to Fellini, that his women are not even
one-dimensional but merely disembodied faces or just parts of the
female anatomy. After all, *City of Women* represents Snaporaz's
infantile view of the other sex. Besides, the film is a comedy. Anything goes—right?

Fellini's defense of *City of Women* seems disingenuous. Why set
out to make a film about feminism, and then show women in consistently unflattering ways? There are "real women"—whole women
—in the world. Why set out to make a film about sexual relations
today, and then show only men and women mutually exploiting
each other? There are mature sexual relationships—warm, loving,
nonexploitative—in our society.

True, *City of Women* is supposed to be a comedy. Fellini's film,
however, isn't funny. The humor remains cheap, tasteless, cruel.
Everyone looks stupid to Fellini. There is not an iota of humane
feeling in the film.

Even the men in *City of Women* are merely cardboard erections
—they bear no relation to ordinary film characters (which at best
are by necessity abstractions), much less to authentic human beings.
Marcello Mastroianni, an excellent actor, is misused (even more so

than Donald Sutherland in *Casanova*) in the service of Fellini's—apparently—own infantile view of women and sex. It is a view we have seen increasingly in Fellini's later films. In *La Dolce Vita* and, especially, in *8½*—both outstanding films—Mastroianni seemed to be a persona for the director himself. The same appears to be true in *City of Women*. Fellini expressed scorn for Casanova, and he could barely manage to shoot a film about him. Yet was Casanova any more of a *stronzo* than Snaporaz? What kind of personal problems has Fellini been trying to work out on the screen for the past fifteen years to the detriment of his art?

By making most of what occurs in *City of Women* Snaporaz's dream, Fellini does more than merely rework an exhausted technique. The dream allows him to escape the consequences of his own choice of material. Instead of facing honestly the challenge of feminism and sexual relations between men and women, whether in the comic mode or not, he distorts everything and then passes off the action on screen as no more than his hero's unconscious fantasies.

In *City of Women* there is no sign of that creative mastery which made films like *8½* and *Juliet of the Spirits* modernist classics. Because there are no characters in *City of Women*, there is no one with whom the viewer can identify. At the center of the film there remains only Fellini's sensibility—or, rather, lack of it. *City of Women* is a hodgepodge of Fellini's obsessions: some of them remembered from better films, where they were integrated with character and theme, others familiar from the more recent past, where they merely highlight the *auteur's* own inability—like the musicians' in *Orchestra Rehearsal*—to subordinate himself to his art. The symbolism is not simply commonplace, like the sunshine breaking through the rain at the end; it often has no artistic justification—the light, for example, at the end of the tunnel. In the film there is not one indication that there is even the possibility Snaporaz will ever grow up. And how could Fellini use a shot of a train going into a tunnel after Hitchcock made such sexual symbolism famous?

City of Women, in my judgment, is Fellini's poorest film—worse than *Amarcord*, worse than *Fellini's Casanova*, worse even than *Fellini Satyricon*.

And the Ship Sails On (1984) is Fellini's eighteenth feature film,* and—surprisingly, after so many bad films—his most impressive work in fourteen years, or since *The Clowns* in 1970. With a budget of six million dollars and a cast of over one hundred and thirty actors, Fellini shot *And the Ship Sails On* using ten of Cinecitta's fifteen sound stages. He had his set designer, Dante Ferretti, build an enormous make-believe ocean liner, complete with pistons to capture the rolling motion of a ship on the sea, the "sea" here being a thousand square feet of cellophane. *And the Ship Sails On* is, then, another of Fellini's "big" films. However, this time bigness is not the result of an inflation of hot air.

Unlike *Fellini's Casanova* and *City of Women* there are no stars. Still, the leading parts are not played by nonprofessionals. Most of the actors have appeared in European theaters. Because the action of the film is set in July 1914, Fellini chose mostly English actors. "For their detached air," he has explained. "And because they were then great world travelers." The nearest character to a protagonist in the film is Orlando, played by Freddie Jones of England's Royal Shakespeare Company. Orlando is a first-person narrator, a chorus-figure who looks directly into the camera and introduces the other characters and comments on the action.

And the Ship Sails On opens as if it were a silent documentary in black and white; slowly color appears, transforming what has seemed to be a mere record of the past on old celluloid into the dramatic present. It is not a new filmic technique, but Fellini uses it skillfully.

The *Gloria N.*, an Italian luxury liner, is embarking on a memorial voyage. On the ship are the ashes of the famous soprano Edmea Tetua, who had asked that her remains be scattered into the Adriatic near Erimo, the island where she was born.

Fellini begins by showing the passengers boarding the ship.

---

*Or nineteenth—if, like Fellini, we count each of his two short films as one full-length film.

AND THE SHIP SAILS ON: *Orlando talking to a fellow passenger on the Gloria N., Fellini's make-believe ocean liner.*

Among them are numerous celebrities from the European music world: singers, conductors, critics, impresarios. Present also is the Grand Duke of Harzock, a fat blond sexually ambiguous-looking youth, and his blind sister, who is having an affair with his prime minister and who may be plotting her brother's overthrow. Brother and sister are accompanied by a large entourage. Then there is the impresario Sir Reginald Dongby (Fellini seems addicted to such names), a foot fetishist, who derives masochistic enjoyment out of his wife's endless infidelities; an old man who likes little girls; and a movie comic who doubles as a medium, and who likes young sailors. Orlando, of course, keeps us informed of all the bizarre events.

There is no plot in *And the Ship Sails On*. Structurally, the film is a series of episodes, most of them truly humorous, unlike those in the wretchedly humorless *City of Women*. In the latter film the maestro's hand was heavy—his touch is lighter in *And the Ship Sails On*. Much of the humor in the film derives from the vanity of the characters, and from their insulated and silly romantic attitudes.

In one scene, for example, the opera singers on board tour the bowels of the ship. Standing on the visitors' gallery of the boiler room, they try to outdo each other by singing bits of arias, much to the enjoyment of the crew, whose sweaty bodies are painted crimson from the coals burning in the furnaces, but whose eyes are filled with adoration for the conceited artists seemingly so far above them.

In their narcissism Fellini's characters are alienated from nature. During lunch one day a seagull enters the salon—flapping from table to table—and Fellini's eccentrics are sent into a panic by the harmless bird. A basso profundo hypnotizes a chicken in the galley in order to demonstrate the power of his singing voice. Meanwhile a rhinoceros lies in the ship's hold, emitting a foul odor; according to the passengers of the *Gloria N.* the animal is not seasick but lovesick—as they all are. Perhaps the most stupidly romantic of the characters remains a former lover of the late diva.

Even as, later, the ship is sinking, even as the sea rises around him, he goes on watching a film showing Edmea Tetua vocalizing soundlessly.

The time, of course, is the eve of World War I. In the Balkans, at Sarajevo, Archduke Franz Ferdinand of Austria has recently been assassinated. Nevertheless a cameraman is aboard the *Gloria N.* to capture the sight of the famous singer's ashes being scattered over the waters.

As usual, Fellini has had much to say about his film. It is, he claims, an attack on "media excesses, news that's inexact and dramatized, made spectacular and administered as an anesthetic." War or no war, the masses long to know what celebrities are up to. But Fellini also wanted "to show a colorful and contented era when the individual was significant, unlike the present when the individual is flattened, and individuality is annulled in groups, categories, collectives."

In *And the Ship Sails On* the era is certainly presented as "colorful," but the odd characters who comprise the dramatis personae of the film scarcely appear "contented"—not with all their sexual peculiarities and frustrations. All the same, Fellini's grotesques are likable grotesques, unlike the grotesques in *Fellini's Casanova*, say, or *City of Women*, and the film is suffused with some of the tenderness that helped make earlier films like *La Strada* and *Nights of Cabiria* screen classics.

The turning point in the action—if one can speak of a turning point in a film without a plot—occurs when an Austro-Hungarian battleship appears. Earlier in the film *Gloria N.* had picked up at sea a group of Serbian refugees. After the assassination of the Archduke, the Austrian police had attempted to arrest the Serbs, who had then escaped on a raft. Now the captain of the Austro-Hungarian battleship demands the extradition of the Serbs. The Italian captain of the *Gloria N.* refuses. When the Grand Duke of Harzock asks the captain of the battleship to allow the *Gloria N.* to proceed, the good ship of Fellini's fools sails on. But after Edmea Tetua's ashes are blown to the winds over the sea, the dreadnought comes back and its captain makes the same demand as before—this time threatening to blow up the *Gloria N.* if he doesn't get the Serbs.

After much discussion the captain of the *Gloria N.* agrees to transfer the Serbs to the battleship. The Grand Duke of Harzock and the people with him also decide to leave. They all get into rowboats. The transfer, however, does not end peacefully. A Serb named Mirko hurls a bomb into a gun turret of the battleship, thus starting off a string of explosions. Before the warship goes down, though, it fires at the *Gloria N.*, which also proceeds to sink. Because this is a comedy and not *Moby Dick*, no one—or almost no one—drowns. We have this on Orlando's authority.

In *And the Ship Sails On* Fellini's characters, in spite of their neuroticisms and perversions, seem far less of a problem than the kind of people who start wars. Since 1914 the world has become increasingly politicized, and therefore remains a much darker and more dangerous place. The assassination of Franz Ferdinand destroyed a style of life that will never come back again. No doubt Fellini intends us to see his ridiculous and overly romantic characters as living in a grand way just before the descent of the West into barbarism. Fellini still has Spengler on his mind.

A romantic himself, Fellini cannot help but identify with his opera singers. Like them, he cares more for art than politics. Art —like Fellini's ship—will sail on in spite of the political climate. The *Gloria N.* may go down, but artists will continue to launch new ships—fresh works of art—to enlighten and entertain humanity. To some, artists may seem frivolous. But Fellini, in spite of the fun he has in *And the Ship Sails On*, doesn't agree. Although art never wholly loses its referential quality, or its link to the real world, the artist confers upon his work a new aesthetic mode of existence. As Aristotle knew, we need art precisely because it is *not* life.

That is why Fellini keeps almost everything resembling what is naïvely called "realism" out of *And the Ship Sails On*. From the beginning we are kept aware that film involves artifice. Even as we watch the silent images in black and white, we can hear the whirring of the projector. Although the *Gloria N.* simulates the movement of an ocean liner at sea, we never for an instant believe that it's a real ocean liner. The ship is as phony as the cellophane sea. "The sunset looks painted," observes one of the passengers on the *Gloria N.*—and the sunset *is* painted. The island of Erimo is papier-maché, and the rhinoceros is likewise obviously fake. Even the Austro-Hungarian battleship looks like gray cardboard with painted smoke curling out of its stacks. To show his contempt for "realism," Fellini even has a Russian name in Cyrillic letters on the warship. When the *Gloria N.* is supposedly on the open sea, we nevertheless catch glimpses of land.

And the Ship Sails On makes the average opera look like something out of Italian neorealism. The actors play every emotion in the broad manner against—oftentimes—stagey backdrops. And the technique of having Orlando and the other characters gaze directly into the camera, or in various ways show awareness of the film being shot, underscores the artificial nature of the proceedings. The music, from Debussy through Schubert and Tchaikowsky to Serbian chants, further augments the film's operatic features. Finally, at the end of *And the Ship Sails On*, Fellini allows us to see his own camera filming the *Gloria N.* as it sinks into the Adriatic.

When Bergman shows us his camera at the end of *Persona* (1966), he is drawing us into the area of epistemology and raising the problematic question: "What is 'reality'?" When Fellini does this in *And the Ship Sails On*, he is drawing a distinction between art and reality; he is saying: "It's only a movie." That might sound superficial —especially compared to *Persona*, which is a great film—but it isn't. One function of art is cathartic: it sends us back to life refreshed. Like Guido at the end of *8½*, Fellini the artist is also saying in *And the Ship Sails On*: "Life is a holiday to be enjoyed. Let us enjoy it together." Perhaps that is a message we need to hear now, as our bloody century moves nearer its end, more than at any time since before 1914.

Part Four

Conclusion

*I don't think a Catholic can ever be entirely free of
2,000 years of authority, although there was paganism
before that, which helps a little. And I don't even
know that I'd want to be free. What else would I
talk about in my pictures? An Italian can never
entirely shake the myth. You can rebel, you should
rebel, but you are completely enveloped in Catholic
guilt all your life no matter what you do or where you
go. It has been stamped on you.*

—FEDERICO FELLINI

CHAPTER 17

Form and Content

The producers, the distributors, and the movie-theater owners have always sold films as though they were products to be consumed and forgotten, like bottles of soda water. And so film audiences think of movies this way. A man who will read, say, War and Peace *two or three times, who will listen to the Beethoven quartets hundreds of times, and who will go back again and again to a museum to look at an El Greco that has captured his interest, will see a film only once—it is the empty bottle of soda he has already drunk. For a film-maker, this is very discouraging.*
—FEDERICO FELLINI

The standard definition of style—how a film director "says" something rather than what he "says"—is misleading because it suggests that form and content are separable components in a motion picture. What we call a film-maker's style is a combination of recurrent elements: the way he shapes reality—or structures it—in order to present it on the screen; the perspective —or point of view—he uses to depict the various levels of that reality; and the fashion in which he shoots a picture—or his visual approach. The artist strives to create a unique world

253

on celluloid: a world with a gallery of characters and related themes, a world coinciding in part with experiential reality yet different from it in its self-ordered comprehensibility. Manner, then, inevitably becomes matter.

If Fellini tends to structure his films in a certain way, the reason is not hard to find: his form expresses a view of life. Fellini's art is both personal and inclusive. Personal, because he has always regarded his own experience as the starting point for a film; inclusive, because his initial solipsism—his egocentric predicament—is invariably overcome in the creative act, in his imaginative and loving encounter with the outside world. In his best pictures, Fellini achieves a balance between dream and "reality," between unconscious spontaneity and conscious architectonics. Ready-made forms will obviously not serve this director's purposes. "When one shows a world that is open, baroque, delirious, demanding, clamorous, multiple, contradictory, a farce and a tragedy," Fellini told Pierre Kast, "there is no reason at all to suppose that it must be less accessible, immediately, than a world enclosed in conventions by force or by usage." Structurally, Fellini's films are open, episodic, rhythmic, shaped by a theme rather than by causal development or logic. Fellini does not go to other artists' work for inspiration; he goes to life. And the viewer responds "immediately" to *what* Fellini shows (the "real" world) and *how* he shows it (the film-maker's singular perception). By design, the story element in Fellini's later pictures has become increasingly attenuated.

Nevertheless, a Fellini film is never without structure of some kind, is never a mere "slice of life." As the director informed Gideon Bachmann: "Always the important thing is to know *who* sees the reality. Then it becomes a question of the power to condense, to show the essence of things." Fellini has normally handled point of view in an imaginative way. Through his choice of "*who* sees the reality," through alternation of personal and public viewpoints on the action, the director has generally given weight to his filmic constructions. As I observed in an earlier chapter, Fellini's statement in a conversation with Enzo Peri—"The really important contribution of neorealism is that it suggested a way to look at things—not with the narcissistic glasses of the author, but with equilibrium between reality and subjectivism"—throws more light on, say, *La Dolce Vita* than on *Shoeshine* or *Bitter Rice*.* In *The White Sheik*, Fellini manages the difficult task of showing experience as the two principal characters respond to it in comic juxtaposition to the way it really is. He does the same thing, but more complexly, in *I Vitelloni*, where the viewpoints of several characters are interchanged repeatedly with a detached approach. *La Strada*, *Nights of Cabiria*, and *La Dolce Vita* benefit both structurally and thematically from Fellini's ability to shift at will from the exterior world, seemingly photographed by an ideal observer, to a vantage point that allows the viewer to feel events as the main characters feel them. *8½* and *Juliet of the Spirits* are much more subjective in technique than previous Fellini films, yet in neither picture is external "reality" completely superseded by an internal one. Of the later films, *The Clowns* stands as a brilliant example of the director's genius for rendering epistemic concepts filmically. Because Fellini is concerned with projecting both subjective and objective happenings—or worlds within a world—his best films possess a wholeness all too rare on the screen.

Although he began as a scriptwriter, Fellini avoids presenting what Hitchcock has often contemptuously referred to as "photographs of people talking." Fellini possesses a vivid cinematic imagination. Unlike many contemporary directors, however, he delights the eye without recourse to visual clichés: he normally resists the temptation to exploit the large number of techniques available to anyone working in the medium—techniques that not infrequently substitute for emotion and thought and personal vision; in other words, techniques that are offered up in place of art. Fellini tends to eschew freeze frames, zoom shots, fast motion; nor is he overly fond of wipes, superimpositions,

* *Shoeshine* was directed by Vittorio De Sica (1946); *Bitter Rice*, by Giuseppe De Santis (1949).

and swishpans. If one technique can be said to recur in Fellini's pictures, it is the moving camera. Since the world remains "open" and "multiple," this procedure seems ideally suited to convey the twin ideas of spaciousness and manifoldness. It would be oversimple to assert, however, that the moving camera enables Fellini to explore the phenomenal domain. "If I wander around the world looking at things, it is only to reassure myself that the world I have invented is true," the director told Doris Hamblin. "For me, the world of my imagination is always closer to the truth than is the truth." Yet in spite of its subjectivity, Fellini's world rarely ceases to remain identifiably "our world." Stylistically, what we call "Felliniesque" cannot be defined in terms of a single technique that any run-of-the-mill director might duplicate; instead, it is made up of various elements that comprise the film-maker's "signature." As Proust contended, style is basically a matter not of technique but of vision.

The key features of Fellini's style include a circuslike atmosphere; processions; theatrical and vaudevillian performances; seriocomic structure; masks and masquerades; the use of grotesques; a fusion of stylization and realism; empty piazzas; the road or the sea as a symbolic landscape; the alternation of noisy scenes and quiet scenes, night scenes and day scenes, or scenes of hysterical action and loneliness, scenes of estrangement and recognition; a nostalgia for childhood innocence, moral purity, sanctity. As we know from *The Clowns*, Fellini fell in love with the circus at an early age, and the flavor of that world has remained with his films. Where the circus—or, for that matter, any kind of performance—appears directly in his pictures, it stands as a metaphor, a device for revealing life as a funny-sad experience with cosmic significance. Masks also derive from performance, and they further help the characters to assume a universal meaning, as do the sundry grotesques. Redemption is probably Fellini's great theme—a theme that can be traced to his Roman Catholic background. The procession as ritual, the juxtaposition of contrasting scenes, the longing for goodness—these elements, as well as some others, derive whole or in part from Fellini's religious upbringing. The film-maker's irony is balanced by humor, his bitterness by sentiment, his pessimism by optimism.

Critics have cudgeled their brains in an attempt to label Fellini's style. "Poetic cinema," "poetic neorealism," "surreal expressionism" are favorite tags. Fellini himself has often been called a "romantic," a "baroque fantasist," an "expressionist," an "impressionist." Fellini's art remains so rich, so various, that it can sustain any number of interpretations. Consequently, there is some correspondence between his films and the definitions cited, just as there is some correspondence between Fellini the artist and the terms in which he has been described. One can perceive a gradual development in Fellini's work, from a delicate balance of realistic and symbolistic elements in the early films—*La Dolce Vita* probably represents a turning point— toward a style that is freer in expression, more spectacular, flamboyant. In his recent pictures, Fellini presents a world less quotidian in some of its aspects than the one shown in *I Vitelloni* or *Il Bidone*; all art is more or less unrealistic, however, and Fellini's later art differs from his earlier in degree, not in essence.

Chekhov once wrote in a letter: "the writers who we say are for all time . . . have one common and very important characteristic: they are going toward something and are summoning you toward it, too, and you feel not with your mind, but with your whole being, that they have some object. . . . The best of them are realistic and paint life as it is, but through every line's being soaked in the consciousness of an object, you feel, besides life as it is, the life which ought to be, and that captivates you."* With obvious substitutions of words like "film-makers" for "writers" and "shot's" for "line's," the remarks just quoted could be applied to the art of Fellini. If the director's later films are more expressionistic than his earlier ones, part of the reason

* *Letters on the Short Story, the Drama, and Other Literary Topics by Anton Chekhov*, ed. Louis S. Friedland (New York: Dover Publications, 1966), pp. 240-41.

lies in Fellini's desire to show (as he once put it to Gideon Bachmann) "not just social reality, but also spiritual reality, metaphysical reality, anything man has inside him."

Although Fellini is rightly suspicious of any label, one could probably make a good case for his art as being "romantic." There is in it a love of mystery; an emphasis on aspiration, wonder, feeling, personality, the inner world, the infinite; an extensive use of symbols and myths; a belief that nature is alive with spirits, or *a* spirit; that nature, since it is part of God, can be a revelation of the truth. Like other "romantic" creators, Fellini believes that the best art is born with as little manipulation by the conscious mind as possible; he sees intellect and intuition at war with each other; he values originality; he has more and more tended to take himself as his hero, or at least as his own protagonist. Fellini continues to be contemptuous of criticism and theory—because both issue from the head—and he manifests suspicion of social forms, religious codes, philosophical schemes—because they block the "natural" development of men and women toward a fruitful, loving, authentic existence. However, much less important than defining Fellini as a "romantic" (or whatever) is seeing his art as basically representing a fusion of the real and the ideal—life as it is, and life as it ought to be.

For the most part, Fellini's "mysticism" is a product of his early religious training. His films reveal a duality in his thinking: a conflict between the positive ideas his quondam faith provided him with—a sense of mystery, an ideal of goodness, the transforming power of love—and the repression of sex, the concept of sin, the morbid concern with death and damnation. "Religion demands of a man that he be morally perfect—which is impossible," Thomas Meehan quotes Fellini as saying. "And when a man fails in his attempts to be perfect, his religion then reacts on his spirits as a destructive force. The myth has filled him with regrets and guilt." Perhaps the clearest expression of the conflict between man's desire to attain perfection and his recognition that there can be no perfection this side of paradise is in *The Clowns*, in the figures of the "white clown" and the *"augusto"* respectively. Despair, however, rarely distinguishes Fellini's outlook on life. Antonioni once remarked: "there is an authentic Catholic nostalgia in Fellini's work . . . there is always hope, or at least there is not that compulsion to look piteously right to the bottom, which is a characteristic secular trait."

Often, Fellini embodies his conception of "hope"—as well as of "mystery"—in a woman; he has observed: "Women are stronger because they are nearer to nature. Intellectuals are lost in pools of anguish for the future. Not the woman—she is here, now." The woman in Fellini's pictures frequently challenges the man to overcome his narcissism, selfishness, brutishness. Gelsomina, the unforgettable heroine of *La Strada*, remains the outstanding example here.

The bipolar presentation of the real and the ideal often appears in Fellini's films. Witness *The White Sheik*, wherein "reality" and "romance" are alike satirized, inasmuch as Ivan, Wanda, and the title character are all equally stupid. In *I Vitelloni*, cheap "romantic" dreams are again ridiculed; but again, "reality" appears in an unfavorable light. Only love and the aspiration to make life better seems to render human existence bearable. As I have already suggested, *La Strada* pits the ideal (Gelsomina) against the real (Zampanò), with the woman being physically destroyed but not without "redeeming" the man from beyond the grave. Throughout *Nights of Cabiria*, the heroine—weighed down by her gross existence—dreams of "salvation" in the form of a loving relationship with a man. Seeking to be reborn, but always disappointed, Cabiria nevertheless goes on hoping.

In *La Dolce Vita*, the apparent "sweet life" is really a sickness unto death. Like Zampanò, Giorgio, and Oscar, Marcello needs the help of a woman if he is to develop in a truly human way. At the end of the film, however, Marcello rejects "salvation" as represented by Paola: he refuses to be reborn. Like Ivan, Fausto, Zampanò, the men in Cabiria's life, and Marcello, the Guido of *8½* is unable to love. Just before shooting himself in fantasy at the end of the picture, the hero—of what is perhaps Fellini's most directly autobiographical movie—calls himself an "incurable romantic." When Claudia vanishes at the conclusion of *8½*, Fellini appears to be "saying" that Guido no longer requires the ideal. However persuasively Guido's rebirth as an artist is presented, his affirmation of love for all mankind strikes a false note.

Iris's message in *Juliet of the Spirits*—"Love for everyone"—carries the theme of *8½* and the earlier films even further. Juliet's illusion is her belief that her husband loves her. Her recognition that in reality he does not care for her sends her off on a search for fulfillment, a search to achieve a balance between the spiritual (the ideal) and the physical (the real). Unlike Guido, Juliet is reborn as a human being, even as Fellini's concern with reality beyond the sense world becomes more manifest. In *Fellini Satyricon*, Iris's message—which even in *Juliet of the Spirits* was misinterpreted by the decadent characters—becomes "love" merely in a sexual sense. The bisexual world of *Fellini Satyricon* reveals what life is like without love, without a sense of the ideal. Here there is no conflict between appearance and reality, or between romance and reality; here, for the first time, the artist looks "piteously right to the bottom." In *The Clowns*, the real is symbolized by the "*augusto*" and the ideal by the "white clown." One can see the clash between romance and reality in *Fellini's Roma*, wherein the artist contrasts the Rome of legend, history, and film with the Rome of modern times. Similarly, in *Amarcord* there is a discrepancy between Gradisca's romantic dreams of Gary Cooper and the real man she finally marries to avoid becoming an old maid. Like *Fellini Satyricon*, *Fellini's Casanova* shows us a world without love or idealism. The same values are missing from *Orchestra Rehearsal*, where "real" translates into "anarchy." Although Snaporaz searches for the ideal woman in *City of Women*, the only reality is a cold ugly world devoid of love. Finally, in *And the Ship Sails On* the ideal is represented by Fellini's artists, and the real—such as it is —by those who wage war.

Since making *Fellini Satyricon*, in which he attempted to be "detached, cold, and impassive"—in a word, *impersonal*—Fellini's art has taken a new direction. Instead of returning after *Satyricon* to the creation of characters like Gelsomina, Zampanò, Augusto, Cabiria, Marcello, Guido, Juliet, and other memorable figures, Fellini has eliminated character in the old sense and projected himself more fully—or rather, more directly—into his work. With the exception of *The Clowns* and *And the Ship Sails On*, the result has not been a happy one. Fellini has lost the "equilibrium between reality and subjectivism" that made his earlier films so haunting; too often, he seems to be gazing at life with "narcissistic glasses." In *The Clowns* and *Fellini's Roma*, Fellini appears on screen; in both films—and in *Orchestra Rehearsal*—we hear his voice on the soundtrack; and the fact that three of his later pictures carry his name in their titles also suggests an increasing subjectivism. True, *8½* is in part an autobiographical film. All the same, there are no Guidos in Fellini's recent offerings.

And speaking of *8½*, one of the themes of that great film was the director's fear of having nothing to say. Most of Fellini's later pictures seem thin in content; indeed, they suggest he is trying to conceal the emptiness within through recourse to spectacle. Oddly enough, in spite of Fellini's increasing reliance on fantastic display, his recent more surrealistic films are much less memorable visually than the earlier masterpieces—derived, for the most part, from neorealism—that originally earned him his reputation. Generally speaking, Fellini's films are most impressive when reality and fantasy (or poetry or surreal expressionism—call it what you will) coexist.

As Fellini's egotism has grown, the quality of his work has deteriorated. *La Strada* represents Fellini's "mythical world." But it is a "world" that has love and compassion in it, qualities that are largely absent from the director's recent films. Although one can now and then still glimpse the values that helped make the earlier films great, the focus has shifted away from sympathetically drawn characters to caricatures, from love to sex, with a resultant loss of artistic discipline. *And the Ship Sails On* shows, though, that Fellini can still make a decent film.

But is Fellini still capable of making a great film? Ingmar Bergman, the Swedish director, believes so. In an interview with John Simon, Bergman says of Fellini:

He is intuitive; he is creative; he is an enormous force. He is burning inside with such heat. Collapsing. Do you understand what I mean? The heat from his creative mind, it melts him. He suffers from it; he suffers physically from it. One day when he can manage this heat and can set it free, I think he will make pictures you have never seen in your life. He is rich. As every real artist, he will go back to his sources one day. He will find his way back.*

All who admire Fellini's best work can only hope that Bergman is right.

In the meantime we still have *The White Sheik, I Vitelloni, La Strada, Il Bidone, Nights of Cabiria, La Dolce Vita, Juliet of the Spirits, The Clowns,* and *And the Ship Sails On*—an impressive *oeuvre*. Fellini's best films will continue to be enjoyed so long as man retains his capacity to feel and to think, to question and to seek, to laugh and to cry, to marvel and to love . . . in short, so long as man retains his humanity.

Ciao, il poeta!

---

*John Simon, *Ingmar Bergman Directs* (New York: Harcourt Brace Jovanovich, 1972), p. 22.

Filmography

1950 *Variety Lights* (*Luci del varietà*)

Direction: Fellini and Alberto Lattuada. Script: Fellini, Lattuada, Tullio Pinelli, Ennio Flaiano. Photography: Otello Martelli. Sets: Aldo Buzzi. Editing: Mario Bonotti. Music: Felice Lattuada. Production: Capitalolium Film. Cast: Peppino de Filippo (Checco Dalmonte), Carla Del Poggio (Liliana), Giulietta Masina (Melina).

1952 *The White Sheik* (*Lo sceicco bianco*)

Direction: Fellini. Script: Fellini, Tullio Pinelli, Ennio Flaiano. Photography: Arturo Gallea. Sets: Fellini. Editing: Rolando Benedetti. Music: Nino Rota. Production: Luigi Rovere. Cast: Brunella Bovo (Wanda), Leopoldo Trieste (Ivan Cavalli), Alberto Sordi (the White Sheik), Giulietta Masina (Cabiria).

1953 *I Vitelloni*

Direction: Fellini. Script: Fellini, Ennio Flaiano, Tullio Pinelli. Photography: Otello Martelli, Luciano Trasatti, Carlo Carlini. Sets: Mario Chiari. Editing: Rolando Benedetti. Music: Nino Rota. Production: Lorenzo Pegoraro. Cast: Franco Interlenghi (Moraldo), Alberto Sordi (Alberto), Franco Fabrizi (Fausto), Leopoldo Trieste (Leopoldo), Riccardo Fellini (Riccardo), Leonora Ruffo (Sandra).

1953 "Love in the City" ("*Amore in città*"): episode in *A Matrimonial Agency* (*Un'agencia matrimoniale*)

Direction: Fellini. Script: Fellini and Tullio Pinelli. Photography: Gianni Di Venanzo. Sets: Gianni Polidori. Editing: Eraldo Da Roma. Music: Mario Nascimbene. Production: Cesare Zavattini. Cast: Nonprofessional actors.

1954 *La Strada*

Direction: Fellini. Script: Fellini, Ennio Flaiano, Tullio Pinelli. Photography: Otello Martelli. Sets: Mario Ravasco. Editing: Leo Cattozzo. Music: Nino Rota. Production: Carlo Ponti and Dino De Laurentiis. Cast: Giulietta Masina (Gelsomina), Anthony Quinn (Zampanò), Richard Basehart (The Fool).

1955 *Il Bidone*

Direction: Fellini. Script: Fellini, Ennio Flaiano, Tullio Pinelli. Photography: Otello Martelli. Sets: Dario Cecchi. Editing: Mario Serandrei. Music: Nino Rota. Production: "Titanus." Cast: Brederick Crawford (Augusto), Richard Basehart (Picasso), Franco Fabrizi (Roberto), Giulietta Masina (Iris).

1956 *Nights of Cabiria* (*Le notti di Cabiria*)

Direction: Fellini. Script: Fellini, Ennio Flaiano, Tullio Pinelli. Additional dialogue: Pier Paolo Pasolini. Photography: Aldo Tonti and Otello Martelli. Sets: Piero Gherardi. Editing: Leo Cattozzo. Music: Nino Rota. Production: Dino De Laurentiis. Cast: Giulietta Masina (Cabiria), Amedeo Nazzari (the actor), François Périer (Oscar), Aldo Silvani (the hypnotist), Franca Marzi (Wanda), Dorian Gray (Jessy).

1959   *La Dolce Vita*

Direction: Fellini. Script: Fellini, Ennio Flaiano, Tullio Pinelli. Photography: Otello Martelli. Sets: Piero Gherardi. Editing: Leo Cattozzo. Music: Nino Rota. Production: Giuseppe Amato. Cast: Marcello Mastroianni (Marcello Rubini), Anouk Aimée (Maddalena), Anita Ekberg (Sylvia), Yvonne Furneaux (Emma), Lex Barker (Robert), Alain Cuny (Steiner), Annibale Ninchi (Marcello's father).

1961   "Boccaccio 70": episode in *The Temptation of Doctor Antonio* (*Le tentazioni del dottor Antonio*)

Direction: Fellini. Script: Fellini, Tullio Pinelli, Ennio Flaiano. Photography: Otello Martelli. Sets: Piero Zuffi. Editing: Leo Cattozzo. Music: Nino Rota. Production: Carlo Ponti. Cast: Peppino De Filippo (Doctor Antonio) and Anita Ekberg (Anita).

1962   *8½ (Otto e mezzo)*

Direction: Fellini. Script: Fellini, Ennio Flaiano, Tullio Pinelli, Brunello Rondi. Photography: Gianni Di Venanzo. Sets: Piero Gherardi. Editing: Leo Cattozzo. Music: Nino Rota. Production: Angelo Rizzoli. Cast: Marcello Mastroianni (Guido), Anouk Aimée (Luisa), Sandra Milo (Carla), Claudia Cardinale (Claudia).

1965   *Juliet of the Spirits* (*Giulietta degli spiriti*)

Direction: Fellini. Script: Fellini, Ennio Flaiano, Tullio Pinelli, Brunello Rondi. Photography: Gianni Di Venanzo. Sets: Piero Gherardi. Editing: Ruggiero Mastroianni. Music: Nino Rota. Production: Angelo Rizzoli. Cast: Guilietta Masina (Juliet), Mario Pisu (the husband), Sandra Milo (Suzy).

1967 "Toby Dammit": episode in *Histoires Extraordinaires*

Direction: Fellini. Script: Fellini. Photography: Giuseppe Rotunno. Music: Nino Rota. Production: Marceau-Cocinor-PEA. Cast: Terence Stamp (Toby).

1969 *Fellini Satyricon*

Direction: Fellini. Script: Fellini and Bernardino Zapponi. Photography: Giuseppe Rotunno. Sets: Danilo Donati. Editing: Ruggiero Mastroianni. Music: Nino Rota. Production: Alberto Grimaldi. Cast: Martin Potter (Encolpius), Hiram Keller (Ascyltus), Max Born (Giton), Capucine (Tryphaena), Alain Cuny (Lichas).

1970 *The Clowns (I clowns)*

Direction: Fellini. Script: Fellini and Bernardino Zapponi. Photography: Dario Di Palma. Sets: Danilo Donati. Editing: Ruggiero Mastroianni. Music: Nino Rota. Production: Fellini, Elio Scardimaglia, Ugo Guerra. Cast: Nonprofessional actors.

1972 *Fellini's Roma*

Direction: Fellini. Script: Fellini and Bernardino Zapponi. Photography: Giuseppe Rotunno. Sets: Danilo Donati. Editing: Ruggiero Mastroianni. Music: Nino Rota. Production: Ultra Film. Cast: Peter Gonzales (young Fellini), Stefano Majore (Fellini as a child), Pia de Doses (The Princess), Renato Giovanoll (Cardinal Ottaviani).

1974 *Amarcord*

Direction: Fellini. Script: Fellini and Tonino Guerra. Photography: Giuseppe Rotunno. Sets: Danilo Donati. Editing: Ruggiero Mastroianni. Music: Nino Rota. Production: Franco Cristaldi. Cast: Pupella Maggio (Titta's mother), Magali Noel (Gradisca), Armando Brancia (Titta's father), Ciccio Ingrassia (Uncle Teo), Nandino Orfei (Pataca), Luigi Rossi (lawyer), Bruno Zanin (Titta).

1976 *Fellini's Casanova*

Direction: Fellini. Script: Fellini and Bernardino Zappone. Photography: Giuseppe Rotunno. Sets: Danilo Donati. Editing: Ruggiere Mastroianni. Music: Nino Rota. Production: Alberto Grimaldi. Cast: Donald Sutherland (Casanova), Tina Aumont (Enrichetta), Cicely Browne (Madame D'Urfe), Olimpia Carliani (Isabella), Adele Angela Lojodice (Doll Woman).

1979 *Orchestra Rehearsal*

Direction: Fellini. Script: Fellini and Bruno Rondi. Photography: Giuseppe Rotunno. Sets: Dante Ferretti. Editing: Ruggiere Mastroianni. Music: Nino Rota. Production: Daimo Cinematographica.

1981 *City of Women*

Direction: Fellini. Script: Fellini and Bernardino Zappone. Photography: Giuseppe Rotunno. Sets: Dante Ferretti. Editing: Ruggiere Mastroianni. Music: Luis Bacalon. Producton: Renzo Rossellini. Cast: Marcello Mastroianni (Snaporaz), Anna Prucnal (Elena), Bernice Stegers (Lady on Train), Donatella Damiani (Ingenue), Iole Silvani (Motorcyclist), Ettore Manni (Dr. Züberkock).

1983 *And the Ship Sails On*

Direction: Fellini. Script: Fellini and Tonino Guerra. Photography: Giuseppe Rotunno. Sets: Dante Ferretti. Editing: Ruggiere Mastroianni. Music: Gianfranco Plenizio. Production: Franco Cristaldi. Cast: Freddie Jones (Orlando), Peter Cellier (Sir Reginald J. Dongby), Norma West (Lady Dongby), Florenzo Serra (Grand Duke of Harzock), Philip Locke (Prime Minister), Janet Suzman (Edmea Tetua).

Bibliography

Bachmann, Gideon, "Federico Fellini: An Interview," in *Film, Book I*, ed. Robert Hughes. New York: Grove Press, 1959, pp. 97–105.

————. "Federico Fellini: The Cinema Seen as a Woman . . ." *Film Quarterly* (Winter 1980–81), pp. 2–9.

Boyer, Deena. *The Two Hundred Days of 8½*. New York: Macmillan, 1964.

Budgen, Suzanne. *Fellini*. London: British Films Institute Education Department, 1966.

Fellini, Federico. "Fellini Talks About the Face of Anouk Aimée." *Vogue*. 150 (October 1, 1967), p. 160.

Friedland, Louis S., ed. *Letters on the Short Story, the Drama, and Other Literary Topics* by Anton Chekhov. New York: Dover Publications, 1966, pp. 240–41.

Hamblin, Doris. "Which Face Is Fellini?" *Life*, 71 (July 30, 1971), pp. 58–60.

Hartung, Philip T. "The Screen" (rev. of *Juliet of the Spirits*). *The Commonweal* (November 26, 1965), pp. 244–47.

Hughes, Eileen. *On the Set of Fellini Satyricon*. New York: William Morrow, 1971.

Kael, Pauline. *Deeper Into Movies*. Boston: Little, Brown, 1973.

Kast, Pierre. "Federico Fellini," in *Interviews With Film Directors*, ed. Andrew Sarris. New York: Avon, 1969, pp. 175–92.

Kezich, Tullio. "The Long Interview," in *Juliet of the Spirits*. New York: Ballantine, 1966, pp. 17–64.

Laurot, Edouard de. "*La Strada*—A Poem on Saintly Folly," in *Renaissance of the Film*, ed. Julius Bellone. London: Collier Books, 1970, pp. 264–76.

MacDonald, Dwight. *On Movies*. New York: Berkley, 1969.

McAnany, Emile G. and Robert Williams. *The Filmviewer's Handbook*. Glen Rock, New Jersey: Deus Books, 1965.

Meehan, Thomas. "Fantasy, Flesh, and Fellini." *Saturday Evening Post* (January 1, 1966), pp. 24–33.

Ortmayer, Roger. "Fellini's Film Journey: An Essay in Seeing," in *Three European Directors*, ed. James M. Wall. Grand Rapids: Eerdmans, 1973, pp. 65–107.

Peri, Enzo. "Federico Fellini: An Interview." *Film Quarterly*, 15 (Fall 1961), pp. 30–33.

Rhode, Eric. "Fellini's Double City," in *The Emergence of Film Art*, ed. Lewis Jacobs. New York: Hopkinson and Blake, 1969, pp. 341–52.

Ross, Lillian. "Profile." *The New Yorker*, 41 (October 30, 1965), pp. 63–107.

Salachas, Gilbert. *Federico Fellini*. New York: Crown, 1969.

Samuels, Charles Thomas. "Federico Fellini," in *Encountering Directors*. New York: G.P. Putnam's Sons, 1972, pp. 117–41.

Simon, John. *Acid Test*. New York: Stein and Day, 1963.

————. *Private Screenings*. New York: Berkley, 1971.

————. *Ingmar Bergman Directs*. New York: Harcourt Brace Jovanovich, 1972.

Solmi, Angelo. *Fellini*. London: Merlin Press, 1967.

Taylor, John Russell. "Federico Fellini," in *Cinema Eye, Cinema Ear*. New York: Hill and Wang, 1964, pp. 15–51.

Walter, Eugene. "Federico Fellini: Wizard of Film." *The Atlantic*, 216 (December 1965), pp. 62–67.

————. "Federico Fellini," in *Behind the Scenes: Theater and Film Interviews from The Transatlantic Review*, ed. Joseph F. McCrindle. New York: Holt, Rinehart and Winston, 1971, pp. 167–71.

Zanelli, Dario, ed. *Fellini's Satyricon*. New York: Ballantine, 1970.

Index